Created and Directed by Hans Höfer

INSIGHT GUIDES

SOUTH TYROL

Edited by Joachim Chwaszcza
Translated by Ginger Künzel

Editorial Director: Brian Bell

APA PUBLICATIONS

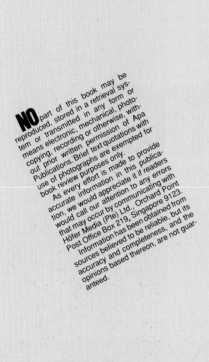
SOUTH TYROL

First Edition
© **1992 APA PUBLICATIONS (HK) LTD**
All Rights Reserved
Printed in Singapore by Höfer Press Pte. Ltd

ABOUT THIS BOOK

When people think of Tyrol they imagine the mountains of Austria. But South Tyrol is, in fact, in Italy. It is more commonly referred to by its Italian name, *Alto Adige*, and it is the northernmost province of Italy lying to the south of the alpine divide and the Brenner Pass.

One reason for South Tyrol's low profile in English-speaking countries is the dearth of readily available literature about it, a lack which the award-winning Insight series set out to address with *Insight Guide: South Tyrol*. Determined to maintain the high standards already set by the 160-strong series, its creator, Apa Publications, set about assembling a team of authors and photographers with expert knowledge of the region.

The Team

Chosen to lead the team was **Joachim Chwaszcza**, a regular visitor to South Tyrol's mountains and valleys. Chwaszcza, a freelance journalist and photographer in Munich, had previously edited Insight Guides to Prague, Yemen and Sardinia. In the course of editing *Insight Guide: South Tyrol* he made numerous trips to the region, speaking to prospective authors and explaining the approach of this affectionate, but at the same time critical, guide. He also took a break from his editing role to research the chapters on South Tyrolean wine and the regional cuisine, subjects close to his heart, and to wander through some of his favourite haunts in the region, such as the Rosengarten and the beautiful Sarn and Ulten valleys.

The turbulent history of South Tyrol is documented by **Christoph Hartungen**, a teacher and author with homes in Bozen and Seis am Schlern. The issues of language and identity which have been central to much of the region's 20th-century history, were tackled by **Florian Kronbichler**, the editor of the *Südtiroler Illustrierten*. Kronbichler also wrote the feature "Bombers and Spies", about the terrorism that rocked South Tyrol in the 1960s, and in the Places section he escorts readers around his home territory in Bozen.

Reinhold Messner, one of South Tyrol's most prominent sons, wrote the introductory chapter, "Back to My Roots", calling on South Tyroleans to protect their beautiful but endangered home. He supports the traditional (today called alternative) methods of farming in the mountains and explains why he has not invested his money in the construction of highly profitable hotels.

Wolftraud de Concini, who has contributed to various other Insight Guides on destinations in Italy, lives in neighbouring Pergine. She wrote the chapters about the Passeier Valley and Vinschgau, and introduces three of history's most famous South Tyroleans: Andreas Hofer, Margarethe Maultasch and Ettore Tolomei.

Arno Makowsky, a cultural editor for Munich's *Süddeutsche Zeitung* newspaper, explains the history and rituals of *Törggelen* (tasting the new wine). In collaboration with **Eva Meschede** from Munich's *Abendzeitung* newspaper, he also wrote the chapters about Sterzing and Ratschings.

Martin Schweiggl works in the Bureau of Land Management in Bozen and is thus actively involved with the national parks and endangered nature of South Tyrol. The author of an excellent book about the Lowlands and the castles of South Tyrol, he was the ideal person to write the chapters on the Wine

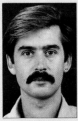

Chwaszcza

Hartungen

Kronbichler

Messner

Road. We also asked him to guide the reader through his hometown region of Magreid.

Dr Dieter Maier, whose major interest is the art history of the alpine regions, was one of the main contributors to *Insight Guide: Austria*. For this guide he wrote the chapters on Brixen, Burggrafenamt and the East Tyrolean valleys.

The recently retired director of the South Tyrol Tourist Office in Bozen, **Dr Siegfried Wenters**, shares his knowledge of Meran, whose famous springs drew the rich and royal of 19th-century Europe, including the glamorous Empress Elisabeth ("Sissi") of Austria.

The Photographers

The project editor's search for 250 of the most arresting images of South Tyrol led him to discover the work of **Othmar Seehauser**, a photographer for the *Südtiroler Illustrierten*, and **Hans-Paul Menara**, who has over 40 books about South Tyrol to his credit.

Apa's publisher, Hans Höfer, who selected the photographs for *Insight Guide: South Tyrol*, was particularly impressed by the pictures of New Yorker **Bill Wassman**, an old hand at Insight. Wassman travelled through the region, for weeks at a time, during all four seasons of the year. Photographers **Jörg Reuther** and **Emanuel Gronau** – who took the cover picture – also made valuable contributions to the book.

Working closely together, this team set about explaining the region and its fascinating history to a worldwide readership.

Südtirol, South Tyrol, is the province's German name. The majority of people who live here are ethnic Germans and, though the region has a distinct whiff of more southern climes, its historical and cultural development is closely tied to events in alpine regions to the north. Before the Treaty of Paris, it was an integral part of the Habsburg Empire; it was parcelled off to Italy as a reward for its support in World War I.

Non-German speaking visitors (generally skiers) will probably be more familiar with the name of the region's mountains (85 percent of South Tyrol lies more than 3,300 ft/ 1,000 metres above sea level); this is where the Alps meet the Dolomites, a range of mountains which look, beside the Alps, said traveller-writer Freya Stark, "as a Japanese garden might look beside the old trees of an English park."

But few skiers bother to explore the villages and towns or the frescoe-covered churches and magnificent castles of South Tyrol and so miss the surprising diversity of this small region. One can stroll along the palm-lined promenade of the spa city of Meran in the morning and hike to a remote mountainside village in the afternoon. One can lunch on Italian cuisine and dine on traditional Tyrolean cooking.

This book was translated from its original German by **Ginger Künzel**, an American journalist who has lived in Munich since 1974. In addition, she wrote the feature on "The Glacier Man", describing the recent amazing discovery of a 5,000-year-old body trapped in the ice of the Similaun glacier. The Travel Tips section was translated by **Susan Sting**, under the direction of translations editor **Tony Halliday**. This edition was completed in Insight Guides' London editorial office under the direction of managing editor **Dorothy Stannard**, and was proof-read and indexed by **John Goulding**.

Schweiggl

Wenters

Wassman

Reuther

History

Features

Maps

TRAVEL TIPS

**For detailed information
see page 289**

Gasthof Rößl

WELCOME TO SOUTH TYROL

On the southern ranges of the Alps, in South Tyrol, the climate is more temperate than to the north. But the culture is no less rich and the landscape no less dramatic. Magnificent peaks decline to rolling vineyards, apple orchards, some 350 castles and churches crammed with frescoes and art treasures. South Tyrol also offers abundant winter and summer sports: daring challenges for climbers, spectacular ski runs through deep powder snow, and hiking trails winding through secluded mountain pastures. It is bordered to the southeast by the Dolomites, a saw-toothed range of mountains which Freya Stark described as "finicky" and which Leslie Stephen described as "Eastern... a fit background for the garden of Kubla Khan."

But South Tyrol isn't all apple blossom, summer wine and *gemütlich*, for it has been racked by ethnic tension several times in its recent past. The conflict between the Italianised Germans and the Tyrolean Italians has subsided since the volatile days of the 1960s (bombs are no longer used to settle disputes); but the two population groups, divided by language, still view each other with caution. In order to understand South Tyrol, one must first understand its turbulent history.

The need for environmental protection and the demands of tourism are also a source of conflict. Europe's most important north-south passage, the Brenner motorway, dissects South Tyrol. Dams, ski lifts and the nose-to-tail traffic on the Bozen to Meran road are the price of tourism. And not all the dangers are evident at first glance. As international mountaineer Reinhold Messner points out, the drive to open the region to tourism must be tempered by the need to conserve natural resources: "To be a South Tyrolean today is a privilege and a responsibility," he says.

Because the official languages of South Tyrol are German and Italian (and Rhaeto-Romanic in some parts) road signs are written in both languages. For this book, it was decided that since the names in South Tyrol are historically of German origin and the majority of locals speak the German language, places should be referred to by their German name; in the "Places" chapters these are followed by their Italianised versions.

Preceding pages: view of the Sella Group; *klausen* in the Eisack Valley; guesthouse *zum Rößl* (the steed) in Kastelruth; antiques and junk in the Grödner Valley. **Left**, downhill ski racer in Vinschgau.

*Having conquered all the world's 26,000-ft (8,000-metre) peaks and battled against blizzards on his trek across Antarctica, the eminent mountaineer **Reinhold Messner** has returned to his native South Tyrol, the region where he learned to climb.*

It never fails. Every time I return to South Tyrol, crossing over the Alps from Austria to the north, a sense of familiarity, of coming home, envelops me. *Gemütlichkeit* is what the thousands of German tourists who stream into this region annually term this sensation. Here there is more sunshine, deeper serenity, a wider sky, a purer light.

As the slopes of the mountains and the solitary farms come into view, a torrent of memories spills over me, of gushing brooks, cool forests and small villages, of paths winding among the trees, of long evenings with friends in dark-panelled pubs, of leisurely walks alongside weathered wooden fences, of exhilarating expeditions up the Dolomite crags.

But in the wake of every gladdening of my heart, a cold shiver runs down my spine. Tourism is killing South Tyrol. Turning the radio dial, I hear one station after another, each trying to outdo the others with their eulogies for the region. The motorway is choc-a-bloc with vehicles from foreign countries, for "Our native land created by God's own hand", as it is called, has become a holiday retreat for almost half the population of central Europe.

If it hadn't been for the Brenner Pass, South Tyrol would have been a very different place – historically, politically and economically. The Celts, Goths, Lombards and ancient Bavarians all settled in South Tyrol. The mountains here have served as a junction rather than a border. Mussolini and Hitler mutually agreed that the Berlin-Rome axis would be linked at Brenner. This was where the Italian border was drawn after World War I.

It is said that when Goethe travelled south, he experienced a feeling of entering Italy as soon as he started crossing the Brenner. It is easy to understand what he meant. The light here is a southern light and the climate is influenced by the Mediterranean – even though the region is populated by several hundred thousand German-speaking residents and outwardly, at least, is very Germanic in character, it has a silky Latin lining.

In earlier times, the Tyroleans referred to their counterparts south of the Brenner as "South Tyroleans", meaning Tyroleans from the south, from the Trentino region. "South Tyrolean" was not a derogatory term – even though it was from this part of Tyrol that the region's tax collectors and travelling hawkers generally came.

In 1918 the Republic of Austria was forced to surrender South Tyrol to the Italians. But it was not until the 1930s that the South Tyroleans became a united German enclave, a minority in a Fascist Italy. After the end of World War II, it remained a tightly-knit group, isolating itself and jealously trying to exclude any other ethnic group from establishing itself in the region. Italians were grudgingly tolerated as holiday guests, but otherwise South Tyroleans wanted nothing to do with them.

With the government's promise of autonomy for the region, reiterated over many years, South Tyroleans became more open in some respects, but egocentric and withdrawn in others. It wasn't until the hordes of holiday-makers started to arrive, in search of peace and quiet, that this attitude changed. The first of these wealthy visitors came from northern Germany and Holland. To begin with they came only in the summer months; now they arrive throughout the year. It seems that the growing prosperity in central Europe has led to disenchantment with urban life and values. As South Tyroleans, we had long considered ourselves oppressed, disadvantaged and poor, but now we realise the value of our deep roots, our home.

The South Tyrol has now become almost a synonym for holiday. South Tyrol is no longer the "Tyrol south of the Brenner Pass", but rather an entity in itself, a profitable invention of tourism. And the people of the region are South Tyroleans – be they Ladins

Left, peasants in the mountains complain that much of South Tyrol is changing for the worse.

(Rhaeto-Romanics), Italians or Germans – bound together despite differences. What was previously a partnership between three language groups is now an integral part of our cultural and economic strength. The transition from "Tyroleans" to "South Tyroleans", accepted by all but the most extreme fanatics, was a path which led to a new understanding of ourselves. The proverbial pride of the South Tyrolean peasant demanding the respect of all visitors is no longer manifested in a brash "we are who we are" attitude, nor in the bombing of masts for high tension electricity cables.

Despite the obstinacy of the population (yes, we South Tyroleans are stubborn) South

us the advantage of being bilingual, if not trilingual (bearing in mind the Rhaeto-Romanic language spoken by the Ladins).

At a time when more and more people find they have no true roots, when feelings of restlessness are contributing to the growth of psychotherapy in Northern Europe, a holiday in a region like South Tyrol can be the perfect tonic. As long as we do not view the politics of Italy with too much intolerance, we can be considered a cosmopolitan resort. Here Germans and Italians feel just as much at home as the Dutch, Americans or the French. I have seen tourists from Hamburg and from Sicily staring longingly at the Rosengarten. Fortunately, they cannot take it with them.

Tyrol has managed to determine its own fate and identity. Nobody would help us, so we did it ourselves. We did it reluctantly and belatedly, after the Tyroleans to the north and the Italians to the south and later than the Swiss in Engadin.

Today we know that our famous industriousness, the beauty of our landscape and the Brenner Pass, the link between north and south, are what give this region its value.

This leads to the question of what we have to offer visitors: a superb climate, our individuality, our labour and our land. The Italian influence has made us different from the Germans north of the Brenner and has given

Many visitors have become regulars, returning year after year, despite the increasing traffic chaos and rising prices. It is no wonder that the tourism industry has expanded so rapidly.

But the South Tyroleans must re-examine their concept of "home" if they want to continue to live from tourism. "Home" does not mean something one can do what one likes with, exploit to suit one's own purposes. South Tyrol needs to be cared for with

Above, the top of the Stilfser Joch Pass looks more like a county fair than a nature preserve. **Right**, a quick snapshot of the Ortler.

environmental protection. It is our duty to gain a better understanding of nature as well as of our cultural heritage. There is a need for self-restraint as well as self-assertion. South Tyrol is not yet as sterile, as built up, as dehumanised as many other resort areas but there needs to be fewer hotels, fewer roads, fewer lifts. Not only for our sake but also for the sake of the guests. "South Tyrol must remain South Tyrol" is the cry I hear daily.

Perhaps the idea that South Tyrol can be rescued from a sad fate is only wishful thinking. It frequently seems that the destruction has gone so far that it cannot be halted. Many old villages have been transformed into bourgeois housing developments. The subsidised chemical industry has wiped out the insects on which many birds used to live. And construction of retaining walls for the mountain streams has become necessary to counter the effects of erosion resulting from the many new roads cut like giant scars through the landscape.

Many people, from poets to public relations experts, have extolled the virtues of South Tyrol. Tourists came to walk alongside the gushing brooks, to enjoy the quaint architecture and hear the song of the lark. But no amount of lovely words could prevent the wounding of the landscape. And the damage is not always obvious to the eye. In many cases, the countryside has become not less beautiful but less healthy.

The only way that the needs of both groups, the tourists and the native population, can ever be accommodated is for the tourism industry and the conservation groups to communicate with each other. At the moment, the concept referred to as "gentle tourism" remains merely a popular phrase in the tourism brochures. Meanwhile, imaginative schemes to build sympathetic architecture and curb excessive city development lie collecting dust in the planning offices, and government subsidies continue to encourage intensified land use rather than ecologically sound agriculture.

South Tyrol's most important asset, its beauty, may soon be depleted. Parts of South Tyrol enjoy a Mediterranean climate, and katabatic winds and fertile soil are found throughout the land. But where are the solar-energy houses, the windmills for electricity and the organic gardens that should be exploiting such advantages? And how many miles of cycle paths are there? In the future, the much vaunted promises of serenity, clean air and good wine may prove empty. The water in the River Etsch reeks, smog is on the increase in the Bozen and Meran basins. Cable cars continue to be subsidised rather than taken out of use and in many people's eyes the "organic farmer" is merely a figure of derision.

The realisation that when we injure the earth, we injure ourselves led to my decision to remain in South Tyrol. To be a South Tyrolean today is a responsibility as well as a privilege. But words alone cannot help, so I have taken constructive action. Rather than investing my money in a hotel, I have pur-

chased a farm, high on the mountainside between the Schnals Valley and Vinschgau. We farm the land ourselves, are self-sufficient and sell the surplus in the nearby restaurant "Schlosswirt Juval" which is open six months of the year.

It is not only bands of hikers who pass by the farm. Foxes and other wildlife also come visiting. Our grapes, free of pesticides, are stolen by the birds, and a pair of eagles have swooped down from Juval and made off with some of our chickens. It is back to nature in the true sense of the phrase. This is how life used to be all over South Tyrol. It is a paradise on earth.

With its mountainous terrain and harsh climate, the alpine region did not provide optimum conditions for early human settlement. Indeed, the earliest signs of human habitation in the high valleys date from only the last Ice Age (120,000–15,000 BC).

It wasn't until the end of this era, the late Palaeolithic Age, that homo sapiens first appeared in South Tyrol. Evidence of man's presence here from 15,000 BC onwards has been provided by the stone tools, mostly cleavers and hand-axes, left behind by groups of hunters on the Seiser Alm, in Naturns and the Jochtal above Vals in the Puster Valley. The density of human settlement began to increase with the arrival of the Mesolithic Age (from 8,000 BC), especially in the Dolomite area, notably at altitudes between 1,800 and 2,300 metres. All these settlements have one thing in common: they were situated on saddles and passes lying well above the level of the treeline.

These natural passes were strategically important for bands of hunters making their way between the lower-lying terrain of the valleys and the high mountain pastures. They established their hunting camps and living quarters beneath large stone boulders and under cliffs.

The Neolithic Age began in the 5th millennium BC and heralded a radical change in man's living patterns. He began to cultivate the soil and practise agriculture. Animals were also domesticated at this time; first dogs, then sheep and goats, followed by cattle, pigs and donkeys.

As man settled down, the itinerant existence of the hunters and gatherers gradually declined and was replaced by a stationary lifestyle. Permanent farmsteads were built and village communities began to emerge. More complex social structures consequently developed. The earliest grave sites date from this period; stone graves, with crouched burial, from approximately 3000 BC, have been discovered in various locations between Verona and the northern flanks of the South Tyrol.

Copper in the Tyrol: From 3000 BC the alpine region witnessed the development of metals; first copper, then bronze and from 800 BC iron. The presence of copper ore in various places in the Tyrol, particularly in the lower Inn Valley, led to increasing communication with neighbouring prehistoric cultures, as displayed by the megalith culture in the Meran Basin with its typical obelisks of stone and dolmen tombs. Some of the columns discovered here are even decorated with figures.

The first European Iron Age (800–400 BC) is named after the town of Hallstadt in Upper Austria, where burial mounds attest to the preference for this material. Finds of Iron Age settlements to the north and south of the Brenner Pass indicate that for the first time a united "cultural province" spanned the main European watershed. There is also evidence that the Tyrolean alpine passes came to be used for long distance trade; it was via these passes that products of the flourishing Greek and Etruscan civilisations arrived in northern Europe.

In the 5th century BC this culture was superseded by an independent culture group whose sphere of influence was limited to the old Tyrolean area. It was named the Fritzens-San Zeno culture after the most important sites of San Zeno in Trentino and Fritzens in the Inn Valley. Archaeologists assume, on the basis of pottery found at these sites as well as the particular style of construction, that the people who lived here were members of a group known as Rhaeti. This is the name which the authors of antiquity (Strabo, Horace, Paterculus, Dio Cassius, for example) assigned to residents of the Alps, although it is questionable as to whether this population was actually one uniform ethnic group. It is now believed that they belonged to the various tribes forced into the remote alpine valleys by the Celts as they pushed down from the north or by the Etruscans and Romans expanding from the south.

The Rhaeti built extensive fortresses to which they could escape in times of trouble. These were embankments situated on ex-

Preceding pages: a famous Gothic fresco in Castle Runkelstein, near Bozen, depicting a scene of daily life. Left, a stone stool, evidence of early settlement..

posed and relatively inaccessible mountain summits. It is probable that they also constructed their religious sites on such summits. One such site is found on the Schlern Plateau where traces of animals burned in sacrifice and shards of earthenware containers have been discovered. The theory that the Rhaeti were united by a common culture is supported by evidence of common written characters. Known as the "Bozen Alphabet", the characters had Etruscan origins. They were used in texts employed for consecration purposes, for names and possibly for exorcism formulas.

Roman times: After the Germanic Cimbri invaded upper Italy, where they remained

deflected the attack. He then stationed six legions along the river to control the frontier. In light of the Germanic attack, the Romans decided that the secure but circuitous route to the Rhine via Gaul must be supplemented by a shorter more direct one.

Thus in the winter of 16–15 BC extensive preparations were made in upper Italy. A new legion was created (the XXI) under the command of Drusus, the young stepson of Caesar Augustus. His adviser was General Nerva, a soldier experienced in mountain campaigns, and by the following spring the Etsch Valley, as far as Meran, had been conquered. During the summer of that year Drusus pushed northwards with his troops

until being defeated in 101 BC by Vercelli, the Romans decided that it would be expedient, for reasons of security, to absorb the southern alpine regions into their sphere of power. Thus, in the last century before Christ, the area which is today Trentino came under Roman control. According to some historians, this region extended as far as the Bozen valley basin and included the Etsch Valley extending to the site of present-day Meran. The northern regions remained, for the time being, outside Roman control.

In the year 16 BC, however, Germanic tribes crossed the River Rhine and invaded Gaul. Caesar Augustus, rushing to the scene,

through the Etsch Valley; at the same time, his brother Tiberius set about consolidating the Roman presence on the northern slopes of the Alps.

Conquest of the Etsch Valley: The tribes of the region (recorded as the Venosti, Isarci, Breoni and Genauni) today known as South Tyrol were caught in the middle. They rebelled bravely, fighting a bitter but hopeless battle. The numerous ruins of settlements and burned fortresses are testimony to the brutal methods employed by the Roman soldiers. All survivors were taken as slaves or forced into military service. A small number of people, the very minimum necessary to cultivate the land, were left in the region as slaves of the occupying Roman forces. In the framework of this new strategic orientation, the Regnum Noricum with its Puster Valley, an ally of Rome for the past century, came under direct Roman sovereignty. Thus the region which would later become Tyrol was now Roman.

Under Emperor Claudius (AD 41–54), the region was placed under control of the civilian administration. The main portion became part of the province of Raetia with its capital of Augusta Vindelicorum (Augsburg); the eastern region, where the Puster Valley was, became a part of the province of Noricum; the south – the Etsch Valley start-

of power. In any event, it was important to have good routes and roads, and in this department the Romans were masters of the trade. In the year AD 46, in the reign of Emperor Claudius, the connecting route from Ostiglia on the Po River to Augsburg and continuing on to the Danube was completed. This route, named Via Claudia Augusta, led through Verona, Trent, Pons Drusi (a military post on shaky ground in the Bozen valley basin), Maia (Mais near Meran), through Vinschgau, across the Reschen Pass and into the Inn Valley. From there it continued over the Fern Pass to the north side of the Alps. A second route across the Alps was also built during Claudius's reign. This be-

ing in Meran and the Eisack Valley south of Klausen – was placed under the administration of the tenth region (Regio X – Venetia et Istria) of Italy.

Tyrol as a transit land: The main function of the mountainous regions during the age of antiquity was as a transit region for goods travelling from north to south and vice-versa, as well as for the military. The latter needed the region as a security buffer to ensure the rulers' sovereignty as well as their position

Left, the remains of a prehistoric settlement in Castelfelder above the Etsch. **Above**, the Roman milestone in the Puster Valley.

gan near today's Venice, passed through Feltre, Belluno and Pieve di Cadore to the Sextner Kreuzberg Pass and from there on to the Puster Valley. From here, the route led through Sebatum (St Lorenzen near Bruneck), Vipitenum (Sterzing) and across the Brenner Pass to Veldidena (Wilten near Innsbruck) and on through Zirl and Scharnitz. The third route across the Alps, the most important one today, was built in the 2nd or 3rd century. It runs from Bozen across the Brenner Pass to Innsbruck and on to Rosenheim.

Colonisation by veterans: For Rome, this region was of minor importance as a land to be settled. Veterans were sent mainly to the southern portion. This explains the numerous town names ending in -*an* or -*um*: Barbian as the estate of a Barbio, Prissian as that of a Priscius, Vöran of a Varius, Eppan/Appianum of an Appius. Tridentum/Trent and Aguntum/Lienz in East Tyrol were larger settlements and were the only two towns which were granted city status by Rome.

Although the region was probably only sparsely populated, there have been many notable Roman finds: jewellery, luxury items, common wares, milestones and small sculptures, to name a few.

One of the longest lasting effects of the Roman occupation was the Romanisation of

the Rhaeti population. This was carried out partially through the deportation of the male population and partially through adaptation by the native population. Over the course of centuries, an amalgamated language developed, the forerunner of today's Rhaeto-Romanic which is still spoken in Grisons in Switzerland, in the Dolomite valleys of Gröden, Abtei and Fassa as well as in Friaul.

Another inheritance from the Roman period, and one which guaranteed cultural and spiritual continuity, was Christianity. It is difficult to say exactly when Christianity first spread to this region, but by the year 380 Trent was already a bishop's see, as was

Aguntum by about 410. Unfortunately, in Säben, the clifftop site of a former bishop's see above Klausen, all traces which might throw light on the date of its founding have been erased, but it has been proved that an early Christian basilica existed on this site in the 4th or 5th century. Its first documented bishop was St Ingenuin around 590. Why Säben became a bishop's see, and from where the bishop fled, are puzzles which have never been solved. It is believed that he may have come from a town in the valley, perhaps Brixen or Sterzing, which had simply become too dangerous.

Pax Romana: After the conquest by the Romans, the people of the alpine regions enjoyed a long period of relative peace, disrupted only occasionally by troops marching through the land. These troops were either on their way toward the vulnerable northern frontier or were hastily heading south from points north during the periodic disputes about succession to the imperial throne.

In the course of the 4th century, however, it became increasingly difficult for the imperial army to repel the onslaught of the Germanic tribes. Again and again these tribes attacked the northern provinces along the Rhine and the Danube, and the central alpine area developed into a region of retreat for the Romanised population which was living north of the Alps.

Left to its own devices, the alpine region was also difficult to retain as a part of the empire. With increasing regularity, tribes marched through the alpine valleys on their way south, wreaking devastation as they went. In the year 406 or 407 the entire Puster Valley was laid waste. Numerous villages, including Sebatum, became severely depopulated. It was not until the Ostrogoth king Theodoric the Great (455–526) came to power that peace returned to the region. Bu it was not to last. In 536–537, Theodoric's successor, King Vitigis, was forced to relinquish parts of the Rhaetian province to the Franks. By about 550, the Frankish domain extended as far as Aguntum. And thus, the sovereignty of the Imperium Romanum, a sovereignty which had lasted for over 500 years, finally came to an end.

Above, a knight's tombstone in the cloisters of Brixen. **Right**, in the parish church of Tramin: Bishop Virgilius.

MADINA

VIRGILLIVS

MAGO

Four tribes, each forced to leave their native regions during the great migrations, now converged in the central alpine region: the Lombards in the south, the Baiuvari (Bavarians) in the north, the Franks in the west and the alpine Slavs in the east.

The Early Middle Ages (600–1000): In 568 the Lombards began establishing a series of duchies in Italy. The most northern of these, Trent, extended as far as Meran. The Slavs, fleeing from the marauding Avars of the Hungarian plains, made their way to the Puster Valley in about 600. Here, however, they soon encountered the relatively young tribe of the Baiuvari which had migrated across the Alps around the middle of the 6th century. Duke Tassilo was victorious over the Slavs in 590, but his son Garibald was defeated in 610 near Aguntum. The task of the Lombard Count of Trent was to secure the northern borders of the Lombard kingdom against the Franks. Several battles were fought before a truce was agreed in 591. This acknowledged the existing boundaries of both parties, including the border near Meran. The Vinschgau thereby came under the sovereignty of the Franks, originating from the Rhaetian bishop's see in Chur. In religious matters, this remained in effect until 1806.

Bavarian rulers: Very little information is recorded about the 7th and 8th centuries. The Bavarians extended their territorial control further and further south. The Lombard scribe Paulus Diaconus recorded a Bavarian count in Bozen as early as 680. Their expansion paved the way for the alignment of the southern alpine regions with those to the north. The Agilofing line of the Bavarian dynasty increased its influence by founding several monasteries. One of the most important was that of Innichen (769), whose monks practised missionary work among the Slavs.

Ethnically, the region remained Latin; only the very upper classes of society were of the ruling Bavarian nobility. The job of this

nobility was to "administer" the country for their dukes. South of the Alps, the land was brought under control more through military action than by mass immigration. However, it can be assumed that the native population was suppressed to a point of finally becoming serfs. The medieval feudal system was about to be born. For the Latins in the region, it was probably more attractive to adopt – farm by farm, village by village, valley by valley – the language of their rulers. This was a long drawn-out process which lasted al-

most 1,000 years (until the 16th–17th century). The Rhaeto-Romanic language survived only in a few remote regions (Gröden, Abtei, Fassa, Buchenstein and Ampezzo).

Under the rule of Charlemagne (768–814), political changes swept through the region of Tyrol. After bringing the Kingdom of Lombardy under his control in 774, Charlemagne forced the Bavarian Agilofings to relinquish their power in 788. For the first time since the fall of Rome, the region was once again united under one ruler, despite the fact that it was divided among separate duchies – Lombardy, Bavaria and Rhaetian Chur (in present-day Switzerland).

Preceding pages: a detail from the vaults of the cloisters in Brixen. Left, Castle Haderburg guards the entrance through the Salurn Defile. Right, gravestone of the lyricist Oswald von Wolkenstein in Brixen.

The future cultural and political development of the region was significantly influenced by the detachment of the bishopric of Säben (Brixen) from the metropolitan association of Aquileia in 798 and its integration into the Bavarian religious province, whose seat was in Salzburg. The alignment with the north was thereby consolidated.

After the death of Charlemagne, the empire was divided among his heirs. The Bozen Lowlands (Unterland) and the Überetsch region were placed under the Duchy of Trent (part of Italy), and the rest of what was later known as Tyrol came under the Bavarian Duchy (part of the East Frankish Kingdom, later to become the German Empire). Since

here, especially vineyards. Thus the links between the regions north of the Alps and those to the south became closer.

The High Middle Ages (1054–1300): The importance of the transit routes of the central alpine region increased with the advent of the Ottonian dynasty. In a revival of Carolingian tradition, Otto I, "the Great" (936–973), re-established imperial rule in Italy, introducing the so-called "imperial processions" in 961. This tradition lasted almost 600 years, ending with the march of Emperor Charles V across the Alps on his way north in the year 1551. Of the 144 treks across the Alps to Italy, 66 were over the Brenner route.

Italy was viewed as a rival power by the East Franks, their interest was in uncontested control of the alpine routes. This was the probable reason behind their decision to strengthen the position of the Säben bishops. In 901, the bishopric was granted the estate of Prichsna (today's Brixen) by Ludwig the Child and in 970 the bishop's see was moved there. From this vantage point, the bishops could begin establishing territorial rule.

The region was divided into fiefs, the history of which is poorly documented. The rulers, members of the Bavarian aristocracy, also had properties in Bavaria. Likewise, many religious institutions owned property

One of the most important political strategies of the Ottonians was to invest religious leaders with more and more secular power. The fact that these leaders were unmarried meant that they had no heirs and so, unlike the head of a dynasty, they had less urge to expand their sphere of influence. And because they had no children, they could not engineer propitious marriages that would extend their territory.

In the year 1004, the Bishop of Trent was invested with a fief. It encompassed today's province of Trentino, the Bozen Unterland and Überetsch as well as the Etsch Valley to Meran. In 1027, the Salian Holy Roman

Emperor Conrad II extended it to Vinschgau and the county of Bozen. Likewise, in 1027, the bishop of Brixen was invested with a fief which included the Eisack Valley to Klausen, the Inn Valley to Arlberg and later (1091) the Puster Valley. Now that these regions were no longer under the control of the imperial marches of Verona and Bavaria, they were able to pursue an independent development.

However, in accordance with ecclesiastical law, the bishops were prohibited from administering their territories themselves. They were thus required to enlist the services of the aristocracy, who served as overseers. This was the basis for the rapid rise of various powerful aristocratic families who,

the Eppan counts out of the county of Bozen, and in 1220 they replaced the Andechs as overseers for the Brixen bishop. Ten years later the Andechs returned to power, but in 1248 the line was extinguished and the counts of Tyrol inherited the right to administer the Brixen properties. With this, Albert III of Tyrol became the most powerful man within the bishoprics of Brixen and Trent. In 1253, however, he died without any male heir and his properties passed to Meinhard II of Görz, who was married to Adelheid, Albert's youngest daughter.

Tyrol becomes a country: Meinhard II continued on a course of territorial expansion right up until his death in 1258. But it was his

through bloody battles and lengthy disputes, relieved the bishops of their property and possessions piece by piece. The counts of Eppan served as overseers for the bishops of Trent, and the counts of Andechs served the bishops of Brixen.

Another aristocratic line emerged at this time: the counts of Tyrol, in 1140. They got their name from their family castle just north of Meran, Castle Tyrol. In 1170, they pushed

Left, the Brixen cloisters contain some of the most magnificent frescoes in all of South Tyrol. **Above**, filigrane carving and winged altars are superb specimens of South Tyrolean sacred art.

son, Meinhard III (1258–95), who founded the state of Tyrol. He staunchly upheld the expansionist policies of his father, usurping control over the city of Bozen in 1277 and acquiring many of the properties of the Trent and Brixen bishops. This led to his excommunication for many years, a punishment he tried to offset by founding a Cistercian monastery in the Upper Inn Valley.

Meinhard was astute in politics. In 1259, he married Elizabeth of Wittelsbach, the widow of the last Staufen king, Conrad IV, who had died in 1254. In 1276 he allied himself with the first Habsburg king, Rudolf, in his battle against Otakar, king of Bohemia.

He also led his country out of the last bonds of allegiance with Bavaria and Görz, although not without relinquishing the Puster Valley to his brother Albert of Görz in 1271.

Under Meinhard, the region prospered, mainly thanks to its flourishing trade and mining industry. The currency of Meran also prospered; the coin known as the *Kreuzer* (used widely until 1871) was first minted during this time. Administration and law were uniformly coded, in accordance with Meinhard's main aim of preventing the existence of a strong aristocracy which could hinder his plans of expansion. In order to achieve this goal, he strengthened the rights of the lower classes by releasing a large

try jointly. But, miserably inept, they depleted the country's resources. Henry governed alone from 1310 to 1335, during which time the sovereign's power declined considerably and the aristocracy once again gained the upper hand. In order to obtain money, Henry was forced to mortgage entire estates. In 1330, he married his 12-year-old daughter Margarethe to the Bohemian prince John-Henry of Luxembourg.

After the death of Henry of Tyrol, Emperor Ludwig (the Bavarian) arranged for the division of Tyrol between Austria and Bavaria. Resistance by the 17-year-old Margarethe and the native aristocracy was supported by her husband's Luxembourg

number of peasants from serfdom. He instituted a sort of hereditary tenure, making the peasants *de facto* owners of their farms. Other landowners, worried that their peasants would stage uprisings, were forced to follow suit. Thus it came to pass that in the 14th century the feudal system in Tyrol (with the exception of a few of the more remote regions) came to an end.

The designation "land Tyrol" also became more and more common, replacing the earlier designation "land on the Etsch and in the mountains".

After Meinhard's death, his sons, Otto, Ludwig and Henry, administered the coun-

dynasty. However, fearing that these outsiders were gaining too much influence in the struggle, she decided to rid herself of her husband. Returning from a hunting expedition in November 1341, he found himself locked out of Castle Tyrol, whereupon he was forced to return to Bohemia in disgrace.

By January of 1342 Margarethe had taken a new husband, Ludwig of Brandenburg, son of Emperor Ludwig. In order to gain acceptance in Tyrol, Ludwig and his father were forced to issue a "Great Decree of Freedom" in which they promised to protect the rights, laid down by Meinhard, for all residents of Tyrol – "the nobility and the commoners, rich and poor" – from the the cities to the villages and hamlets.

A land excommunicated: The church did not recognise Margarethe's second marriage and excommunicated the entire country of Tyrol, a state of affairs which lasted until 1359. As fate would have it, it was during these years that Tyrol experienced a series of disasters – plagues of locusts, a severe earthquake in 1348 and a plague epidemic in 1348–49. These catastrophes were interpreted as manifestations of God's wrath for the actions of Margarethe and Ludwig.

Nevertheless, Ludwig was an efficient ruler. He built new trade routes and instituted measures to lift the country out of the deep

inheritance. Rudolf IV of the Austrian Habsburgs also expressed an interest in the country and, travelling through deep snow across the alpine passes, he hurriedly made his way to Tyrol where, on 26 January 1363, he was granted sovereignty over the land. He was forced to take an oath guaranteeing that the existing rights of the Tyroleans would be preserved, that he would ensure the support of the Brixen bishop and convince the Bavarian Wittelsbachs to relinquish all claims to the land. The latter was not accomplished until 1369, the year in which Margarethe Maultasch died.

Tyrol was now Austrian and, with the exception of the southern half of the land,

economic crisis which came in the wake of the plague. At Ludwig's death, his son Meinhard II was only 17 years old. He had married a Habsburg at the age of 15, but had never developed the stature of a ruler, and in January of 1363, barely 19 years old, he died.

Margarethe resumed the regency. She came under great pressure from the aristocracy, who demanded more and more privileges, and from Bavaria which was calling for its

Left, South Tyrol - Land of Castles. <u>Above</u>, the minstrel Walther von der Vogelweide on Walther Square in Bozen (left). Crucifixion group from the church in Innichen (right).

remains so to this day. For the Habsburg dynasty, it served as a valuable bridge for its expansionist campaigns in Alsace and Breisgau and as a base from which it could suppress the Swiss movement for independence. For Tyrol, the new status meant a shift in the focal point from the Etsch Valley (Meran) to the Inn Valley (Innsbruck).

Although nominally Meran remained the capital until 1848, the centre of power was actually in Innsbruck. This was due to its position on the main transportation artery as well as to the fact that from the late 14th century a line of the Habsburg dynasty took up residence in the city.

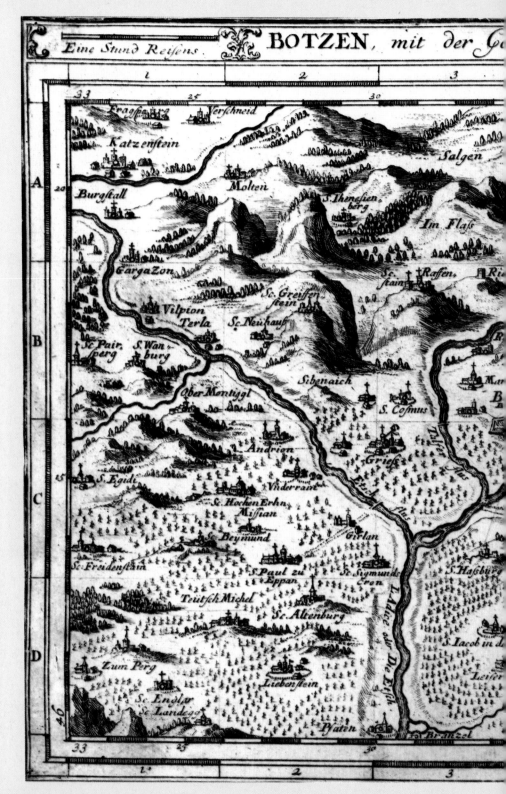

Fragss   Verschneid
Katzenstein
Burgstall   Molten   S. Ihenesien berg   Salgen   Im Flass
GargaZon
S. Greissen stein   Sc. stain   Raffen   Ri
Vilpion   Sc. Neuhaus   R
Terla
S. Pair sperg   S. Wan burg   Sibenaich   Mar   B
Ober Montiggl   S. Cosmus
Andrion   Griess   Etsch Flus   Thal er Flus
S. Egidi   Viderrant
Sc. Hochen Erhn   Missian
Sc. Beymund   Girlan   S. Hassburg
Sc. Freidenstain   S. Paul zu   St. Sigmunds   L Adice oder Die Etsch
Eppan   Cron   S. Iacob in d.
Teutsch Michel   Sc. Altenburg   Leiser
Zum Perg   Liebenstein
Sc. Englar   Prantzol
Sc. Landegg   Pfaten

auf 2 Stunden. Eine Gemeine Teutsche Meil.

Cam Pidell

carnthal

S. Niclas in Assing

Reineg

Colmann
Saubach

Gericht Ritten

Mittelberg
Sissan

S. Iohannes

Wangen

Lengenstein

Oberstein
zum Teütsch

Aichach

S. Peter

Stein

Anrlatt

Langsmos

Im Leitach

unkhlstein

Preibach

Sc. Carneid

Im Leitach

Feigenburg

Fluss

Bissackh

Sch. Campen

Carlautt

Steinegg

S. Vigili

S. Martin

Petersperg

Teutschnosen

Prandten Thal

Weisenstein

ELISABETH

One of the more outstanding figures of the Habsburg family was Frederick IV (1406–39), otherwise known as "Frederick with the Empty Pockets". He was at odds with Emperor Sigismund in matters of foreign policy and coveted the crown for himself. At the Council of Constance, in 1415, open conflict broke out between the two men and Sigismund banished Frederick from the empire, forcing him to flee to Tyrol. There the burghers and peasants offered him their support and with their help he soon regained his former power. It was during this phase that he earned his nickname.

However, he did not endear himself to Tyrol's nobility. They rejected Frederick's policy of centralisation, viewing it as progressive encroachment upon their own powers and privileges. The burghers and peasants, on the other hand, preferred a single powerful sovereign to numerous battling aristocratic families and readily aligned themselves with Frederick.

During his reign, the people's representatives met increasingly often, serving as an advisory body to the sovereign. Frederick, however, ensured that the cities and towns, which served as a counterweight to the aristocracy, were also represented. From 1420 onwards, times were more peaceful and it was a period of economic prosperity, based on increased mining of silver and copper. Innsbruck became the official residence of the sovereign as well as the administrative centre of Tyrol. When Frederick died in 1439, he left a country in good order and a treasury of filled coffers.

Frederick's son, Sigmund the Wealthy (1439–90), first arrived in Tyrol in 1446 at the age of 19. From the start, his court was known for its luxury and splendour. Parties, hunting expeditions and magnificent buildings (Sigmundsburg, Sigmundslust, Sigmundsfreud, Sigmundsegg as well as Tyrol's largest fortress – Castle Sigmundskron near Bozen) were all built during his reign. He kept a vast court and had numerous

Preceding pages: a17th-century map of Bozen and environs. Left, statue of Empress Elisabeth in Meran. Right, the Tyrolean coat of arms.

favourite ladies. It is said that he had more illegitimate children than weeks in a year – but, alas, no legitimate heirs.

Political conflicts broke out in 1450 between Sigmund and the philosopher Nicholas Cusanus, bishop of Brixen. Cusanus was also a cardinal and a reformer. The sovereign's court was the last pocket of the fabulous luxury that had characterised European society in the Middle Ages, a pomp financed by mining, an industry then in its prime. In Schwaz, around 55,000 lbs (120,000 kg) of

silver were mined from 1480 to 1490 and, by 1492, 4,000 people were employed in the industry. But although this generated much wealth in the country, it also led to higher prices, especially for food. Meanwhile Sigmund, in order to finance his excesses at court, was forced to lease more and more of the mines to Germans from the north. They transferred the profits out of the country, and all that was left for Tyrol was the rising cost of living.

But the income from leasing the mines also proved inadequate. An appeal was made to the ruling Bavarian Wittelsbach dynasty for financial aid, a request which they eagerly fulfilled, thereby cementing their influence in Tyrol. Sigmund was even prepared to sign over his country to Bavaria upon his death. But now the representative council intervened, forcing the retreat of the "evil advisers". In the end Sigmund was removed from power by his cousin Emperor Frederick II and his son, the future Emperor Maximilian I, though he was astute enough to secure a guarantee of income and privileges until his death in 1496.

Restless times: Maximilian I, termed by contemporary sources as the "last knight", now became the sovereign of Tyrol and, in 1493, the German Emperor. Thanks to his father's penchant for ruinous wars, providing finances for his reforms as well as his numerous military campaigns.

Tyrol was involved in several of these campaigns. The year 1499 marks one of the bloodiest defeats in Tyrol's history. Over 4,000 men died in the Battle of Calven fought against the Grisons troops in upper Vinschgau. This was followed by an eight-year war with Venice, resulting in important territorial gains in Trentino in 1516. Tyrol's newly drawn southern boundaries remained uncontested for the next 400 years.

Further territorial expansions included the addition of the Puster Valley in 1500, when the line of Görz counts expired, and that of Kufstein and the surrounding area in the year

Maximilian came to the throne virtually bankrupt and he embarked on an energetic policy of expansion to try and rectify the matter. Tyrol served as an important base for his territorial expansion to the west – he had acquired Burgundy by his youthful and highly lucrative marriage to Mary of Burgundy – and to the south. Mary died at an early age in a riding accident and Maximilian then married Bianca Maria Sforza, daughter of the Duke of Milan, who, though regarded as an arriviste, was also wealthy. He thus secured this duchy for himself. At the same time, the Tyrolean mines (silver, copper and salt) were reaching their optimum level of production, 1503. Tyrol expanded to a size which was, with the exception of minor additions at a later date, to be its largest.

However, to meet the financial demands of Maximilian's imperial politics this small but wealthy country was ruthlessly plundered by German trading concerns. Discontent aimed specifically against Maximilian escalated. In 1518 the city of Innsbruck even refused to allow the old and failing emperor to enter its walls; the authorities insisted that he must first pay the debts from his last stay there. Maximilian was thus forced to continue to Wels in Upper Austria, where he died in 1519.

The Renaissance: In the following two years, during which Tyrol was a country without a ruler, all of the problems which had attended Tyrol's transition from the Middle Ages into modern times came to a head. The country was in the midst of a deep financial crisis. Inflation – fuelled by the various mining interests – led to sharp increases in food prices. Many landowners experienced financial difficulties and consequently demanded increased payments from the peasants. The peasants were concerned by the rulers' attempts to replace the old medieval common law with a new codified one aimed at increasing control from above. Concurrently, a widespread mistrust of Church and State

same time, he started planning his revenge.

He met his match in the peasant commander Michael Gaismair (*ca* 1490–1532) from Sterzing. Gaismair had led the rebels from the Brixen bishopric and was considered the leader of the revolution. He was treacherously lured, with a promise of safe conduct, to Innsbruck where he was imprisoned. Escaping to Switzerland, he began planning new revolts in the winter of 1525–26. This time Ferdinand was prepared for the onslaught and made no secret of his intention to quash even the slightest hint of rebellion with whatever means necessary. The peasant leader and his followers were forced to flee to Venice where they successfully aided the

was developing. The common man was becoming increasingly unwilling to accept the authority of these two institutions.

When the brother of Emperor Charles V, the future Emperor Ferdinand I, took over the regency in the year 1521, he continued along the path of reform. But the population was seething and in 1525 the Peasants' War erupted. Ferdinand, surprised and alarmed by the level of discontent, quickly accepted almost all of the demands presented by the peasants in the "Meran Articles". But, at the

Left, fresco from the church in Dorf Tyrol. **Above**, Nativity scene fresco in Hocheppan.

Venetian Republic in its war against the Habsburg troops. When Gaismair thereafter requested Venetian support for a repeated attack on Tyrol, however, it was to no avail. Bitterly disappointed by the lack of support, he resigned himelf to failure. He moved on to settle in Padua, where he was murdered on 15 April 1532 by Emperor Ferdinand's men.

Religion as revolt: Elements discouraged by the failure of the revolts now turned their efforts toward seeking freedom of religion. The movement known as the Anabaptists, believers in baptism of adults rather than children, gained more and more support. In the Tyrol, the movement's spiritual leader was Jacob Huter from Moos near Bruneck and the group came to be referred to as the "Huterish Brothers". Huter was executed in Innsbruck in 1536.

This was a radical movement, but one which was completely non-violent. It totally rejected all Church hierarchy and preached a strict policy of communal property. It was for these reasons that the movement was bloodily persecuted by both Church and State. About 600 members of the Anabaptists died for their cause, and most of the others emigrated to Moravia, where they were initially tolerated. In the 17th century, however, the Counter-Reformation spread to Moravia and the remaining Anabaptists were

ginning was marked by the Council of Trent (1545–63).

The "Holy Land of Tyrol": After the defeat of the Hungarians at the hands of the Turks in the Battle of Mohacs and the death of their king, Ludwig II, Ferdinand I inherited the Bohemian and Hungarian thrones. The focal point of the empire thus shifted once again to the east, and the main preoccupation over the next two centuries was the repulsion of the invading Turks.

The Italian and Burgundian territories passed into the hands of the Spanish line of the Habsburg dynasty and the role of Tyrol as a link between the various parts of the empire in the east, west and south became a

forced to move to the Ukraine. When military conscription was introduced in 1874, they emigrated to Canada and the USA. Settlements of Anabaptists still exist in North America, still following their beliefs and still preserving their dialect (Tyrolean with Carinthian influence).

Classic Protestantism, on the other hand, met with virtually no sympathy among the people of Tyrol. Most of the few existing Protestants were from northern Germany who were only working in Tyrol. They never found a broad basis of support. What did, however, take firm root in Tyrol was the Counter-Reformation, an epoch whose be-

minor one. Tyrol was now on the lee side of the political storms stirring around Europe.

After the death of Ferdinand I in 1564, several minor lines of the Habsburg dynasty took up residence in Tyrol. The first of these was Ferdinand II (1564–95), known for his passion for collecting and his marriage to the commoner Philippine Welser, a beautiful and wealthy woman, but nevertheless one below his station. In the political arena, Ferdinand's main interest was in establishing the Counter-Reformation.

Catechistic control: The Counter-Reformation in Tyrol was pursued particularly zealously. All employees of the Church and State were required to report any people considered to be "religiously suspect" and to ensure that regulations pertaining to fasting and the correct receiving of the sacrament were folowed. Baptismal registers, confessional papers and confessional registers served as a control. Anyone who refused to confess to Catholicism was forced to leave the country. During the so-called "book visits", hundreds of printed works which were not approved by the Catholic Church were confiscated from people's homes and later burned. This interference by the sovereign in religious matters was an attempt to establish and enforce the government's absolutism.

The religious modernisation – as specified

ices, as well as the processions, served to reinforce pride in the Church. Rosaries and "40 hours of prayer" were diligently followed. Thus the modernisation of the Church, combined with the measures instituted by the worldly rulers, led to Tyrol's transformation during the 17th century to the "Holy Land of Tyrol".

Bozen's Golden Age: The fact that Tyrol now occupied a less than central position also played a major role in this transformation. The important political, military and economic currents were no longer felt in Tyrol. The axis of Europe had changed from a north-south (Mediterranean) orientation to an east-west one. But with the final decline

by the Tridentine doctrine – affected all areas of life. Regular visits by the priests ensured the necessary control. Seminaries to educate "worthy" clerics were established. New religious orders – for example, the Jesuits for the intellectuals and the Capuchins for the common folk – came into existence. The newly authorised catechism ensured a basic religious education for believers, and the magnificent baroque churches and church serv-

Left, Gothic peasant altar in a tiny church above St Peter in the Villnöß Valley. **Above**, the Schnatterpeck altar of Lana, the largest and most beautiful Gothic winged altar in South Tyrol.

of the mining industry, handling the trade to and from Italy remained South Tyrol's most important source of revenue since the agricultural industry, although able to feed the majority of the population, was never sufficient to support the entire economy. This trade reached its peak in 1619 when some 12,000 tons of goods crossed over the Brenner Pass.

The main transfer point for these goods was Bozen which held four trade fairs annually. This period was the city's golden age, and in 1635 a mercantile council was established to take control of trading matters. It was set up by Archduchess Claudia de Medici, daughter of the last duke of Urbino, wife of Leopold of Tyrol (who died an early death) and regent for her young son Ferdinand Karl from 1632 to 1646.

Mercenaries from Tyrol: With the outbreak of the Thirty Years' War (1618–48), trade decreased sharply. Owing to its geographical location, Tyrol suffered no major damage during the war, but great numbers of troops marched across its soil. With them came the plague, whose outbreak in 1630 resulted in a large loss of life. The population recovered relatively quickly, but the war ushered in a period of general stagnation which lasted for over a century. For this reason a large portion of the population be-

sion (1701–14), the first major European war, battles were fought in Germany and in upper Italy. In 1701, imperial troops marched through Tyrol under the command of Prince Eugene of Savoy, destined to become Austria's most famous soldier, who had been victorious against the Turks. Via small remote paths across the mountains, they took the French troops in upper Italy completely by surprise and swiftly defeated them.

In the summer of 1703, the Bavarians, allied with the French, attempted to march into Tyrol. The regular troops of the Austrian imperial army were quickly defeated but the Bavarian campaign was nevertheless crushed by the Tyrolean militia who were able to use

gan to migrate (at least seasonally) in order to find work. They sought employment as masons, marble workers, traders of toys and carved items (Gröden), bird merchants (Vinschgau and Upper Inn Valley), picture and book dealers (Trentino) or rug and blanket salesmen (East Tyrol). Some sought work as mercenaries.

After the Tyrolean line of the Habsburgs died out (1665), the land was administered by a governor appointed by Vienna. Tyrol nevertheless retained its autonomy. The European concert of powers and their battles for hegemony brought Tyrol once again into the limelight. During the Spanish War of Succes-

their intimate knowledge of local geography to great advantage. This was the first successful engagement of the "Tyrolean Defence Force", which had first been codified by decree of Emperor Maximilian. The decree, issued in 1511 and continuously adapted thereafter, granted the Tyroleans the responsibility for defending their own country by means of conscription. Depending on the military threats involved, they were allowed to call up 5,000, 10,000 or 20,000 troops. Correspondingly, they were freed from having to serve in the imperial army, unless, of course, they wanted to volunteer.

Under the last two male Habsburg emperors, Joseph I (1705–11) and Charles VI (1711–40), absolutism once again took root. The rights of the four Tyrolean classes – nobility, clerics, burghers, peasants – became increasingly limited. Eventually the monarch even triumphed over tax concessions. It was now no longer a question as to which taxes must be paid, but how much.

The battle against Enlightenment: Despite the fact that the 18th century was a stormy one for most of Europe, the quiet corner of Tyrol was barely touched by the overwhelming movement toward modernisation, the Age of Enlightenment.

This was in marked contrast to the city of Vienna. Austria had come to the conclusion, as a result of numerous crises which had threatened the state (Austrian War of Succession 1740–48, Seven Years' War 1756–63), that a thorough reform of the government was the only way to avoid a "Polish fate" – the partitioning among expansionist neighbours. These reforms were begun under the reign of Maria Theresa (1740–80) and accelerated under her only son, Joseph II (1780–90). They were more restrained under Emperor Leopold II (1790–92), who favoured a course of more cautious reform, and abruptly abandoned under Emperor Francis II (1792–1835), who was anxious to turn the ship around in the opposite direction.

Reform was particularly enlightened under Emperor Joseph II, who was and a student of radical French philosophy. He abolished the feudal system in 1781, issued the Edict of Toleration for Protestants and adherents of the Orthodox Church in 1782; and proclaimed toleration for Jews in 1783 (until then Jews had had to identify themselves by wearing yellow stripes). Among his other reforms, he prohibited purely contemplative monasteries, reduced the number of the regular clergy by more than half and eliminated papal dispensations for marriage.

That the old circles of power felt threatened by such measures was ignored by Joseph for too long. These circles were so successful in counteracting reform that many of them never gained a foothold. If the implementation of the reforms was difficult at the centre of the empire, it was almost impossible in

Left, this rifle target, dating from 1689, depicts the middle-class summer resort of Ritten. **Right**, view of Castle Tyrol.

peripheral or remote areas. The Church in the "Holy Land of Tyrol" was especially successful in suppressing most of Joseph's reforms. Its policy was simple; it played on the anxieties of the common people. They had traditionally found security in the Church and were worried that it was being undermined. The State was able to offer no new values to replace the old ones.

In order to avoid a popular revolt, Joseph's successor, Leopold II, was immediately forced to repeal military conscription and state control over the education of priests in Tyrol. He was also compelled to establish a parliament to debate the repeal of other reforms implemented by Joseph. Between 22

July and 17 August 1790, the 580 delegates presented about 2,000 complaints, mainly dealing with religious matters but also, to a lesser extent, with judicial and tax issues (for example, the taxation of land owned by the aristocracy). Although Vienna was willing to compromise on some minor issues, it would not concede any ground on issues affecting the government's policy of centralisation. Nevertheless, the main representatives of enlightened absolutism were recalled from Tyrol and replaced by more moderate civil servants who were not particularly strict in their enforcement of the reform laws.

ISABELLÆ MARIÆ, PHILIPPI BORBONII PARMÆ DUCIS F.
IOSEPHUM AUSTRIÆ ARCHIDUCEM SPONSUM
ex Italia Feliciter adeunti,
Collegium Mercatorum ad Bulsanenses Nundinas Confluentium.
Francisco Ferdinando Bayero Rosacensi
Bartholomæo Bortoletto Veronensi   } Consul·
Francisco Todeschio Roboretano
Andrea Olivetto Veronensi   } Consil·
Ioanne Iacobo Ienischio Campidonensi
Melchiore Maria Menzio Bulsanensi
Francisco Iosepho Rosminio Roboretano Cancellariæ Direct·
                    D.   D.   D.
        XIII. Cal· Octobr·   CIƆIƆCCLX.

One of the most critical opponents of the enlightened reform policies was the so-called "Bozen Party". Bozen had historically been the centre of the transit-trade. But in recent years, most of the trade had moved to the Trieste–Graz–Vienna route, thereby circumventing Venice and ensuring that all trade was carried out within the borders of the empire. Additionally, Joseph II had instituted a protectionist customs duty to encourage development of domestic industry. These factors, of course, damaged the transit-trade. Bozen's trade fairs and markets were still well attended but the volume of trade decreased – and this during a period when the overall trade volume in Europe had increased by 200 percent.

The heathen age: The year 1792 was decisive in determining the outcome of the French Revolution. On 20 April, the National Assembly in Paris declared war on Austria, introducing an age of rebellion and the spread of seditious ideas throughout Europe, right up to the Tyrol's doorstep. In 1794, a club of Jacobins was discovered, consisting of 31 students, at the University of Innsbruck. These students, mainly from Trentino, were not, however, considered a serious threat to the established order and were let off with relatively light sentences.

In the spring of 1796, the French, under Napoleon Bonaparte, who was then commander of the French army in Italy, threatened Tyrol's southern border. A state of war was declared and the troops were called out. On 1 June, Tyrol joined in an alliance with the "Most Holy Heart of Jesus", for protection against the Godless revolutionaries. Napoleon called off his attacks on Tyrol and turned instead to conquering the Papal States.

In March 1797, the French moved into Tyrol to protect Napoleon's flank during his Venetian operations. Bloody battles ensued around Brixen before the French moved on to the east. This first war ended in the same year, but the peace did not last. Again and again Tyrol was threatened. One result was that, in 1803, the religious principalities were annexed to various other states in compensation for the territories lost to France. Austria was granted, among other regions, the religious principalities of Brixen and Trent. They were placed under the jurisdiction of Tyrol, resulting in a further expansion of the country. These borders now remained fixed until the year 1918.

The War of the Third Coalition broke out in 1805. Napoleon sealed his victory on 2 December in the Battle of Austerlitz, and Austria was forced to relinquish sovereignty over Tyrol to France's most loyal ally, the newly formed Kingdom of Bavaria. This was mainly a strategic move on France's part to ensure that the shortest route between the two most important zones of deployment, the German plains and the Po plains, remained in the hands of a French ally.

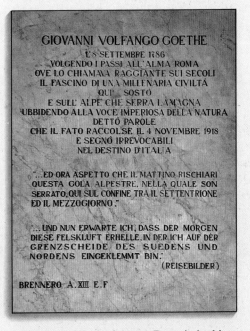

Bavaria and the resistance: Bavaria had instituted major reforms at the turn of the century, becoming one of the most modern states in Germany. It was felt that the newly acquired province should also benefit from the process of modernisation. The Bavarian administrative system, geographically much closer than that in Vienna, implemented its policies step by step. The Church was brought under state control, taxes were doubled and the administrative bodies were consolidated and made directly responsible to Munich, the capital of Bavaria. In 1808, a Constitution was drawn up dissolving the state of Tyrol. The Tyroleans became subjects of the

<u>Left</u>, festive reception of the Princess of Parma in Bozen. <u>Above</u>, memorial plaque for Johann Wolfgang von Goethe at the Brenner Pass.

Bavarian king and were forced to serve in his army. This quickly led to a flurry of local insurrections.

When Austria formed a new coalition against France in 1809, urging the Tyroleans to stage rebellions behind the enemy lines, the Tyroleans jumped at the chance of regaining their former status. The war began in April of 1809 and within three weeks the Tyrolean troops had ousted the detested enemy. In the course of three victorious battles on Mt Isel near Innsbruck, the Tyroleans entirely quashed French hopes of reconquering the region. However, in July of that same year, Napoleon's troops decisively defeated the Austrian army in the battle of

liberal, was closed down. City residents who were thought to have leftist leanings were closely monitored and persecuted. Dances other than those at weddings and church festivals were strictly forbidden, and ladies who attired themselves in the latest "Empire" *decolleté* fashions, exposing too much flesh on the arms and chest, were subjected to a more sober dress code.

But Hofer's victory was not to last. After the signing of the Treaty of Schönbrunn on 20 October, massive numbers of troops began marching toward Tyrol from all four directions. Despite desperate attempts at defence, during the fourth battle at Mt Isel on 1 November the rebellion was bloodily

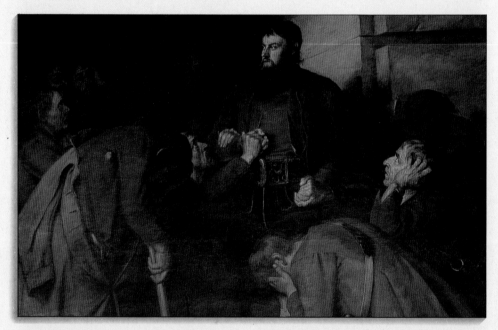

Wagram and the Tyroleans were left to face the enemy alone.

Freedom fighters: The Tyroleans, under the leadership of Andreas Hofer, innkeeper and horse-dealer from the Passeier Valley, placed their trust in God and resolved to carry on their fight for freedom. These rebels met with initial success, and Hofer marched triumphantly into Innsbruck on 15 August 1809 as the victor.

During the following two months, Hofer established a regime which was in direct opposition to the government's policies of enlightenment. Jews were robbed and persecuted, and the university, considered far too

crushed. It had lasted just three months. Andreas Hofer was betrayed and, on 20 February 1810, he was placed before the firing squad in Mantua.

Because Bavaria had not been able to fulfil its task of keeping Tyrol under control and thus guaranteeing a secure route between north and south, Tyrol was now divided into three departments. Trentino and the Bozen Basin (extending approximately to the old Roman boundaries) were granted to the Kingdom of Italy and came to be known as "Dipartimento Alto Adige". The larger portion of Tyrol, the Inn sector, remained a part of Bavaria, while the eastern Puster Valley was annexed to the Illyrian provinces (whose capital was Ljubljana), which the French had obtained from Austria at the Treaty of Schönbrunn.

Now, divided between three states and armies, the Tyroleans were forced to fight in the Russian campaigns (1812) for the preservation of the Napoleonic system, a system which was destined to disintegrate in 1813. In 1813–14, Austria once again took possession of Tyrol militarily; and in 1815 the Congress of Vienna granted Austria political control over the land.

In the grip of Metternich: Under the protection of a ruling dynasty once again, the Tyroleans thought that things would return

Freedom of the press was swept away and political activity was totally prohibited. Secret police were introduced to spy on the population. Tax pressures were increased. The aristocracy was resuscitated but given no power other than that of relaying requests to the emperor (a guileless imbecile firmly in Metternich's pocket). Even the exemption from military service, a privilege for which the Tyroleans had fought valiantly in 1809, was abolished with the establishment of the imperial rifle regiment.

Nevertheless, no revolts took place, due to the fact that both of the major groups responsible for the 1809 insurrection – the clerics and the nobility – had regained most of their

to how they had been in the past. But they were wrong, because in the meantime the authoritarian political leadership of Metternich had transformed Austria into a tightly organised, centralist police state where special privileges for various regions had absolutely no place. This was particularly true in light of the new and important strategic role which Tyrol now played as the link between Austria and its newly acquired territories in upper Italy.

Left, the Tyrolian national folk hero Andreas Hofer. **Above**, fortifications in the Dolomites dating from World War I.

privileges. In 1837 about 400 Protestants from the Ziller Valley were deported by the leaders of the conservative Bozen Party and the Brixen curia.

Tyrol suffered only minor effects from the revolution of 1848. The representatives sent to the various national assemblies (Frankfurt, Vienna) were conservative and saw their main task as the preservation of religious unity within the country and the suppression of the wishes of the liberal Italian-Tyrolean representatives pressing for autonomy. This sowed the seeds of conflict, one which would have a decisive impact on the coming decades. In any event, troops of volunteers were sent to the southern border in order to protect it from any Italian guerrillas who might attempt to attack.

Abolition of the feudal system: The revolution of 1848 brought in its wake one very important change. The levies and aristocratic rights over property were abolished, putting a final end to serfdom throughout Austria and thus throughout Tyrol. Aside from this fact, however, everything else remained unchanged during the Age of Neoabsolutism (1850–61).

This period came to an abrupt end, paving the way for the introduction of the era of parliamentarianism. In Tyrol, too, a parliament was convened in 1861, one in which the

liberal minority and the conservative majority stood in bitter opposition to one another. The liberals were drawn mainly from the cities and were led by Bozen's mayor, Streiter (1861–70). The main support for the conservatives, whose leader was the Brixen prince-bishop Vinzenz Gasser, was drawn from the rural regions.

The most obvious sign that the age of modernism had arrived was the construction of a railway linking Tyrol to the European railway network. In 1858, tracks were completed through the Inn Valley as far as Innsbruck, in 1859, Bozen and Verona were linked to the network, and in 1867 the Bren-

ner railway went into service, establishing a direct connection between Germany and Italy. In 1871, the line Puster Valley–Carinthia–Vienna was opened, making the transportation of goods through the region an important economic factor once again. With this development came the advent of tourism. Europe's population had discovered the alpine and spa resorts.

Politically, the conflicts of these times revolved around three themes: admitting Protestants into the country; State (rather than Church) control over the schools; and marriage as a civil rather than religious institution. The conservative clerics were particularly unwilling to compromise on this last issue, but were unable to gain the upper hand against the majority in the government in Vienna. Austria set a firm course down the path of constitutionalism with the establishment of the constitutional laws of 1867. Bitter battles were fought within the country until 1891 when the almost 30-year long cultural disputes were settled by means of a compromise on the education issue. It appeared to be a victory for Vienna, but in reality the church had succeeded in placing its stamp on the educational system.

Bozen as a German bulwark: The year 1866 was decisive for Tyrol. Not only did Austria leave the German alliance after the defeat at Königgrätz but it also lost its last upper Italian province (Venice). This province had given Tyrol a strategic advantage as it extended into the territory of the young Kingdom of Italy. The nationality disputes with the Italian minority in Tyrol, the Trentinos, became increasingly radical. South Tyrol, and especially Bozen, "the southernmost German city", took on an important role as the German bulwark against "Italian arrogance". Nationalism became an increasingly explosive force within the Austro-Hungarian empire.

A clear expression of the nationality conflict was the erection of two statues. The first was of Walther von der Vogelweide, erected in Bozen in 1889. He was situated facing south as though in warning. As a countermeasure, Trent erected a statue of Dante in 1896 with his hand raised against the north.

Above: memorial plaque for the imperial riflemen who lost their lives in battle. **Right:** view of Bozen around 1800.

When the Austro-Hungarian Empire used the assassination of the Archduke Franz Ferdinand in Sarajevo in June of 1914 as an excuse to attack Serbia, thus sparking World War I, the men of South Tyrol were duly called up. By August of 1914, four imperial rifle regiments, three infantry regiments, two regiments of territorial reserves and an artillery regiment had been despatched to Russia and Serbia where they were almost totally wiped out. The war which Austria had originally dismissed as "walk-over" proved, in

In the autumn of 1918, however, Austria and Germany capitulated to the Allied forces. The Austrian army surrendered in Italy in November, and the centuries-old Austro-Hungarian Empire crumbled into various national states. On 7 November 1918, the Italians reached Bozen and by 11 November they were on top of the Brenner Pass.

The outcome of the war was a bitter blow for the Tyroleans south of the Brenner. From being an integral part of the Habsburg Empire, they had now been relegated to an

fact, to be anything but that.

Very few troops remained in South Tyrol itself. And when the former ally, Italy, came into the war on the side of the Allies in May 1915, the only people available to build a front line of defence along the southern border were those who had not been conscripted. Together with the "German Alpine Corps", they formed the Tyrolean High Mountain Front, known as the "Dolomite Front", which they managed to hold until they were joined by regular military units that autumn. This completely new type of warfare in the high mountains won the respect of the Tyroleans and took on the flavour of a "popular war".

unprotected minority. In return for supporting the Allies, Italy had been guaranteed the region all the way up to the Brenner.

Benito Mussolini usurped power in Italy with the "March on Rome" on 28 October 1922. For the Fascists there was only one state and one nation. Minorities were not tolerated and there was therefore only one way in which to proceed: the forced assimilation of foreign-speaking subjects. From 1923 measures were taken to give the South Tyrol an Italian appearance. Even the name Südtirol was forbidden and replaced by the designation Napoleon had used: Alto Adige. The school system was Italianised and private German lessons forbidden; Italian became the only official language. Signs now had to be written in Italian; all place names, Christian names and numerous surnames were converted into the Italian language.

The limits of Italianisation: While these measures were outwardly successful, there was no way in which the internal unity of the South Tyroleans could be broken. The dictatorship therefore resorted to radically altering the population balance in South Tyrol. With the settlement of large industrial enter-

oppressed South Tyroleans now pinned their hopes. As early as July 1933 the illegal "South Tyrol People's Front" (VKS), modelled on National Socialist principles, was established. Over the years this organisation spread and became the force behind all aspirations of "liberation" through Adolf Hitler.

Hitler, however, had other plans for the South Tyroleans. In order to ensure the support of Mussolini, he guaranteed the inviolability of the Brenner border. On 23 June 1939, the Fascists and the National Social-

prises in the area from the mid-1930s, tens of thousands of Italians poured in. By the beginning of the 1940s, their numbers had swollen to over 100,000 (in 1921 there were 21,000 Italians to 230,000 Germans).

In the meantime another development had begun to preoccupy the ethnic Germans south of the Brenner. With the rise to power of the National Socialists, Hitler's Germany became the country on which many of the

Preceding pages: the decorations on this house have little to do with Rhaeto-Romanic tradition. Left, rally of the Italian Fascists in Bozen. Above, parades in traditional costumes are common.

ists reached an agreement: the South Tyroleans could choose whether they wished to remain in Italy or emigrate to Germany.

The population split into two irreconcilable camps. The majority supported the VKS, enthusiastic campaigners for the Third Reich. A minority wanted to remain in the homeland, for religious as well as patriotic motives. The result was a clear victory for the VKS: 86 percent declared their willingness to emigrate and only 14 percent opted to remain. By the end of 1942, when emigration was interrupted by military developments, one third of the "German opters", about 75,000 people, had left South Tyrol.

In September 1943, Italy surrendered to the Allies. As part of the Alpine field of operation South Tyrol came under German control, but, in deference to Mussolini, and to the dismay of the South Tyroleans who had emigrated, the region was not annexed.

South Tyrol was now subjected to the brutality of the Nazi regime. There were more victims between 1943 and 1945 than there had been in the 20 years of Italian Fascist oppression. There was resistance on the German side, notably by the Andreas Hofer League, and on the Italian side by the "National Liberation Committee" (CLN). For the South Tyrol, the war ended with the capitulation of the German army in Italy, on 2 May 1945.

The road to compromise: After the war, the ethnic Germans established the "South Tyrolean People's Party" (SVP), while the Italians joined the Italian national parties. Both sides watched each other with a certain degree of mistrust; for the one group supported a return to Austrian rule while the other demanded that South Tyrol remain under Italian sovereignty. In 1946, delegates to the Allied Peace Conference in Paris signed the Treaty of Paris, also known as the Gruber-De Gasperi Agreement. Under the terms of this treaty, South Tyrol remained a part of Italy, but both sides – Austria and Italy – agreed to guarantee minority rights. This remains the basis for South Tyrol's autonomy.

On 31 January 1948 Italy's constitutional assembly passed the Statute of Autonomy for the Trentino–Tyrolean Etschland region. The fact that Trentino had been included meant that the balance of population now tipped in the Italians' favour. Nevertheless, this incomplete administrative autonomy was accepted and a phase of rebuilding began.

After the emigrations before and during the war, the German-speaking population was now only a fraction of what it had been. While most of the rural population had remained behind, many of the townsfolk had left. It was now predominantly Italians who lived and worked in the major centres. It was this "division of labour" that was the root of the crisis of the late 1950s. The young people of rural South Tyrol, finding no employment, felt forced to emigrate, and the SVP feared that this emigration would lead to the decline of the ethnic Germans as a population group. Thus, starting in 1957, protests were staged, aimed at forcing the government to embark on a more conciliatory course.

But Rome did not react, and the SVP thus decided to entrust the issue to the Austrians. The Austrian government went before the General Assembly of the United Nations in 1960 to plead the case. After exhaustive negotiations, the UN demanded that both sides seek a peaceful solution.

When negotiations began in 1961, they were accompanied by hundreds of bombings and assassination attempts, which between 1961–1972 resulted in 19 dead and dozens of injured. But the ball had begun rolling. The government recognised the existence of a "South Tyrolean issue" and announced its willingness to seek a solution. In 1969, a legislative package was presented, containing 137 measures designed to protect the South Tyrolean minority. On 29 November that year, the SVP accepted the package.

This second, expanded, autonomy statute came into effect on 20 January 1972, although a small number of the provisions (six out of 137) have still not been fully implemented. Nevertheless, the statute has led to widely expanded powers for the province South Tyrol/Alto Adige, as it is now known. Now all government administrative offices must operate bilingually – even trilingually in the Rhaeto-Romanic villages. Ethnic quotas have been established, under which the hiring of public employees must reflect the strength of the three ethnic groups. Presently, 66 percent of the population is German, 29 percent is Italian and 5 percent is Rhaeto-Romanic.

Quotas regulate relationships: It was the implementation of these quotas which led, in the 1980s, to new tensions. While the German and Rhaeto-Romanic elements of the population profited from these new measures, the economic security of the South Tyrolean Italians declined. This led to the rapid growth of the neo-Fascist party, the MSI. However the new generation of the SVP, in conjunction with a more flexible application of the autonomy provisions, especially of the ethnic quota system, is contributing to a gradual relaxation of tensions.

South Tyrol could become a model for a successful and peaceful solution to ethnic conflicts all over the world.

Right, Bozen is now one of the most expensive cities in Italy.

FUNIVIA SEILBAHN
SASS PORDOI
SELF SERVICE
RESTAURANT
SOLA
SOLA
ACQUE MINERALI
S.MARTINO IN RIO - RE
SOLA

The word for language in Italian is *lingua*, a word which also means tongue. But if any self-respecting 20th-century South Tyrolean had been around when the Italian language developed, he would never have permitted more than one meaning for the word language. Or, at the very least, he would never have stood for the coupling of the word "language" with "tongue". If a dual meaning had to be assigned, then he would have ensured that the second meaning was anchored closer to the heart.

est ethnic group. Their language, today spoken only in the Dolomite regions, as well as in Friaul and Grisons in Switzerland, stems from the mixing of the Rhaetian language with Latin.

So far the Ladins have preferred to stay out of the language conflict, an attitude which extremists in the German population like to denigrate as typical of their passive character, even contending that people or groups who refuse to take a stand in language disputes have no place in their society. In fact,

German, Italian, Rhaeto-Romanic: The relationship of the South Tyrolean people to language is a complicated one. Throughout South Tyrol, you will frequently see cars sporting the bumper sticker "South Tyrol – German for the past 1,200 years". South Tyroleans never like to waste any opportunity to reiterate their claim that they were in South Tyrol first, and that their rights are thus more important than those of the Italians, who have been in the region for, at the most, 60 years.

In fact, the original inhabitants of the region known as Tyrol were the Rhaeto-Romanics, known as Ladins, today's small-

the Ladins have ensured the survival of their language simply by continuing to use it in their daily lives. Despite the invasion of tourism, and despite the fact that there are no Ladin schools in South Tyrol, a remarkable 80 percent of the residents of the Grödner and the Gader valleys still speak the Rhaeto-Romanic language.

I speak, therefore I am: South Tyrol is composed of three language groups: the Germans, the Italians and the Ladins. The government's policies on almost all issues, including subsidies and jobs, are always designed to reflect the needs of these groups. The fact that language is a means of communication is of secondary importance to the South Tyroleans. Its main function is to define who a person is and to which group he or she belongs.

It is for this reason that the statistics relating to the language groups are important. The population comprises 65 percent Germans, 30 percent Italians and 5 percent Ladins. Each adult individual in South Tyrol is obliged formally to declare to which of the three officially-recognised language groups he or she belongs. This is done every 10 years, during the general census.

German kindergarten, an Italian primary school, followed by a German senior school. He may eventually go on to the University of Bologna.To which language group does he therefore belong?

Secondly, there are often more important reasons for not stating the truth. Government hiring is based on a strict quota system whereby the jobs available are divided among the language groups in direct proportion to their size. Thus there is never any question as to how many Italian secretaries, German

years, during the general census.

The authorities must assume that every person is truthful when they fill in their census, but although most people would like to be, it is not always easy. Firstly, the truth is not that simple. The language groups have always intermarried. A child might speak German with his German mother and Italian with his Italian father, and he might attend a

public health officials or Ladin forest rangers will be hired over the next 10 years until the next census is held. With regulations such as these, nobody can blame an ambitious Ladin doctor for declaring that he belongs to the German language group if it helps him to secure the job he desires and is fully qualified to do. And a rural German with his heart set on being a forest ranger may well declare himself Ladin in order to secure the necessary training.

Thus the policies that attempted to force a trilingual registration throughout the land at the beginning of the 1970s were beset by problems. There were too many exceptions to the rule. What about those who considered themselves cosmopolitan? Or simply a mixture of German-Italian? Those who wanted to sabotage the system were very inventive, but the bureaucrats were ever ready to meet their ruses. Now, anyone who declares that he is German must take all his employment examinations in German. At one point attempts to classify the different groups went too far: one regulation, for example, stipulated that an Italian child who wanted to attend a German kindergarten had to take a language test. Such policies began to earn the system a bad name.

Why so much fuss?: The jungle of regulations which ensnares South Tyrol was origi-

tween 1920 and 1950 as civil servants and factory workers in a land which had been annexed. The indigenous population showed animosity toward these newcomers, who understood neither their language nor their culture yet unlike most "immigrants" had a passport to many of the best jobs, and the two groups studiously avoided one another.

The state, rejected by the German-speaking population as a government of occupation, proceeded to cement their hold on the region by importing more and more civil servants, military personnel, factory and construction workers from elsewhere in Italy. With centres such as Bozen and Meran, they established an urbane Italian society parallel

nally designed to protect the German and Ladin ethnic minorities in Italy. And if one takes a look at these two minorities today – by and large prosperous, self-assured and on the road to success – it is obvious that these protective measures have served their purpose. In fact, nowadays it is among the Italians rather than these minorities that one hears complaints.

The Italians in South Tyrol have had to overcome their own problems. For some years now the region's youth have felt a duty to make amends for wrongs carried out against the South Tyroleans by their parents and grandparents, many of whom arrived be-

to the German one.

Each ethnic group ignored the other for as long as possible. An Italian housewife who settled here could go about her daily business without ever confronting a South Tyrolean. It was like living in a ghetto.

But it wasn't possible to live in total isolation. The Germans were soon dependent on the Italians. Every farmer, at some point, had to pay a visit to a state bureau, every male youth had to serve in the military and the

Above, participants in a shooting tournament sport Italian and Tyrolean dress. **Right**, a result of Tolomei's efforts: Ausserpichl/Colle di Fuori.

ETTORE TOLOMEI

On 9 March 1979, in the cemetery of the tiny village of Montan, someone desecrated the grave of Ettore Tolomei, a man who had been dead for 27 years. It was an act of violent revenge. Tolomei's goal had been to transform South Tyrol from an historically German-speaking region into an historically Italian-speaking "Alto Adige".

Ettore Tolomei was born in 1865 in Rovereto, a town in the Etsch Valley, south of Trent. At that time the region was still part of the Habsburg Empire, but the Irredentist movement, advocating the recovery and union of all Italian-speaking districts, was beginning to gain a foothold.

In 1890, Tolomei founded a weekly newspaper with the ominous title *La Nazione Italiana*. In the newspaper's first edition he wrote of Bozen: "...a lovely and lively town in which over 4,000 Italians live, a frontier post of the 'Italianità'. The German population is friendly, but led astray by a feeling of Pan-Germanism..."

In following editions of the paper, he repeatedly defended the "watershed theory" which saw the region south of the Alps as belonging to Italy. He disputed the historical and geographical existence of Tyrol. It quickly became obvious to the paper's readers that Tolomei was attempting to achieve the Italian annexation of South Tyrol.

During the course of World War I, Tolomei and his followers changed 17,000 South Tyrolean place names into Italian in an attempt to Italianise the region "all the way to the most remote farmhouse", as an entry in Tolomei's journal from October of 1917 noted. Some of the names were changed by adding an Italian suffix (for example, Brenner became *Brennero*, Bruneck was changed to *Brunico*). Others were simply translated; for example Kaltenbrunn, meaning cold fountain, was given the Italian name *Fontanefredde*, and Pflughof ("Plough Farm") became *Maso dell'Aratro*. Sometimes an Italian name was simply pulled out of the hat *ad hoc*, thus Gossensass became *Colle Isarco* and the Grasleiten Pass was renamed *Passo del Principe*. Similarly, the 9,557-ft (2,913-metre) high Glockenkarkopf which rises in the remote extremes of the Ahrn Valley became, in Italian, *Vetta d'Italia*.

It is debatable whether or not Tolomei's efforts had any effect on the post-World War I negotiations over the position of the Italian borders, but one thing is certain. The American president Woodrow Wilson, who later admitted that he had not had a clear understanding of the South Tyrolean situation, was presented with inaccurate, even falsified, maps. These maps showed the Glockenkarspitze as *Vetta d'Italia*, leading Wilson to the false assumption that the region was a predominantly Italian-speaking one.

With the advent of the Fascist regime, Tolomei's ideas flourished further. His *Prontuario dei nomi locali dell'Alto Adige* (Handbook of Names and Places in South Tyrol) was employed by Benito Mussolini as a guide for his Italianisation of maps as well as a foundation for the compulsory measures he intoduced in the region. In 1936, however, Ettore Tolomei published a work which made foreign scholars suspicious of his plans. The work, *La restituzione del cognome atesino*, listed about 5,000 German surnames with suggestions for substitute Italian names, noting that the goal was to "restore the altered or foreign family names". Under Tolomei's proposals even the poet Oswald von Wolkenstein was to be rechristened; his new name was *Osvaldo di Selva*.

After World War II, the Treaty of Paris stipulated that all family names which had been Italianised under the Fascist regime should revert to their original German form. But the Italian names for towns and places remained and are still in use by the Italian government, in spite of a United Nations proclamation stating that all place names should be viewed as historical monuments to the language.

But even in Italian circles Ettore Tolomei's ideas have been discredited. The Italian historian and politician, Gaetano Savemini, has referred to Tolomei as the man "who discovered the most refined tools of torture to be used on the ethnic minorities in Italy".

railway was state-owned; the need to speak Italian was imperative. The Italians did not learn to speak German because the Germans could speak Italian. The Germans soon felt they were being discriminated against, and they were.

The democratic conscience of Italy was rudely woken at the beginning of the 1960s by a series of bombings and other terrorist activities. Tensions between Austria and Italy rose. The Italians believe that the Austrian authorities were not taking energetic measures to stop terrorists from using Austrian territory as a base for their activities in South Tyrol. Eventually a statute of autonomy for South Tyrol, giving it more power in the

bureaucratic superstructure. The reality of everyday life was something completely different. Harmony between ethnic groups cannot be achieved through legislation but must come about gradually.

Indeed, over the years and with increasing prosperity, people on all sides of the language divide began to see the positive side of living with the other language groups. Nowadays the German-speakers in Bozen, when not self-consciously parading their pride in being German, do everything in their power to be mistaken for Italians, who are considered chic. In their cuisine and their fashion the Germans want to appear Italian. Their children's loyalties lie with the Italian

economic and cultural fields and in public order, was passed and the guarantee of minority rights, a provision of the 1946 Treaty of Paris, was instituted. Under these terms the German and Ladin populations were granted more rights and some of the privileges of the Italians were eliminated. The right to subsidised housing, jobs within public administration and the right to communicate in their mother tongue were accorded to the minorities.

These changes proved to be painful. But although their significance was emphasised by every South Tyrolean public official, the modifications actually affected only the

soccer teams – if for no other reason than to annoy their father.

Among the Italians, a feeling of "interethnic" attachment to the region is taking root. The grey *Sarner*, the original South Tyrolean knitted jacket, is now a coveted fashion item among young girls from all three language groups. And the Italians, formerly disparagingly referred to as "city slickers" or "spaghetti eaters" by the Germans, have become enthusiastic hikers and experts in preparing liver dumplings and other local specialities. Although the Germans are perhaps not quite as fluent in Italian as the Italians, almost all are bilingual, despite the fact that a few are still too stubborn actually to admit it.

Problems of identity: Nowadays the language barriers have almost disappeared, but other problems have arisen in their place. As the cultures grow closer together, new alarm bells ring. People worry that the two cultures are on the verge of merging completely. They find themselves once again confronted with the same question, "Who am I?" Both cultures have taken on a duality and there is an urgent need for the population to search for a common identity that embraces both ethnic groups.

The obvious manifestation of this paranoia is the German-speaking South Tyroleans' fierce protection of Germanic traditions. Immigrants, converts, social climbers and the *nouveaux riches* have a reputation the world over for being zealots.

But the people of South Tyrol have further grounds for zealotry, for they have a very special regard for customs and community spirit, a fact which the South Tyroleans themselves are proud to admit and is evident to every tourist. Nowhere else in the alpine region is there such an assortment of marching bands, church choirs, companies of volunteer firemen and amateur riflemen. Nearly every village has its own sports club, agricultural organisation and amateur theatre group. Practically every male villager in South Tyrol belongs to one or more of the above groups. The importance placed on tradition by the South Tyroleans may be attributed to their dislocated history. Almost nowhere else is there so much talk about identity and its loss, about customs and attachment to the homeland.

The separation of South Tyrol from the Austrian portion of Tyrol has accentuated the desire to preserve the German language and traditions. Some people may join the church choir as a way of lauding God, others

might join the local marching band because they enjoy music – but, in the end, the fundamental purpose of these organisations is to preserve the ethnic folk group. The volunteer firemen are confident in their ability to defend the land, and the amateur riflemen, although prohibited from bearing arms, see themselves as the incarnate protectors of South Tyrol's innate Germanism.

The need to preserve traditions is most acute when the internecine troubles are greatest. But in recent times this has not been the case. The region is prosperous, the survival of the German language group is guaranteed and Italy is no longer seen as the

Left, a rural display of piety. **Right**, jovial exuberance.

enemy (indeed, it is positively fashionable to be an Italian). Now the South Tyroleans are suffering from an identity crisis, unclear what it is that still needs to be defended. For a while, the sense of being threatened was deflected against communism, but these times have now also passed.

"What still needs to be defended?" is the question. Tradition is the obvious answer. Upholding tradition in South Tyrol is central to religion and rural life, on which South Tyrol's present image is based. The motto "Holy Land of Tyrol" is taken literally, and for a "true" South Tyrolean, the adjectives Christian and Tyrolean are practically interchangeable.

that he was avenging a "disgrace to the village". He claimed that the native inhabitants, whose beliefs and morals had degenerated, no longer had the strength of character to do it themselves. Thus, although he was a newcomer, he had felt compelled to perform the task for them.

A show of piety: Every good Tyrolean sees himself as a good Christian, at least in principle. But because this is no longer the reality, if indeed it ever was, the authorities have taken practical steps to enhance the image of religiosity. For instance, church services are no longer held in German as was the case after the second Vatican Council, but are again sung in Latin, and the long-forgotten

The following incident clearly illustrates the point: in the summer of 1990 in a small mountain village in the Puster Valley, a Jehovah's Witness died. The Catholic priest buried him in a cemetery and the people of the village expressed the same sentiments as they had when the man was still alive: "Let him be." But there was one person, a newcomer to the village, who could not let the matter nor the Jehovah's Witness rest. He went to the cemetery during the night and desecrated the grave, because in his opinion the man had "wandered from the path of true Christian faith".

Later, at his trial, the offender declared

pilgrimages and ways of the Cross have been revived.

But it isn't for the benefit of the South Tyroleans alone. During the Christmas season, the tourist offices arrange visits to midnight Mass in the tiny churches of mountain villages just as they might organise a sledding party under the full moon. And on village squares snow sculptors carve a crib from piles of artificial snow specially imported for the purpose. Carefully sprayed with water

Above, traditional *Schuhplattler* dance on the zebra crossing. **Right**, the results of an attack on the pipes of a hydro-electric power plant.

BOMBERS AND SPIES

During the night of 11 June 1961, loud explosions were heard in several dozen towns in South Tyrol. All over the land bombs placed at the bases of the high tension electricity pylons were exploding. This particular Sunday, the Feast of the Sacred Heart, almost a national holiday for South Tyroleans, was specially chosen as the date for the "night of fire". The attack was the first in a series of terrorist incidents by sections of the region's German-speaking population.

The day marked the transition from peaceful to violent measures in the ethnic struggle in South Tyrol. The results of 10 years of discussions were indeed pitiful: despite proclamations of autonomy, the province was still under an Italian administration. In effect this meant that for any German-speaking South Tyrolean, employment with the government, be it with the postal service, the railway or any other state agency, was virtually impossible. And subsidised housing was reserved almost entirely for the Italian population. Massive military and police presence on the streets, along with arbitrary decisions by civil servants, had become a way of life.

A sense of frustration and resentment had developed, which eventually proved explosive. Countless utility masts, the most concrete expression of remote-controlled repression, were toppled. As a result, all the lights went out in the industrial metropolises of Upper Italy.

One month later, a further wave of terrorist attacks occurred. Again the bombs were planted on the high tension masts. The "bashers", as the terrorists were called, were careful to ensure that human life was not endangered.

Shortly afterwards, South Tyrol became an occupied province. House searches were carried out, masses of people were arrested and some prisoners were tortured. Sepp Kerschbaumer became the first South Tyrolean patriot to die as a result of torture. Group trials were held to sentence the "bashers", which again placed South Tyrol in the international headlines, and Kerschbaumer became a martyr for South Tyrolean freedom, a modern day Andreas Hofer.

Although the political representatives of South Tyrol distanced themselves from these terrorist activities, they were not entirely displeased by the violent background to their political discussions. The bombings continued, despite the fact that the main leaders of the armed resistance had been rounded up and placed in jail.

However, the South Tyroleans began to lose control over their mission. Increasingly, extremists from Austria and Germany infiltrated protests. Border and police stations were attacked, and human life was no longer sacred. There were even rumours of infiltration by agents from the Eastern Bloc. The Italian secret service sent spies.

The ordinary South Tyroleans were repelled by this violence and much of the support and sympathy they had initially felt for the terrorists began to evaporate. Gradually the "peaceful path to autonomy for South Tyrol" began to have some success. In 1969 the provincial assembly of the SVP accepted the "South Tyrol Package".

But the ethnic problems of South Tyrol were by no means solved. At the beginning of the 1980s, a time of economic prosperity for the region, terrorism once again reared its head – this time organised by Italians. Cable cars in the tourism centres, the source of South Tyrol's new-found wealth, were bombed. It was an echo of the German death march hysteria of the early 1960s. Italian nationalists issued a protest against the sell-out of the Italian province of Bozen.

The bombing soon died down, but, among the Italians, the air of discontent remained. It was they who now felt that they must band together in a national collective. It was achieved under the banner of the neo-Fascist party.

As a countermeasure, at the end of the 1980s a group of ethnic German nationalists campaigned for the return of South Tyrol to Tyrol. Autonomy was, for this small minority, no longer sufficient. This campaign, which found no support among the general population of German-speaking South Tyroleans, came to a tragic end when two "freedom fighters", inexperienced in handling explosives, blew themselves up with their own bomb.

and turned to ice, this sculpture remains fixed until the end of the season, there for locals and visitors to admire, proving to all the tourists what an important role Christianity plays in the lives of the pious people of South Tyrol.

In some regions, residents still participate in religious processions, dressed in their native costumes – women with flowers and silk-coloured bows in their hair, the men wearing traditional jackets and belts embroidered with threads of peacock quills. Tourists are bussed in from far and wide to witness the processions. Törggelen (sampling the new wine; *see page 87*) has become a round-the-year "industry", no longer limited

wives also worked on the farm. A political irony: the status of women, in what is a distinctly anti-feminist region, was suddenly raised simply because the politicians refused to accept that this farming province had so few farmers.

But the government also employs more direct methods to ensure that South Tyrol remains a farming province, namely its introduction of "farm aid". Nowhere else in the European Community has there been so little migration to the cities as in South Tyrol. The primary goal of farm aid here is to keep the farmers on their farms. The more remote a farm lies and the higher it is perched on a mountain, the more important it is that it

to the autumn months.

Too few farmers: The second pillar of identity, rural life, is no less corrupted. Statistics for the number of farmers and farm labourers in South Tyrol are always exaggerated. According to the authorities, 15 percent of the workforce is employed in the agricultural sector. At the end of the 1970s, people working on a development programme for the province discovered that the percentage was rather less. Perturbed by this, the politicians manipulated the statistics so that the 15 percent figure stuck. The government was forced to defend its position. It argued that most farmers were married and invariably their

should be preserved.

So that their policy should succeed the government invested a great deal of time and money in "consciousness-raising" among the farmers, i.e. stressing the cultural value of the region's farming roots. Their policy was extremely successful. Working the land in South Tyrol has a much greater significance than mere numbers indicate. Farmers constitute only "15 percent" of the population and more than half that number must rely on outside jobs to supplement their income. Nevertheless, after hours, on weekends and during the holidays, people return to the land. Ask people what they do for a living and the majority will reply that they are partially farmers.

But the true farmers are not the ones upholding tradition. Since the introduction of farm machinery and the consequent loss of farmhands, farmers have had little time for customs and traditions, which are economically unviable. They are dismayed by this but unable to remedy the problem. Consequently, as has been pointed out by some only slightly tongue-in-cheek observers, meetings of local agricultural groups have turned into psychological self-help groups whose purpose it is to boost the morale of the farming community.

Playing at tradition: In many cases, the task

harvest and numerous customs derived from Germanic traditions.

If a competition were held to determine which town has the most tradition-conscious inhabitants, then the winner would undoubtedly be Haslach, a modern settlement on the outskirts of Bozen, home to the bulk of the region's civil servants. The inhabitants of Haslach work all week for the government in Bozen, but return at weekends to their villages, where they serve as community officials and ensure that the age-old traditions of South Tyrol are preserved.

After World War II, when it became clear that South Tyrol would not be returned to Austria, the people of the region had other

of preserving rural traditions has fallen to people who grew up on a farm but who now work in factories, public administration, as teachers or as waiters and chambermaids. Such jobs offer them little sense of identity; no trade unions or working class movements have developed in South Tyrol. They thus invest all their spare energy in reviving their "lost identity", in particular in the "traditional rural events" listed in all tourist brochures. These include pilgrimages to pray for the right weather conditions or a good

<u>Left</u>, summer festival. <u>Above</u>, a nun educated in herbal medicine; distinctive headgear.

priorities than upholding customs. It was not until the 1970s and 1980s that they woke up to the value of their cultural traditions. The realisation was prompted by the arrival of tourists. Customs were rediscovered – and exploited.

This, of course, has introduced a whole range of new fears. Many people view everything South Tyrolean – be it an evening of folklore, a procession in national costumes, or a festival of regional cuisine – as something that ought to be shielded from mass tourism. The South Tyroleans are still trying to guide their oh-so-precious identity to a safe harbour.

The coach, packed with some 50 eager tourists, winds its way along the serpentine road beyond the mountain village of St Andrä above Brixen. Suddenly, from behind one of the bends, the vast inn "Mair am Bach" comes into view. The passengers let out a chorus of delight. "Wow! Just like in the tourist brochures," one of the men exclaims as the coach draws to a halt outside.

These coach passengers are about to embark on the *Törggelen*, or sampling the new wine. The term comes from the word *Torkel*, which, in South Tyrol, means a wooden grape press. The original form of the ancient custom of *Törggelen* was a far cry from the huge tourist attraction it has since become. The inns where the tradition is still practised now attract coachloads of tourists from all corners of Europe.

"In earlier times," the waiter explains as he placed the first pitcher of the fermented grape juice on the table, "*Törggelen* was basically a private affair between neighbours and friends. After the harvest had been gathered in, the vintner would invite a few friends for an evening of wine tasting. The wine was traditionally served with oven-roasted chestnuts and home-made sauerkraut, a selection of cured sausages and cold cuts from the cattle which had recently been herded down from their summer pastures. Imagine the taste!"

The cold cuts of ham and the roasted chestnuts which traditionally accompany the new wine are still served. But the vintner's circle of friends has expanded. Whereas in earlier times it was common to set up just one or two tables specially for the occasion, many of the "Törggele Inns" of modern South Tyrol have evolved into enormous dining halls.

But Mair am Bach, operated by the son of an old Brixen vintner family, has managed to maintain its original charm, despite the occasional inundation of tourists. The tiled oven provides a cosy atmosphere in the vaulted inn, and the wooden tables are worn and stained from many years of use. The wine is still served in simple pitchers and not, as in many of the other guesthouses, in fancy stemmed goblets.

The wine varies in taste according to the level of fermentation. "It tastes sticky-sweet," one lady proclaims. She is describing the famous *Suser* or *Sauser*, the young cloudy wine in the first stages of fermentation. The wine in this stage is harmless, really just a tangy grape juice. Wine in the next stage, however, termed *Federweisser*, plays mischievous tricks on the unsuspecting drinker. It goes down like grape juice, but packs a terrific punch, as many a poor soul has discovered too late.

As the noise level rises in proportion to guests' level of intoxication, many switch to the ripened wines from previous years. A few of the hard-core imbibers even decide to sample the local *schnapps*, a course of action guaranteed to produce a raging hangover. But the South Tyroleans know the perfect antidote: they take a stiff walk both before and after the drinking spree. The fresh mountain air accompanied by physical exercise works wonders.

It takes many hours to sample all the delicacies that a typical South Tyrolean guesthouse has to offer, often until the early morning. Chestnuts are an integral part of such an evening. Purists claim that areas where it is too cool for chestnuts to grow cannot be considered real *Törggelen* regions (Franzensfeste is the most northerly point where the climate is still mild enough). While numerous *Törggelen* inns are found in the town of Sterzing and the surrounding area, for example, one would be hard pressed to find a genuine South Tyrolean in any of these establishments.

In recent times, a movement has grown up in opposition to the over-exploitation of this age-old tradition. Some inn-keepers in remote villages refuse, as a matter of principle, to admit large groups of tourists. There is one proprietor near Vahrn, for example, who only allows native residents to sample his wine. But outsiders should not be discouraged. There are still plenty of places where they can experience a pleasant evening of *Törggelen*.

Preceding pages: the elders still gather for a glass of wine. Left, essential accompaniments.

A change has been detected in European drinking habits in recent years. The days when the ready availability of cheap wine in two-litre bottles was an attractive prospect are over. Interest in quality wines, however, is booming. It took a long time for this trend to be realised in South Tyrol; in general, most tourists came to ski or hike and, afterwards, to enjoy long, convivial evenings in the local bars. For this, quantity rather than quality was what mattered.

The first vintners in Italy to compete with the French in producing high quality wines were the growers of Tuscany and Piedmont. Wines such as Brunello di Montalcino, Tignanello and, of course, Chianti – all from Tuscany – and Barolo, Barbaresco or Grignolino from the Piedmont region were the first to appear on international lists of top quality wines. They were quickly followed by wines from several other regions, such as Friaul and Venice.

South Tyrol eventually followed suit. About 15 percent of the land in South Tyrol is used for wine growing. The annual production is over 1.5 million hectolitres, of which some 60 percent is classified as D.O.C. wine. Over 35 percent of the wine is exported abroad, making South Tyrol one of Italy's top wine producers. Despite the emphasis place on volume, the region produces a number of excellent wines, although it should be said that, with a little more effort and a bit more control, the quality could reach even higher standards.

A new image: As the quality of Italian wines gradually improved, vintners wanted to advertise the fact to the world. Thus, in the Chianti region, the world-renowned bottles encased in bast were replaced by 0.75-litre bottles sporting a fashionable designer label. A similar trend is underway in South Tyrol; the red-nosed mountain peasant with his quaint hat and look of drunken stupor who formerly appeared on the labels has been replaced by more artistic motifs.

Equally most of the diluted, sweetened

wines of the past were replaced by more refined products. The view that South Tyrolean wines should be accompanied by an aspirin for the inevitable headache has now almost disappeared and international trade publications such as Veronelli, Vinum or Johnson have all turned their attentions to the region.

Wines from South Tyrol are designated DOC (*Denominazione Originale Controllata*), which is an all-encompassing regional designation. This stamp of quality, recognised throughout Italy, is accompanied in some regions by a G for *Garantita*. The following wines, all on the international market, bear this designation:

Red Vernatsch wines: The most famous of these is the Lago di Caldaro, Lake Kalterer (grown on the land around this lake), a wine which still suffers somewhat from the poor reputation it acquired in the past. Wine sold under this name is made mainly from the red Vernatsch grape (*Schiava*). It is light red in colour, sometimes verging on rosé, with a relatively smooth taste. It should be served chilled and drunk when it is young (within three years). The designation *classico* is

<u>Left</u>, for years South Tyrolean wine was equated with mass production. <u>Above</u>, a wine tasting in Castle Rametz near Meran.

given to wines made from grapes grown in the immediate vicinity of the lake. Those with a minimum of 10.5 percent alcohol are termed *classico superiore*.

Another simple red wine made of the Schiava grape is the Colle di Bolzano. This ruby-red wine, made from grapes grown on the hillsides around Bozen, should not be kept longer than three years.

The Santa Maddalena, also called Sankt Magdalener, is known far beyond South Tyrol. Formerly, it was, along with Barolo and Barbaresco, one of Italy's most famous wines. It is produced from the Schiava grapes grown around Bozen. Mixed with Lagrein and Blue Burgundy grapes, it develops its typical vio-

let aroma with a light almond taste. The quality is quite good despite the fact that some 4 million litres are produced annually. Wines made from grapes grown in the direct vicinity of Santa Maddalena are classified *classico*.

The Meranse di Collina, also produced from the Schiava grape, comes from the vineyards around Meran. It is a smooth-tasting wine ranging in colour from light to ruby-red and has a lightly aromatic bouquet. The name Burggräfler is also applied to this wine, although, strictly speaking, it specifically refers to a small number of vineyards in one particular region.

Tips for the connoisseur: The Marzemino, grown in Trentino, is less well known but definitely worth discovering. It is a full-bodied dry red wine. The leading *fattoria* (place of production) for Marzemino is still Simoncelli near Rovereto.

Another Trentino wine, but one which is also found in South Tyrol, is the Teroldego. This dark ruby-red wine with plenty of character is produced only in the region between Mezzolombardo and S. Michele all'Adige in the Noce Delta. To enjoy it at its best, it must be aged for at least two to three years before it is drunk. Both these wines, the Marzemino and Teroldego, are practically unknown outside South Tyrol and Trentino.

Dark Lagrein and Merlot, Cabernet, Pinot Nero (red Burgundy) and Malvasia are types of grapes grown in the DOC region and often marketed as simple table wines under the designation "Alto Adige". However, in the overall production of wine, they play a relatively minor role. Only about six percent of land devoted to vineyards is used for the production of red wine such as Lagrein (mainly in Girlan or St Anton near Bozen). And only four percent of vineyards in South Tyrol is planted with Pinot Nero (mainly in the south).

White wine: Although about 80 percent of vineyards produce only red wine, it is actually South Tyrol's white wines which deserve special attention. These wines are wonderfully fresh and fruity; they are clear and age extremely well. Above and beyond the mass-produced grape Chardonnay, marketed and exported under the title "DOC Alto Adige", are several top quality products worthy of mention.

One of the most important representatives of this class is the Moscato Giallo, or golden muscadine, an aromatic and surprisingly dry table wine. Pinot Bianco and Pinot Grigio are also noteworthy examples. In fact, the quality is so good that vintners from the Veneto region have started buying these grapes to upgrade the quality of their own wines. Both Pinots are youthful wines with an exquisite bouquet. The vineyard Zeni has had such overwhelming success with its Chardonnay Zaraosti that a number of other vintners in the region have also started producing this wine, helping it to achieve widespread recognition.

Tramin is the home of the renowned

Gewürztraminer, a grape which wine connoisseurs mainly associate with the Alsace region. When it is young, it is a fruity, usually yellow-gold, wine. It improves greatly with age as the aroma and flavour continue to develop. When purchasing this wine, however, it is important to distinguish between the simple Traminer and the Traminer Aromatico as there is a huge difference in quality between the two.

Sparkling wine and hard liquor: Spumante is another wine that has attained an exceptional level of quality. It is made from the Chardonnay, Pinot Bianco, Pinot Grigio and Pinot Nero grapes. A group of producers of varying sizes and backgrounds have joined to-

too, quality has been much improved in recent times. Whereas this drink was, in former times, known for its rotgut character, it has now been refined to a point where it is a fine-tasting clear alcohol. The best places to buy this high-proof product are Zeni or the Neustift Monastery.

Sampling and selling: Vintners are keen to invite visitors to sample their wines, particularly during the *Törggelen* season (*see page 87*). Whereas in simple guesthouses the house wine may not be of the highest quality, in the more upmarket dining establishments one usually finds a very palatable house wine in addition to a comprehensive choice of top regional wines. In Bozen, the Rote Adler has

gether to form the *Consorzio Spumante Trento Classico*, similar to the cooperatives formed by wine producers. All of these consortiums or cooperatives, both in wine and sparkling wine production, guarantee quality. The top Spumante producer is the Vineyard Ferrari, owned by the Lunelli brothers in Trent, which produces some three million bottles annually.

This chapter cannot be closed without a short mention of the popular drink grappe, also known in South Tyrol as *Treber*. Here,

Left, the grape harvest. **Above**, the freshly-planted grape vines are watered with wine.

an excellent wine list, as does Johnson & Dipoli in Neumarkt. Both restaurants are also known for their cuisine. Along with Bozen's Adler (at the fruit market), Zum Gostner offers a good wine selection. They also sell wine by the bottle, although their prices are higher than in the shops.

Trade groups from the wine industry can participate in organised wine-tasting sprees, and for the normal public many wine villages offer annual wine days or weeks. It is hoped that the trend towards quality wines will continue and that the popular red table wines will attain a reasonable level of palatability right across the board.

Detractors complain that South Tyrol's gastronomy is a mixture of every-day plain cooking and bland "international" fare put out for the tourists. The reason, it is said, is that the tourism industry takes its customers for granted, and assumes they will eat whatever is set before them. The clientele, they claim, demands quantity not quality, therefore plates are piled high and prices are kept reasonable.

But there are many older dining establishments with a long tradition of serving high-class cuisine, and these have been joined in recent years by several new restaurants of distinction. They are not catering for the masses of tourists arriving in cars and coaches from northern Europe, but for a discerning Italian clientele. For the Italians, quality is more important than cost. Visitors to South Tyrol who want to dine well have everything to gain from this development.

Basic principles and differences: Genuine South Tyrolean cuisine is a marvellous mixture of hearty Tyrolean dishes and traditional Italian specialities (*nouvelle cuisine* has barely penetrated South Tyrol). A good example of this culinary interchange are the *Schlutzkrapfen*, known among the German population as "spinach pockets" and among the Italians as *ravioli* – a far cry from the versions served in most London trattorias. Topped with lightly browned butter and freshly grated Parmesan cheese, they are delicious.

One of the most famous regional dishes, included on almost every menu, is dumplings (*Knödel*). Proof of the long and distinguished career of the dumpling in South Tyrol is provided by the Romanesque fresco in the Castle Hocheppan, depicting what is popularly known as the "Dumpling Eater".

There are many varieties of dumpling, including some incorporating bacon or spinach. Sometimes dumplings are served sweetened as a dessert, and sometimes sour with sauce or gravy or in soups. The dumpling is an integral part of the South Tyrolean

Left, stalwarts of Tyrolean hospitality: the bacon dumpling and wine. **Above**, a robust peasant meal: polenta with bacon and cheese.

cuisine. The specific consistency of a dumpling is determined by the skills of the individual chef rather than South Tyrolean preference. Thus one may be served a soggy lump, a tough, hard-to-digest cannonball or, ideally, a mouth-wateringly light and tender delicacy.

Nocken also come in many guises. They may incorporate spinach, cheese, semolina or liver. The Italians have their own variety, known as *gnocchi*, often served with tomato sauce. It is a difficult dish to make, but a

perfect *Nockerl* is one which is light and easy to cut with a fork.

Where roast meats (known in Italian as *arrosto*) are concerned, the method of preparation depends on the nationality of the chef. If he is Tyrolean, he will serve a crispy pork roast with dumplings or *Brätern* (roast potatoes). If he is Italian, on the other hand, he will probably produce thin slices of meat seasoned with rosemary. (Bear in mind that if you order roast meat, side dishes must always be ordered separately.)

The best of Brixen: There are two restaurants in Brixen which are especially recommended. These are the Finsterwirt and the Elefant.

(The latter is also one of the leading hotels in South Tyrol.) In the Elefant, be sure to request a table in the "Zirbelstube" room: the other rooms are more modern and have less character. This restaurant's menu ranges from traditional Tyrolean specialities such as *Käsnocken* (delicious cheese dumplings) to a luxurious fish risotto, a dish less typical of the region. The range of meat entrées includes such dishes as tender lamb medallions fried in a potato crust until crisp. The house wines, including Magdalener and Eisacktaler, are excellent.

The Finsterwirt is less elegant than the Elefant, but, with its dimly-lit, cosy dining room, it is an ideal place for an intimate

served on a board), should head for the wine cellar in the nearby Neustift Monastery. Here, under ancient vaulted ceilings, simple meals are accompanied by the monastery's own delicious wine.

The heart of good cooking: The city of Bozen is very much the centre of the region. This also holds true for its cuisine. If you do not want to dine in the Hotel Greif at Walther Square, where most visitors in search of good food end up, then you should try the Rote Adler (Goethestrasse 3). This restaurant is small (seats only 40), so reservations are essential – at least for those who want to choose from the extravagant seven-course menu. Alternatively, if you are not hungry

evening with friends. Here, too, the menu ranges from traditional Tyrolean dishes to more refined Italian specialities. Be sure to sample the house speciality, *Eisacktaler Weinsuppe* (Eisack Valley wine soup).

Another recommended dining establishment in Brixen is Restaurant Fink, Unter den Kleinen Lauben 4. It is run by Hans Fink, who has published his most acclaimed recipes in a cookbook. In Stufels, near Brixen, pay a visit to Restaurant Dominik.

Those who are only passing through Brixen and merely want to stop for a light meal, such as *Kaminwurz'n* (a tasty smoked sausage) or *Speck am Brettl* (South Tyrolean smoked ham

enough or rich enough for that, try the adjoining bistro, which offers a wide selection of light meals. This is a good place to unwind over a glass of wine after exploring the town.

Just a few steps away, through the fruit market and on the right side, is the bistro Zum Gostner (Oxnschmid). It has a dining room and a bistro. Three daily specialities are offered (costing about 10,000, 14,000 and 17,000 lire), all served with a fresh salad. On Saturdays, the chef prepares traditional liver dumpling soup (*Leberknödelsuppe*) or goulash with liver dumplings (*Gulasch mit Leberknödeln*).

Those who want only a slice of pizza

should carry on past the fountain at the market. On the right-hand side is a small pizza shop. In complete contrast is the celebrated Park Hotel Laurin with its *belle époque* restaurant, which can be recommended for those desiring something more substantial – and expensive.

Fine cooking and peasants' soup: The unspoilt Sarn Valley, stretching northwards from Bozen, contains three good, if very dissimilar, restaurants. The so-called "Sarn Valley speciality weeks", organised by the two leading restaurants, Bad Schörggau (just a few miles from Sarnthein) and Bad Rungg directly in Sarnthein itself, are well known. These two restaurants alone make a visit to the region worthwhile. Their menus represent a mixture of traditional Sarn Valley cooking, accompanied by a selection of typical side dishes (such as buckwheat noodles), and more sophisticated Italian cuisine. The *Latschenschnapps* (alcohol distilled from local dwarf-pines) is made at Bad Schörggau. This delicious drink makes an ideal *digestif*.

Anyone who likes hearty home cooking should follow the winding road leading to Durnholz, where the parish guesthouse (Pfarrgasthof Durnholz) is located. One glance at the huge frying pan of sizzling potatoes or the hand-rolled bacon dumplings in the kitchens is enough to stimulate the most jaded appetites. The best time to visit is Sunday morning, when the villagers don native dress.

In the picturesque Ulten Valley, it is possible to sample the entire range of South Tyrolean cuisine. A few miles beyond St Gertraud on Lake Weissbrunn is il Godio, which has reaped numerous accolades from food critics (the other restaurant here is really just a canteen for package tourists, so beware). Il Godio's "ploughman's soup" (*Bauernsuppe*), made of fresh cream, bacon, onions and cabbage, is superb. Appetisers range from the Italian favourite *carpaccio*, thin slices of marinated raw beef, to homemade liver pâté to mushrooms. (Do not be deterred by the unpromising exterior of the building; it was once part of the power plant of the hydro-electric dam.)

The founder of the Hotel Villa Mozart and

the Restaurant Andrea in Meran is Andreas Hellriegel. Although he has now delegated the responsibility of running the restaurants to one of his pupils – while he turns his attention to satisfying the appetites of diners in New York – the quality of food and service has remained the same. The Villa Mozart (St Markusstrasse) is a favourite among gourmets; reservations are therefore essential.

Visitors who do not have a hearty enough appetite for a full-blown meal might try Meran's Bistro Seibstock, popular purveyors of tasty snacks and a variety of sausage, ham and cheese specialties. Another place well worth visiting is Restaurant Flora in Laubengasse 75.

Burgeis in Vinschgau tempts visitors with hearty home cooking. Gasthof Zum Mohren, run by the Theiner family since 1665, serves typical Tyrolean dishes ranging from the daily barley soup (*Gerstesuppe*) to the weekly platter of freshly-slaughtered meats (*Schlachtschüssel*). The desserts, too, are recommended.

Those travelling through the southern regions (Unterland) might try Marklshof in Girlan and Rose in Eppan/St Michael. Marklshof, a traditional restaurant frequented by Bozen residents, serves first-class food and its own wines. It occupies a prime position on the region's "wine road".

Left, at the riflemen's festival, beer has replaced red wine as the liquid refreshment. **Above**, sides of ham and *Kaminwurz'n*, smoked sausage.

THE GLACIER MAN

Should South Tyrol remain under Italian sovereignty or be reunited with Tyrol, thus becoming once again a part of Austria? This debate, often heated, has been going on ever since the region was severed from Austrian Tyrol and placed under Italian rule at the end of World War I. But in September 1991 a man turned up in South Tyrol who surely never gave a moment's thought during his lifetime to the issue of national sovereignty. He was neither Italian nor Austrian, neither Tyrolean nor South Tyrolean. For this man, known as *Homo tirolensis*, made his home in this region more than 5,000 years ago, long before the emergence of

discovery, a number of amateur "archaeologists" arrived on the scene and poked about the remains, resulting in some damage to parts of the anatomy. Who could the man in the ice be? At first it was thought that the body was that of an unfortunate mountain climber who had met an untimely death in the recent past. However, coroners called to the scene soon proclaimed that this was no ordinary cadaver, but one dating back to prehistoric times. Experts were immediately summoned to supervise a proper exhumation.

In addition to the body, several weapons and tools were also found. The corpse was transported to Innsbruck for examination by an international team of experts while the artifacts were sent to the Roman-Germanic Central Museum in Mainz to be studied. Although scientists, anthropologists and

such national designations. In his lifetime this man was mainly concerned with the problems presented by day-to-day survival.

Homo tirolensis, also known as the "glacier man" or more affectionately as "Frozen Fritz", was discovered by Erika and Helmuth Simon, two German tourists holidaying on a farm in the Schnals Valley. Returning from an hike up Mt Finail, at an altitude of nearly 11,000 ft (3,350 metres), the couple spotted something protruding from the Similaun Glacier. Upon closer examination, they realised that this was a human corpse, so they hurried to the nearby Similaun Hut and announced their find to the proprietor, who immediately notified the Italian as well as the Austrian authorities.

Unfortunately, during the first hours after the

historians will need years to analyse all of the findings, a number of theses have already been offered about who the glacier man was, what his lifestyle was like and exactly when he lived.

At the University of Innsbruck the body was placed in a room with a temperature of 22° F (minus 6° C) in order to ensure the same conditions which had preserved it for thousands of years. In the first days after the spectacular find, sceptics pointed out that, due to constant movement within the glacial ice, it was highly unlikely that a body could have been preserved intact for that long. They also noted that the oldest remains previously found in a glacier were only 50–70 years old. Their verdict: the mummy was a macabre hoax staged by publicity-hungry pranksters.

But careful research and examinations, including carbon dating, soon proved that the body was indeed some 5,000 years old.

The ice had served as an excellent preservative for *Homo tirolensis*: skin and muscle tissue were still intact in some places. It has been determined that the man was between 20 and 40 years old when he died of an – as yet – unknown cause. His teeth were worn down, indicating that he probably lived on a diet of meat and ground grains. The internal organs of the glacier man were extremely well preserved, as were parts of his clothing. His boots, made of leather, were filled with hay for added warmth and his clothing was made of tanned animal skins pieced together in a patchwork fashion and joined with threads made of animal tendons and leather. Additionally, the clothing showed

metres) long, a rather amazing length considering that he himself was only 5 ft 2 inches (1.6 metres) tall. It is probable that the bow was not yet a finished product, experts say. Its surface was still rough and no evidence was found to prove that it had ever been strung. The 14 arrows, too, were only half-finished. Other finds included a quiver, a flintstone knife and a copper hatchet.

As scientists and experts from different countries work together in an atmosphere of cooperation to solve the mysteries presented by this unique find, Italian and Austrian statesmen battle over where the mummy should find his final resting place. The site where he was originally found was close enough to the Italian-Austrian border to make it questionable as to which country had jurisdiction. The Italians, unaware that the corpse

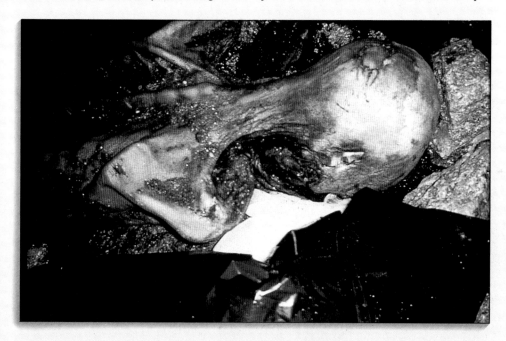

evidence of crude repairs with threads of grass, a fact which leads experts to believe that he may have been living by himself in the mountains for an extended period of time.

It can also be deduced, however, that *Homo tirolensis* was not always a loner. Scientists point out that he had tattoos on his back which would have been impossible for him to have executed himself. Two kernels of grain found in his clothing also indicate that he had contact with the people in the valley settlements where crops were planted.

The ice man's bow was approximately 6 ft (1.8

Left, Homo tirolensis, released from the clutches of the Similaun glacier. <u>Above</u>, closer examination revealed wounds to the head.

was of such historical significance, agreed to let it be transported to Innsbruck. Now South Tyrol's capital city of Bozen is dreaming of the day when the mummy might find its way into that city's museum. However, the scientific research on the ice man is expected to continue for at least 10 years, and the decision as to which country can claim him as its own may take just as long.

It is ironic that *Homo tirolensis*, who knew no national boundaries, who probably crossed what is today's border between Austria and Italy countless times during his life, is being fought over by these two countries. Austria claims him as a Tyrolean; Italy claims him as a South Tyrolean. And, if he could speak for himself, he might point out that he was neither.

It would be incorrect to say that the South Tyroleans welcomed the idea of setting up national parks. When the Mussolini administration decided to establish the Silfser Joch National Park in 1935, for example, the Vinschgau residents viewed this act with deep suspicion. They saw the park as a pretext; popular speculation was that the government's true goal was to undermine people's livelihoods.

In fact, their suspicions proved to be well-grounded, for the villages of the valley were also subject to the park's restrictive regulations. Consequently, much later, in 1975, when the Schlern National Park was opened, the music of the attendant marching bands was not as vigorous as is usual on civic occasions. In fact, many of the musicians boycotted the festivities in protest against the newly instituted protective measures. Farmers were worried that they wouldn't be able to use their mountain pastures, hunters worried about whether they would be allowed to hunt, and hotel owners saw their future plans for splendid new amenities and ski lifts quashed.

But initial distrust has now abated. For the Schlern National Park, like all the other parks, has proved to be a big draw for visitors. Hotels include pictures of it in all their glossy brochures.

In many ways, the park has been a victim of its own success. It has succeeded in producing conditions which are the complete antithesis of what was originally intended. As more and more hikers tramp the paths, the flanking vegetation recedes further and further. Many of the paths are now as wide as streets, and roads, lifts and ski trails have bored deeper into the mountains. In many cases bitter disputes have arisen between the tourism bodies and local environmental protection groups. The Alpine Club has made valiant attempts to plant new vegetation, and several "environmental construction sites" have been established.

Preceding pages: view of the Drei Zinnen (Three Pinnacles); graffiti in stone in the Sexten Dolomites; the nest of a wood grouse; first flowers of spring. Left, Lake Karer with Mt Latemar.

The Dolomites were formed over a period of some 30 million years. During this time, more than 200 million years ago, the region lay under a tropical Mediterranean ocean founded on volcanic stone – Bozen quartz porphyry and Puster Valley phyllite. Today, fertile plateaux, such as the Seiser Alm, are evidence of the prehistoric volcanic activity. The warm waters of this ancient sea were teeming with life forms. Plant remains and animal shells accumulated on the sea floor, developing into coral reefs and limestone banks. The volcanos spewed their lava into the sea, and the reefs and banks grew higher and higher.

About 50 million years ago, the Alps emerged from the sea. Scree slopes at the base of rock faces, stony expanses, gorges and subterranean chasms filled with gushing brooks are all testimony to the effects of water and ice erosion over the millennia.

The concept of the national parks: Together the eight national parks provide a cross-section of the various landscapes of the province. The tourist offices and the Landesamt für Naturparke (39100 Bozen, Cesare Battististrasse 21) can provide visitors with information about the parks. The concept of the national parks is to provide a basis for conservation, environmental education, recreation and research. For this reason, no new permanent settlements, ski lifts or hydroelectric projects are allowed. The inhabitants of the region may, however, use the land for farming and lumbering, as well as for hunting and fishing.

All minerals and fossils, animals, plants and mushrooms are protected species within the park. This means that cars are banned and campfires and camping are prohibited. This is taken seriously and violations are punishable by law. Visitors are well-advised to remain on the marked trails.

Schlern Nature Reserve: This park encompasses the communities of Kastelruth, Völs and Tiers and spans 14,455 acres (5,850 hectares) of land. The Seiser Alm Plateau, over 12,000 acres (5,000 hectares) in size and lying just outside this park, is a prime example of what can happen to a landscape visited by too many people. Here, where orchids, gentian, primroses, edelweiss and a wide variety of other wildflowers once carpeted the landscape, it is now nothing but monotonous green. Roads and lift facilities cut through the landscape. Everywhere one looks there are hotels.

But those who search beyond the main routes can still find unspoilt corners in the park, particularly in the southern regions of the plateau. The contrast between the gently rolling meadows of the plateau and the massif of the Schlern is startling. Traces of ancient cults dating back thousands of years have been found here.

One of the best routes to take to enjoy the Schlern is to begin at the Völser Weiher

of Gröden and Alta Badia are in the immediate vicinity.

At one time this paradise was threatened by plans for a massive new ski resort in the Vilnöss Valley, at the foot of the majestic Geisler Peaks, Sass Rigais and Furchetta (9,925 ft/3,025 metres). Fortunately the scheme was thwarted by environmental pressure groups.

The expansive pine forests (well stocked with game) of the northern sector of the park stretch to the Geisler Peaks and Mt Peitlerkofel (9,465 ft/2885 metres). Golden eagles circle the summits of these mountains. The pine forests descend to a landscape of gently rolling pastures, quaint villages

(Völs Pond) and follow the Knüppelweg trail, hikes through the wild Schlern Gorge up to this Schlern Plateau. The panorama is breathtaking.

Puez-Geisler National Park: The town of Wolkenstein (Selva), lays claim to having the highest-lying formerly inhabited fortress in Europe. It shares the 22,758-acre (9,210-hectare) square Puez-Geisler National Park with the villages of Villnöss, St Christina, Corvara, Abtei and St Martin in Thurn. Here contrasts are extreme. Looking out over the bare, windswept heights of the Puez Plateau can feel like standing a million miles from anywhere – even though the modern centres

and farmhouses.

Fanes-Sennes-Prags National Park: The park surrounding Abtei, Wengen, Enneberg, Olang, Prags and Toblach is much larger than the Puez-Geisler National park; it covers 63,454 acres (25,680 hectares). The expansive high mountain pastures of Fanes, Sennes, Fosses and Plätzwiese, lying above the tree line, offer even novice hikers wonderful opportunities to experience the thrill of the Dolomite peaks. Bubbling Karst springs, lush mountain pastures and secluded mountain lakes make an appropriate setting for the Rhaeto-Romanic legends of the Fanes kings. Down below, however, long traffic jams clog the roads to Lake Toblach and Prags Wildsee.

Sexten Dolomites National Park: What is probably the world's most impressive sundial can be seen in the Sexten Dolomites National Park, a park covering some 28,750 acres (11,635 hectares) surrounding Toblach, Sexten and Innichen. The densely packed peaks were used as orientation by early astronomers. Thus the peaks of the Sexten Mountain Sundial, towering almost 10,000 ft (3,000 metres) above sea level, were called the Nine, Ten, Eleven, Twelve and One (*Neuner, Zehner, Elfer, Zwölfer* and *Einser*). In the latter part of the 19th century, mountaineers from all corners of Europe came to

ters, fortifications, artillery sites, dug-outs and military trenches. On Monte Piano and on Mt Fanes, the Peace Trail (*Friedensweg/Via della Pace*) is a memorial to the horrors of all wars. The victims of World War I are buried in the military cemetery in the Höhlenstein Valley.

The Innerfeld, Fischlein and Rienz valleys lead us to the base of the mountain Drei Zinnen ("Three Pinnacles", 9,843 ft/3,000 metres), one of the major landmarks of the Dolomites. A road heads up the mountain from the south, making it accessible even for non-hikers. Consequently during the main tourist season, it is possible to run into more people wandering around up here than pac-

scale these mountains, establishing a network of trails and mountain huts which are still in use today.

During World War I this area was crucial to the Tyroleans' attempt to fend off the invading Italian troops. Some 10,000 soldiers occupied the mountains, even during the iciest winter months. As the cannons thundered, whole sections of the peaks toppled into the depths below. To this day, one can see the remnants of underground shel-

ing city pavements.

The Dreischuster Group (10,341 ft/3,152 metres) and Mt Haunold (9,731 ft/2,966 metres) are much less overrun. The spectacular flower-covered meadows flanking the entrance to the Innerfeld and Fischlein valleys demonstrate the positive effects of proper land usage.

Rieserferner Group National Park: Between Sand in Taufers, Gais, Percha and Rasen-Antholz, a nature reserve in the truest sense of the word unfolds over 50,852 acres (20,580 hectares). Chamois, deer, marmots, alpine hares, golden eagles, heath- and mountaincocks live here in almost total peace. Visitors

Fossils (left) and lizards (right) are just two of the natural phenomena found in the national parks of South Tyrol.

tend to visit the high-lying valley around Rein in Taufers. The ridge-top trail from the Hochgall Refuge into the Ursprung Valley is very popular.

Ancient gneiss rock (rusty brown colour with an "elephant hide" appearance), mixed with the "merely" 30 million-year-old paler-coloured stone, tonalite, form Mt Schnee-bigen Nock and Mt Hochgall (11,017 ft/ 3,358 metres and 11,270 ft/3,435 metres respectively). Their spectacular glacier snowfields and icy lakes prompted plans to turn the area into a glacier ski resort. Fortunately these have now been stopped.

The high-lying pine forests on **Tristennöckl** (8,087 ft/2,465 metres) are the highest

Trudner Horn National Park: Those who are willing to forego colossal scenery in favour of a little solitude should head for the 16,460-acre (6,660-hectare) Trudner Horn National Park, between the towns of Truden, Altrei, Montan, Neumarkt and Salurn. Although close to the densely populated Etsch Valley it is blissfully peaceful. Dark forests of beeches, spruce and fir trees carpet the mountains, to be replaced at higher elevations by flower-filled larch meadows and peaceful moorland.

It is here that the light grey Dolomite meets the brownish volcanic Bozen quartz porphyry. But the flora and fauna are the real attractions of the area, and the park is a mass

in the Alps. A hundred years ago, this was a region of glaciers, but today the region is covered with bushes and shrubs.

The melting snow produces a magnificent network of brooks and waterfalls, of which the Reinbach Falls and Pojer Falls are the most celebrated. As George Meredith said in a letter to his friend Frederick A. Maxse: "This land abounds in falling waters, brooks, torrents, all ice cold." The power industry would love to harness this natural source of energy. The Rieserferner Group, together with the neighbouring Hohe Tauern National Park, form a nature preserve of enormous proportions.

of fruits and blossoms for 10 months of the year. Here sub-Mediterranean plants and shrubs are at their most northern zone. Lizards, preying mantises, the chirping cicada – which, in the words of George Meredith, "goes all day like a factory wheel" – and a wide variety of rare butterflies are just a few of the creatures encountered.

Texel Group National Park: In Meran, senior citizens holiday under the palm trees and flowering magnolias, but above an icy wind whips around the snow-covered peaks. Just a few miles from the spa town of Meran, between Schnals, Naturns, Partschins, Algund, Tyrol, Riffian, St Martin in Passeier and Moos, the Texel Group National Park stretches over 82,604 acres (33,430 hectares). It is an unspoilt mountain wilderness. The heart of the park can be reached only by crossing over the Passeier and the Pfelderer valleys or via Schnals and the Pfossen Valley with its variety of wildlife. From here, you can see Mt Similaun (11,831 ft/3,606 metres), Hohe Wilde (11,424 ft/3,482 metres) and Texelspitze (10,883 ft/3,317 metres) with their ice-covered peaks. The famous Meran Ridge Trail is a five-day hike from hut to hut along a 60-mile (100-km) path circumventing the Texel Massif.

An information centre, open from April to October, can be found in the school in

action is taken, they may gradually die, a prospect which would inevitably mean massive landslides.

The water which runs off these mountains is caught in ancient canals used to irrigate the dry slopes of the Sonnenberg in Vinschgau. A hike up to the seven Sproner Lakes, nestling in a landscape of mountain pastures, moraines and glacial boulders, is well worth the effort. In the Schneetälchen (small snow valley), spring does not arrive until late, but when it does, usually in August, it is truly magnificent.

Sarntal Alps National Park: This park, almost 99,000 acres (40,000 hectares) in size, is covered with fields of dwarf pines and pine

Naturns. It provides useful information about all the parks of South Tyrol.

In the Schnals Valley, you can find farms at altitudes of over 6,500 ft (2,000 metres). If it were not for the larches, the landscape would be a desert of rocks. However, as it is, as well as being a beautiful spectacle – bright green in spring and a brilliant yellow-gold in autumn – these trees hold the soil in place on the steep mountainsides. Unfortunately, they are endangered by the ever-increasing pollution and it is feared that, unless preventive

Left, glacial lake on Mt Rieserferner. Above, the Pragser Wildsee in eastern South Tyrol.

forests. It is possible to wander through the the park without meeting a soul, even though it lies in the heart of the most popular part of South Tyrol. Its alpine fauna live almost undisturbed.

To the west lies the idyllic Lake Durnholz. To the east lie the virgin regions of the Flagger Valley and the water-rich Schalder Valley leading into the heart of the Samtal Alps National Park. The hike up to Lake Puntleid, situated in deep woods, is long and steep, a fact which helps keep it free from masses of tourists and souvenir shops.

The mountain pastures of the Rittner Horn stretch out above Barbian, Villanders,

Latzfons and Feldthurns. In earlier times, when the inhabitants' survival was dependent solely on the harvest, every square inch of barren pasture was precious, as is shown by the many disputes and battles over land documented in medieval court records. The remains of stone walls wind for miles across the landscape, a result of the need to restrain cows from wandering on to the neighbouring farmer's land.

Today, times are rather better, but the subsidies received from the provincial government have encouraged farmers to drain and level the land and use chemical fertilisers to increase grass production. Inevitably this has disturbed the balance of nature.

The expansive *hochmoor*, nonetheless prevails. This plant serves as a natural sponge, helping to prevent floods and drought in the agricultural lands below. Here dwarf pines, alpine roses and berry bushes grow with other moorland vegetation. It is important not to walk over the moorland, as this vegetation is extremely sensitive.

Pilgrims still make their way to the Latzfons Holy Cross, pitched at an altitude of 7,546 ft (2,300 metres) and Tyrol's highest place of pilgrimage. It was here that people used to come to pray for protection from lightning, hail and sudden cloudbursts. According to superstition, the mountains were the dance floors for witches and weather gods.

The region around the Totenkirchl, between Villanders and Reinswald in the Sarn Valley, is totally deserted. This was not always the case: in prehistoric times the region was mined for copper, and in the Middle Ages, people prospected for valuable minerals above Klausen. It is one of the rare regions of South Tyrol from which mankind has retreated, giving nature a chance to regenerate itself.

Stilfser Joch National Park: The South Tyrolean part of the park encompasses 132,200 acres (53,500 hectares) around Stilfs, Taufers in Münster Valley, Mals, Glurns, Schluderns, Prad, Laas, Martell, Schlanders, Latsch and Ulten. As already mentioned at the beginning of this chapter, when this park was originally established in the 1920s the German inhabitants of the region were sceptical, mistrusting the motives of the then Fascist government.

Nowadays, it is the environmentalists who have grounds for mistrust as more and more land is turned into plantations, roads are extended right up to the mountain pastures and hydro-electric plants are built (for instance in the Ulten and Martell Valleys). Ski resorts have mushroomed in Sulden and on the Stilfser Joch (9,045 ft/2,757 metres), which gave the park its name. With its large hotel complexes and glacier skiing, Stilfser Joch is more like an alpine Las Vegas than a nature reserve.

But in spite of such developments this park remains impressive. Together with the neighbouring Swiss National Park, it encompasses a total area of over 331,000 acres (134,000 hectares). The region around the ice-encrusted Ortler (12,795 ft/3,900 metres), Zebrú (12,270 ft/3,740 metres) and Königsspitze (12,661 ft/3,859 metres), together with the bordering Swiss region, forms one of the most important protected environments in Europe.

The park can be approached from the Martell or Ulten Valley, both dotted with old farmhouses, or from the Trafoi or Sulden valleys, both of which earned a reputation for tourism as long ago as the turn of the century. Mountain trails lead to moraines and lakes and the bizarre ice formations of the expansive glacier, the source of the foaming brooks rushing down toward the valley. In many places in the Vinschgau region the difference in altitude between the valley and the peaks is more than 8,200 ft (2,500 metres). As a result, the vegetation is very varied. In the valley, there are vineyards and orchards which enjoy a temperate climate; on the peaks, the climatic conditions resemble those in Scandinavia.

The seemingly endless forests with their firs, larches and pines extend to an altitude of over 7,400 ft (2,250 metres). Deer are so abundant here that tree destruction has become a serious problem (hunting is strictly forbidden in this national park and the natural predators of the deer – for example, bears, wolves and lynx – have long since died out in South Tyrol). Nonetheless it is a marvellous natural habitat. Magnificent chamois and ibex climb among the rocky cliffs while the droll marmots graze untiringly in the grassy heaths, building up a thick reserve of fat to tide them over during their eight long months of hibernation.

Right, a panoramic view of the Geissler peaks.

According to legend, the Rosengarten Massif was once the realm of the dwarf king Laurin. It was a splendid kingdom: the crystal walls inside the mountain sparkled like diamonds, while a magnificent garden of fragrant roses adorned the grounds outside. A golden cord wrapped around the mountain kept trespassers out.

But when the fierce warriors of Theodoric the Great, known in German legend as Dietrich of Bern, descended on Laurin's magic realm the golden cord proved useless. They ripped it away and trampled the roses into the ground. Neither Laurin's magic hood nor belt could save him from his fate. He was led away in chains, humiliated, and the treasures of his kingdom were plundered. Before leaving, he placed a magic spell on his ravished garden, turning it into stone: "Neither by the light of day nor in the dark of night shall the eyes of a human ever see your magnificence again!"

But Laurin forgot the hours of twilight. And so, shortly before sunset on most days, the Rosengarten still glows red above the dark forests. The sight is so intensely beautiful that onlookers are drawn to it as though under a spell, to be released only when the colour of the massif slowly fades from a glimmering red to a pale grey.

Another local story features the mythical city of Gand, supposed to lie between Eppan and Kaltern. According to the tale, the inhabitants of the city were excessively arrogant: they ignored God's 10 commandments, derided the pilgrims who passed through the region and committed various unholy practices. But on one occasion they carried things too far. During a Shrove Tuesday feast, they skinned an ox alive, and Nature took her revenge. Lightning struck, hail pelted down, and an earthquake shook the nearby cliffs, sending them thundering down upon the city. Nature took over where civilisation had failed. The place where Gand is supposed to have fallen is a mass of mysterious ice holes. The entire region is officially protected as a nature preserve.

The moral of both of these tales, of course, is that man should be wary of his power to destroy, but this lesson is illustrated not only

by myths. For example, up until the 1970s, Schnals was a virgin valley. For the inhabitants, life was difficult, and many of the young people, seeing no future in the valley, left to make their fortunes elsewhere. However, one young farmer, whose farm was the highest-lying in Kurzras, opted for a different course. He built Italy's biggest glacier cable car network and an enormous hotel next to the mountain hut used by climbers. Skiers came in droves. From then on the majority of Schnals residents earned their

livelihood from tourism.

Meanwhile another resident, Leo Gurschler, turned his farmland into a huge hotel and holiday flats complex. To begin with, his venture was successful; but a period of economic stagnation sent his empire tumbling and Gurschler lost everything, from his cows to his helicopter. But new investors started other projects, and today the valley is once again packed with tourists all the year round.

But the entrepreneurs aren't governed by economic factors alone. Man hasn't entirely suppressed the natural environment of South Tyrol. There is always the chance that natural forces will reclaim the mountains and valleys, and sometimes this happens with devastating consequences. On 15 February 1990, in upper Vinschgau, for example, a huge avalanche swept away the entire ski resort of Haideralm. "The revenge of the mountain" some called it.

The resort's proprietors had to fight for survival, but they wasted no time in rebuilding the skiing centre. The result was even larger and more modern than before. The provincial government invested enormous sums of money to guard against future disas-

ters, installing iron beams to hold back avalanches. Before the year was over, skiers were once again racing down the slopes. The wildlife which had begun to reassert itself in the valley retreated once again.

Today, skiers rule these regions. Their needs and desires govern much of local policy and spending. They want to arrive by modern motorway and to climb the mountains with the aid of a modern ski lift. They want prepared slopes, cleared of all trees. They

Left, most fans of the great outdoors arrive by car. Above, the establishment of national parks does not prevent rubbish heaps.

want snow cannons for the days when the sun is shining as well as heated swimming pools and solariums for the days when it is not. And in the summer months those seeking unspoilt natural environments are encouraged to venture into the remotest regions to find what they are after. In so doing, even the best-intentioned hikers inevitably destroy what they seek.

Fortunately, there are still parts of South Tyrol which haven't lost their original character or way of life. Outside the clusters of farms squeezed into narrow valley locations, where the farmers are forced to compete with the European Community's agriculture industry, and outside the major centres of tourism, where the population and traffic triples during the main tourist seasons, traditional rural practices survive. But the crowds are a constant threat, even in the remoter areas. The first public underground garage in South Tyrol is being planned, not in Meran or Gröden as one might expect, but in Kasern in the far reaches of the Ahrn Valley, where the tourists come to glimpse the glacier.

South Tyrol is a region of short distances. In a matter of a few hours it is possible to hike through all the climatic zones, beginning with palm trees and ending with edelweiss. Yet it is not unusual to hear visitors bragging that they have driven over 100 miles (160 km) in one day, without stopping, crossing all five of the major Dolomite passes. They gain little sense of the real South Tyrol this way and leave nothing behind but clouds of carbon monoxide.

Water pollution is another serious threat to the natural environment. The hotels of the region all have crystal-clear swimming pools, but in the picturesque brooks running alongside their grounds the fish are steadily dying from pollution, for most of the mountain villages have no proper sewage systems. If hotel guests inquired into such things as sewage systems as much as they do about ski lifts and swimming pools perhaps something would be done. Such inquiries are bound to be taken much more seriously than the protests of local environmental groups. After all, here the guest is king.

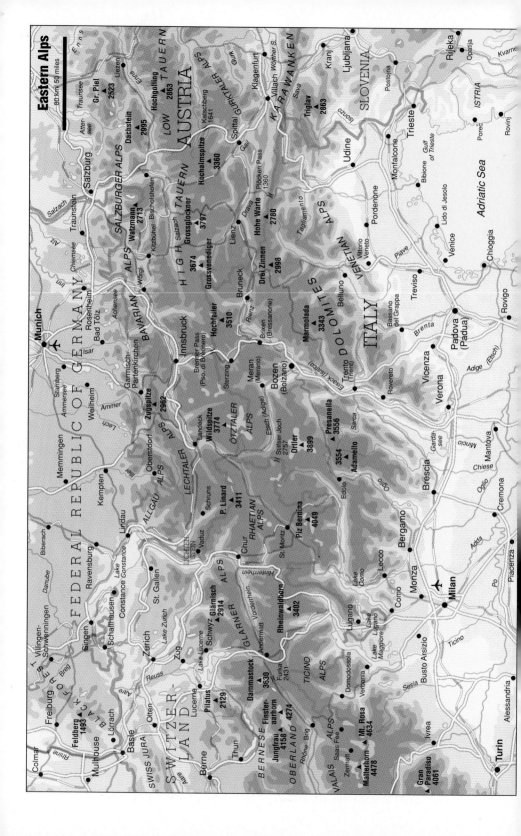

PLACES

This section has been arranged to reflect the most common tours of South Tyrol, beginning with the Brenner Pass, the main gateway to Italy and the entrance to the region from the north. Immediately beyond the Brenner lies Brixen (Bressanone) and the winding Eisack Valley (Valle Isarco).

South Tyrol is a varied and beautiful region. The lush Ahrn Valley, the rugged peaks of the Drei Zinnen (Three Pinnacles), castles and churches, remote wooded valleys and unexpected high-lying lakes are just some of its attractions.

The guide proceeds south to the region's capital, Bozen (Bolzano). Ringed by mountains – Ritten, Salten and Schlern – as well as the Eggen Valley and the Rhaeto-Romanic Grödner Valley with its Sella Massif and the peaks of the Langkofel, Bozen is a microcosm of South Tyrol as a whole. From here, the "Wine Road" leads south through the villages of Kaltern (Caldaro) and Tramin (Termeno). The rolling hills, covered by vineyards and orchards and commanded by castles, are ideal for hiking.

The third part of the journey leads through the western regions of South Tyrol. It begins with a visit to the Burggrafenamt region, followed by the spa town of Meran (Merano) and then the Sarn and Passeier valleys. Vinschgau is the centre of "disc-spinning", a tradition rooted in pagan ritual . The last chapter treks through the rural Ulten Valley, crosses the Mendel Pass and returns to the starting point, the Eisack Valley.

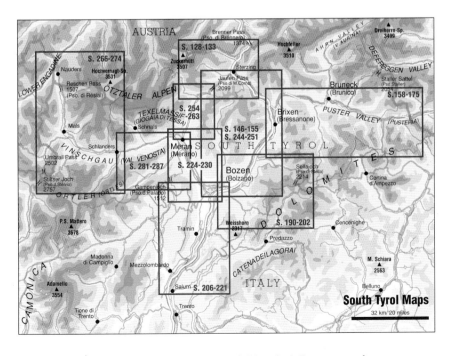

Preceding pages: at the Puez Alm; at Stilfser Joch Pass; memories are made in neon-colours and picture postcards; in the pub of Durnholz.

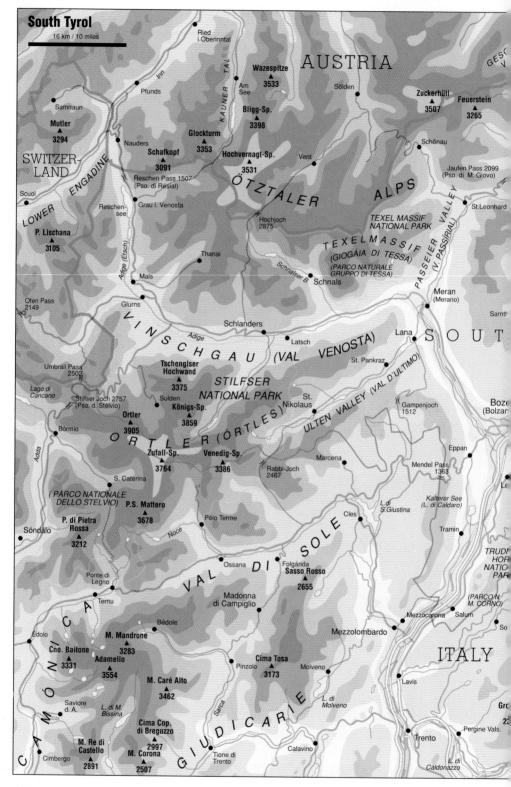

South Tyrol

16 km / 10 miles

Ried
i.Oberinntal

AUSTRIA

GESCH
V

Inn

Pfunds

Wazespitze
▲ 3533

Am
See

Sölden

Zuckerhütl
▲ 3507

Feuerstein
▲ 3265

Samnaun

Bligg-Sp.
▲ 3398

Mutler
▲ 3294

Nauders

Glockturm
▲ 3353

Schafkopf
▲ 3091

Hochvernagt-Sp.
▲ 3531

Vent

Schönau

SWITZER-
LAND

ENGADINE

KAUNER TAL

Jaufen Pass 2099
(Pso. di M. Giovo)

Scuol

Reschen Pass 1507
(Pso. di Resia)

Reschen-
see

Grau i. Venosta

ÖTZTALER   ALPS

St.Leonhard

LOWER

P. Lischana
▲ 3105

Adige (Elsch)

Hochjoch
2875

TEXEL MASSIF
NATIONAL PARK

Meran
(Merano)

PASSEIER VALLEY
(V. PASSIRIA)

Ofen Pass
2149

Thanai

TEXEL MASSIF
(GIOGÁIA DI TESSA)

Sarnth

Glurns

Mals

Schnalser B.

Schnals

(PARCO NATURALE
GRUPPO DI TESSA)

Schlanders

Adige

Latsch

Lana

SOUT

VINSCHGAU (VAL VENOSTA)

St. Pankraz

Umbrail Pass
2502

Tschenglser
Hochwand
▲ 3375

STILFSER
NATIONAL PARK

ULTEN VALLEY (VAL D'ULTIMO)

Gampenjoch
1512

Boze
(Bolzar

Lago di
Cancano

Stilfser Joch 2757
(Pso. d. Stélvio)

Sulden

Königs-Sp.
▲ 3859

St.
Nikolaus

Eppan

Le

Bórmio

Ortler
▲ 3905

ORTLER (ÓRTLES)

Marcena

Mendel Pass
1363

Adda

Zufall-Sp.
▲ 3764

Venedig-Sp.
▲ 3386

Rabbi-Joch
2467

Kalterer See
(L. di Caldaro)

S. Caterina

L.di
S.Giustina

(PARCO NATIONALE
DELLO STELVIO)

P.S. Mattero
▲ 3678

Péio Terme

Cles

Tramin

Sóndalo

P. di Pietra
Rossa
▲ 3212

Noce

VAL   DI   SOLE

Ossana

Folgárida
Sasso Rosso
▲ 2655

TRUDI
HOR
NATIC
PAR

Ponte di
Legno

Ternu

Madonna
di Campiglio

Mezzocorona

Salum

(PARCO N.
M. CORNO)

So

Bédole

Mezzolombardo

ITALY

Edolo

M. Mandrone
▲ 3283

Cno. Baitone
▲ 3331

Adamello
▲ 3554

M. Caré Alto
▲ 3462

Pinzolo

Cima Tosa
▲ 3173

Molveno

Lavis

Gr
2

CAMÓNICA

Saviore
d. A.

L. di M.
Bissina

Sarca

L. di
Molveno

GIUDICARIE

Cima Cop.
di Breguzzo
▲ 2997

M. Re di
Castello
▲ 2891

M. Corona
▲ 2507

Tione di
Trento

Calavino

Trento

Pergine Vals.

Cimbergo

L. di
Cáldonazzo

125

STERZING

The town of Sterzing (Vipiteno, 3113 ft/ 949 metres) is the first settlement of any size on the south side of the Brenner Pass, and as such can be regarded as the northern gateway to South Tyrol. Historically, Sterzing's fortunes have been inextricably linked with the trade route over the Brenner Pass, one of the most important north-south lines of communication in all Europe. Even today, the town is closely associated with this mighty thoroughfare traversing the alpine divide.

Centre of pilgrimage: The emblem of the town, the pilgrim with the tall hat under the Tyrolean eagle, was first depicted on the town seal in 1328. In 1524 the pilgrim was incorporated in the coat-of-arms, holding a crook and with a garland of roses decorating his head. But even centuries before this the city was associated with travellers. From the 3rd century, when the Roman staging post of Vipitenum (hence the official Italian name Vipiteno) was established here, pilgrims and travellers were Sterzing's most important source of revenue. They remain so today. Some experts even trace the origins of the town's name back to the so-called *Sterzer*, as pilgrims were once known in these parts. According to local lore, the first pilgrim to arrive in the town was the hunchbacked "Sterzli", who decided to settle here.

Today's visitors tend not to stick around Sterzing quite so long. Most people, governed by tight schedules, just flash past on the motorway, in an attempt to catch up on the wasted time spent queuing at the toll booth. People travelling from the south tend to stop to spend the last of their lira on *grappa*, and those coming from the north, from Munich and elsewhere, perhaps down for a day's skiing, have very little time for breaks.

At first glance, it might seem that they are justified in neglecting Sterzing, for the town appears to have little to offer visitors. But, in fact, anyone who makes a point of stopping in Sterzing will not come away disappointed, especially if they enjoy shopping. The claim by locals that the choice of goods on sale in Sterzing is "almost on a par with that in Milan" might be a little exaggerated, but there is an extraordinarily wide range of goods on offer: notably Italian fashions, quality leather shoes, wines, schnapps and noodles alongside South Tyrolean ham, sausage, bread and sports articles imported from Germany.

There are bars offering fragrant Italian coffee and mouth-watering Austrian cakes as well as restaurants serving Neapolitan pizzas and local sweet specialities such as the *Eisacktaler Schlutzkrapfen*, a kind of doughnut.

According to the people of Sterzing, the town is sometimes as busy as Riccione or Rimini. This is certainly the case when Italian and German holidays coincide and the two-way traffic is at its worst. The chaos is compounded by the volume of heavy goods vehicles on the pass. Then, regardless of which side of the pass they live – Austria or Italy –the

inhabitants of the communities along the Brenner complain bitterly. To save money and the need to queue, many of the motorists avoid the toll, "legalised banditry" as some refer to it, by turning off the motorway. This means they must crawl bumper-to-bumper through the narrow streets of the villages, creating a parallel queue to the one already on the pass. It becomes impossible for locals to get anywhere fast.

Sterzing is the last port of call before the steep climb up to the Brenner Pass. Even in ancient times, when the route was nothing more than a narrow trail a few feet wide, people must have paused for rest and refreshment in this area. In Roman times the path was developed into a proper track broad enough to take carts and during the Middle Ages it was further widened to become the famous Imperial Road.

Eventually, the old trunk road, the B12, could no longer cope with the ever-increasing volume of traffic, and so the present motorway was built, more than 65 ft (20 metres) wide and sup-

ported by gigantic concrete piers. The travellers that subsequently poured over the pass brought not only marks and schillings but also 24-hour noise and exhaust fumes, which soon permeated every nook and cranny of the valley. It is often the case that on winter weekends people hoping to escape to the **Ratschings ski area** are disappointed; sometimes the access road has to be closed because even by midday the car parks are full.

For skiers and hikers: It is therefore advisable to explore the attractions of the **Ratschings Valley** when things aren't quite so busy – i.e. on weekdays. Hikers are drawn here by the wide and wild landscapes dissected by fast mountain streams. Climbers, on the other hand, tend to head for the rather more challenging routes, such as the **Gilfenklamm**, where a shelf of marble hidden for a length of 6 km (4 miles) under the **Mareiter Stein** emerges.

The number of hiking routes available in summer is matched by the network of pistes of the Ratschings Valley

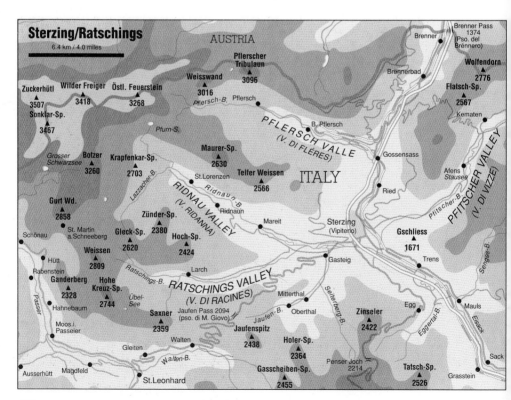

in winter. Locals, however, tend to prefer the quieter slopes under the forests, and so often head for their local mountain, the **Rosskopf**. The cable car to the summit of Monte Cavallo (this mountain's Italian name) trundles over the motorway all the year round.

As well as benefiting from trade, Sterzing once derived much wealth from the mining of iron ore, then plentiful in the area. But providing hospitality for the many travellers and merchants has played an equally important part in the local economy. In the 14th century the town was granted the "privilege of hospitality", acquiring a local monopoly on the provision of accommodation and care of travellers. On numerous occasions this privilege became a bone of contention between the people of Sterzing and the miners living in nearby **Gossensass,** who liked to claim that they were able to provide much cheaper lodgings for passers-by.

The town's sites: A leisurely walk through the old part of town provides plenty of evidence of Sterzing's former importance and glory. On the southern edge, for example, some distance off the high street, is the unmistakable parish **church of Our Dear Lady**. It owes its existence to the sizable revenues derived from silver mining at the beginning of the 15th century. The church was built behind the town houses so that the miners would have less distance to walk to Mass.

Building work began on the church under the supervision of local masters Hans and Friedrich Feur around 1420. Hans Feur, the architect of the chancel, was one of the most accomplished master builders of the late-Gothic style in the Tyrol region, as is evident in the chancel's exquisite star-vaulting supported by flying buttresses. Feur learned his craft by working on the construction of the cathedral at Ulm in Bavaria, the spire of which remains the tallest church spire in the world. The Feurs built a similar spire on this church in Sterzing; unfortunately, however, this came crashing down.

In 1456 the Ulm sculptor Hans

Castle Reifenstein in the Eisack Valley.

Multscher was summoned to work on the high altar of the church. Unfortunately, the 40-ft (12-metre) high altar fell victim to baroquisation in 1781, but the five main figures remain intact: Mary with Child and the saints Barbara, Ursula, Catherine and Apollonia.

Segments of the original altar can be admired at the **Multscher Museum** which occupies the former Hospital of the Holy Ghost. The work occupies an important place in the history of art because here, for the first time, the strict conventions that had hitherto governed sacred art were relaxed and the artist incorporated figures displaying local characteristics.

Lying south of the church is **Neustadt** (new town). Colourful houses with oriel facades line both sides of the pedestrian precinct, and an avenue of trees provides shelter for window shopping should it be raining or snowing. The people of Sterzing completely rebuilt this part of town after a disastrous fire in the 15th century.

This vigorous period of building work included the construction of the town's best loved landmark, the tower known as the **Zwölferturm**, again the work of the famous Hans Feur. His work in the town did not end there, for from 1468-72 he erected the **Town Hall**, in front of which stands a **statue of St John of Nepomuk**, put there as a talisman to protect the townsfolk from the ravages of flooding.

Ancient and modern: In the courtyard of the town hall it is still possible to detect traces of the Roman settlement. The famous **Mithras Stone**, cult object of the Persian god of the same name revered in the early Roman Empire, is thought to have been brought here by Roman soldiers; the Mithras cult was predominantly a military one. Some Sterzing inhabitants still claim that the stone possesses special powers. Next to it is a Roman milestone dating from the 2nd century, which was discovered during excavations in 1979.

In line with various other environmental initiatives in the city, and like many similar places elsewhere in Eu-

The Brenner motorway, Italy's most important link to the north.

rope, the **Town Square**, behind the Zwölferturm, is no longer accessible to motorised traffic. This "salon of the old town" as locals affectionately refer to it, is now an integral part of the pedestrian precinct. On warm summer evenings it becomes the most animated spot in the city, with theatre performances, concerts and even fashion shows. In the winter months the town's children come here to play in the snow.

But there are limits to how many new ideas the people of Sterzing are prepared to accept. This fact was clearly demonstrated by the townspeople's reaction to the building of an ultra-modern bookshop, the **Athesia Book Shop**, slapbang in the middle of the old quarter of town. Traditionally-minded people immediately denounced the steel and glass edifice with its futuristic facades, claiming it was an eyesore, and campaigned to have it torn down. However, local people gradually got more used to the building and emotions have now calmed down – in fact, the controversial building has become a tourist attraction.

Formal dress is rarely required.

Poets and discothèques: The **Gasthof Krone**, the inn in the centre of the old town, has been famous since the 15th century. Italian emissaries sang its praises and even Goethe came here to sample its attractions. It remains a popular place for locals and visitors alike, who come in particular to savour the atmosphere of the Kronenkeller. In winter it is frequented by skiers and in summer climbers come here to celebrate their latest feat.

Sterzing offers visitors plenty of entertainment, right into the early hours of the morning. There are four discothèques to choose from, of which the **Derby Club**, a pizzeria-cum-discothèque (upstairs) on the outskirts of town, seems to be the most popular. It doesn't matter who one asks, this is the place to go in Sterzing. Most people, however, like the town's older generation, are drawn to Sterzing by the call of the mountains rather than the sound of rock music. Their usual course of action is to retire early to bed in preparation for an early morning start.

BRIXEN

At the point where the **River Rienz** (Rienza) flows into the River Eisack (Isarco), the valley widens into the Brixen Basin. Here the distinctive southern character of South Tyrol first becomes apparent. The basin is enclosed by three narrow gorges: the Brixen Gorge in the north, the Mühlbach or Haslach Gorge to the east and the so-called Star Chasm, or "Southern Brixen Chasm", in the south.

The first two gorges are characterised by hard Brixen granite, composed mainly of plutonic rock comprising quartz, feldspar and mica, which are capable of withstanding many of the extreme forces of nature, a quality important during the Ice Age. Throughout the region's history these gorges have made ideal locations for road blocks, not least for the customs houses collecting tolls.

Here travellers arriving from the north

catch their first glimpse of southern vegetation. Chestnut groves, orchards and bushy-tipped vineyards, as well as stands of cedars and cypress trees, dot the landscape. The surrounding mountains, Plose (8,215 ft/2,504 metres) and the 8,507-ft (2,593-metre) Schrotthorn, tower above the valley. Elsewhere in the world, mountains of such terrific height as these might intimidate; but here they merely enfold and shelter.

Travellers with an interest in art and architecture should be sure to allocate plenty of time for a visit to Brixen. The town contains some splendid architecture, ranging from Gothic, Renaissance, baroque, rococo and Biedermeier all the way to neoclassical and Art Nouveau.

Brixen's warring bishops: Brixen (Bressanone) has a long and turbulent history, closely tied to the activities of its bishops. It first became significant in the early 10th century, when the Bishop of Säben (Sabiona) who lived on a barren cliff above the town of Klausen (Chiuso), was presented with the "Meierhof Prichsna", a prosperous dairy-farming estate in the valley, by the German king Ludwig the Child. In 970, Bishop Albuin decided to move his see here and ordered the construction of Brixen's first cathedral.

Conrad II founded the sovereign diocese of Brixen in 1027. With the aid of bishops loyal to the German emperor, he created a powerful base from which to protect the vital route through the Eisack Valley. In 1179, when the diocese was granted currency, trade and customs rights by Frederick I, as well as its own exclusive jurisdiction, Brixen's future development as a major town was assured.

In the middle of the 15th century, Nicholas Krebs, son of a German vintner, was named Bishop of Brixen under the name of Nicholas Cusanus. This illustrious man, after whom the Academy of Arts in Brixen is named, played a central role in the region's fortunes. Immediately after being made bishop, he became involved in a dispute with the province's secular ruler, Sigmund the Wealthy. In principle, the dispute was over the rights to the office of the bailiff for the Sonnenburg Monastery in Pustertal (Val Pusteria), but in reality it involved the right to sovereignty over the monastery in general.

The bishop lost the support of the population when he tried to institute a series of laws designed to curb wicked sensual pleasure; they included such unpopular measures as the prohibition of dancing at weddings. Such controls proved totally obnoxious to the local population and ultimately the bishop was unsuccessful in implementing his authority. Eventually, after 10 years as bishop, he admitted defeat and retired to the Vatican.

During the Reformation in the 16th century Brixen was affected by the Peasants Wars that were sweeping through Europe from southwest Germany. Following a series of executions in 1525, the frustrated peasants stormed the city and occupied it for two months. In the end the rebellion was crushed and its leaders were beheaded in the cathedral square.

From 1806 to 1814, the Bavarians ruled the city, for the December 1805 Treaty of Bratislava, signed after Napoleon's victory over the Habsburgs, had forced Austria to relinquish sovereignty over Tyrol to Bavaria, a French ally. The religious-political measures instituted by the Bavarians on top of the open battle between the churches shocked the conservative population of Tyrol. They managed to stage a successful revolution against the Bavarians (1813–14), and Brixen subsequently returned to Tyrolean rule. The bishop's see for the diocese of Brixen-Bozen remained in Brixen until 1964 when it was moved to neighbouring Bozen.

The bishop's see of Brixen: Although the bishop no longer resides in Brixen, the town's most interesting sights all stem from the town's history as an esteemed bishop's see and important German fief. The Prince-Bishop's Palace and the cathedral complex, the chapel of St John, the famous cloisters and the parish church are the main buildings of interest in the city centre. But the attraction of Brixen lies in the ambience as much as

In summer, the cathedral square is filled with tourists.

138

the sights. Narrow streets lined with attractive arcades, former patrician and church officials' homes, flower-filled nooks and crannies and some of the top guesthouses in the region (for example, Fink and Finsterwirtmake) make it a very appealing town in which to wander.

Among the best hotels is the Zum Elefanten (*see Restaurants chapter, pages 92–95*), an establishment famous far beyond South Tyrol's borders. The hotel acquired its somewhat curious name in 1551 when an Indian elephant, a gift from the Portuguese king to Archduke Maximilian of Austria, was stabled at the inn on its journey across the Alps to the royal palace in Vienna.

To the cathedral: To get a proper sense of the chronological development of the **cathedral buildings**, it is preferable to enter through an unobtrusive door at the rear of the complex, across from the Café am Gries on the street called Rundgartgasse. This leads directly into the Romanesque cloisters which, in turn, lead to the chapel of St John, the cathedral proper and the parish church dedicated to St Michael.

The **Gothic cloisters** are a real architectural jewel. They were built around 1200 as part of the original Romanesque cathedral which stood on this site. Unfortunately, when the Gothic arches were constructed in about 1370, the existing Romanesque paintings were totally destroyed, partly by the new construction and partly by the extensive use of whitewashing.

The frescoes which you can see today were painted between 1390 and 1509, generally at the behest of wealthy members of the cathedral chapter. Of the 20 arcades, 15 are extensively embellished with frescoes. Thus the Brixen cloisters present a complete history of the development of Gothic painting in Tyrol. A walk through the cloisters is tantamount to a walk through art history.

In the 15th century, a Brixen school of painting developed, distinguished by a late Gothic realism, which after 1430 replaced the elegant "court" style which had previously been in vogue. The new school represented true-to-life painting and was characterised by a penchant for dramatic exaggeration, especially in the subjects' faces.

One of the most prolific masters of this school was Master Leonhard, who was responsible for a veritable flood of frescoes, altars and altar panels in and around Brixen from 1454 to 1473. It did not seem to bother his patrons that Leonhard understood little about perspective and totally ignored the artistic developments current at the time. The painting of pure Gothic frescoes was still common in Brixen at a time when the rest of South Tyrol was being heavily influenced by the Renaissance.

At the southern end of the cloisters is the late Romanesque **chapel of St John**. Invariably this is locked, and obtaining the key from the sexton is not an easy task. However, it is perfectly satisfactory to peek into the chapel through a small side window from the cloisters. Built at the beginning of the 13th century as a baptismal church, it has a 14th-century square nave with cross vaults and a chancel with an arched cupola construction.

On the Eisack Bridge in Brixen.

The interior of the chapel is almost completely covered with frescoes dating from the High Middle Ages. These represent some of the most valuable examples of this type of art in the entire alpine region. Depicted on the upper walls of the nave are the throne of Solomon and Sophia in majesty, surrounded by the prophets and the righteous, patriarchs and ecclesiastical fathers. It is thought that this fresco was completed around 1250 and represents the first signs of the early Gothic linear style. The chancel contains a splendid fresco cycle with scenes from the life of John the Baptist, various saints, the Adoration of the Magi and a noteworthy Crucifixion scene.

The Romanesque nave of the Brixen cathedral, built around 1200, and the Gothic chancel, completed in 1472, are still standing. The other parts of the cathedral, built in a simple Lombardian baroque style, were constructed between 1745–55. The two western towers were built in Romanesque style, though completed in the 17th century.

The monumental single-nave interior, with its side altars and short transepts, is dominated by a series of ceiling frescoes by the artist Paul Troger (the altarpiece on the Cassian altar is also by Troger). The neoclassical vestibule houses numerous Gothic gravestones of Brixen bishops from 1374 to 1521. A plaque commemorating the famous poet and knight, Oswald von Wolkenstein, is found on the cathedral's northeastern exterior wall.

Cathedral treasury: The **cathedral treasury**, located in the former granary of the old cathedral chapter, can be reached from the cloisters. It contains precious sacral robes, shrines and magnificent monstrances. Among the most valuable pieces are the robes of Byzantine purple with a pattern of eagles, the Hartmann robes and accompanying mitre of woven silk from Asia Minor (dating from *circa* 1150) and the papal gloves, made around 1200. Large reliquary busts of figures, a relics coffer dating from the 13th century and a 12th-century Venetian cedar shrine, deco-

Left, in the monastery's library; **right**, the Stufels coat-of-arms.

rated with gold, are just some of the pieces found here.

The unassuming parish church, dedicated to St Michael, lies directly to the north of the cathedral. It was built around 1500 and incorporated the existing steeple (1459). The interior, remodelled in baroque style in 1757, contains magnificent ceiling frescoes. The altars, built in neoclassical style, have altar-pieces from the baroque era. The most valuable piece is the *Fall of the Angels*, painted by Franz Frank in 1681.

In the southwestern corner of the old town lies the **Palace of the Prince-bishops**, the original of which was completed in 1270. The current building was built by Albrecht Lucchese between 1591 and 1600 in the style of a Renaissance palace. The outwardly plain structure contains an interesting inner courtyard with a three-storey loggia with arcades. It is adorned with 24 terracotta statues made by the German Hans Reichle around 1600. The interior rooms are decorated with magnificent coffered ceilings, portals, stucco decorations,

panelling and tiled ovens. A **collection of nativity scenes** (some 100 exhibits) occupies part of the main floor. The upper floors house the **Diocesan Museum** containing outstanding works of sacred art.

A tip from the bishops: The three stone statues of the bishops Ingenuin, Cassian and Albuin on the facade of the cathedral's vestibule have been given more secular significance, at least by jocular locals. According to them, the sculpture depicts the bishops in the midst of an important midday discussion: Ingenuin places his hand on his heart and moans about the heat and Albuin asks Cassian what they can do about it. Cassian, the figure in the middle of the group, is the patron saint of Brixen. He points with his outstretched hand toward the narrow cathedral lane and the sign **Zum Finsterwirt**.

Those who follow the bishop's advice will find themselves in a cosy inn with a long and venerable tradition. Here, in former times, the wine of the cathedral chapter was dispensed, but

The "Elephant" in Brixen.

only under the condition that imbibing ceased as soon as darkness fell. Furthermore, use of artificial light to circumvent the stricture was forbidden. The name of the pub, which means "inn of darkness", gives a good clue as to how the innkeeper managed to flout the restrictions without getting into trouble. Anyway, it is a convivial place in which to adjourn for a drink.

The old town: Brixen, South Tyrol's oldest city, has a wealth of interesting historical sights, particularly in the way of architecture. Narrow lanes of arcades, smart patrician homes, dignified churches and narrow buckling bridges all date from the Middle Ages. Most of the facades with their arches, oriel windows, parapets and stepped gables, date from the 16th and 17th centuries.

The houses were frequently decorated with frescoes. Those on the house at Zinggasse 8 and those on the old town hall are particularly remarkable. The most handsome patrician house is the Goret House at Pfarrplatz 1. Built in 1581, and a mixture of Gothic and Renaissance styles, it is a typical Tyrolean town house.

The old town is small and it is easy to see the whole area on foot, but rather than try to cram everything into one day it is best to stop overnight in one of the many stately guesthouses. Be sure, too, to sample the Eisack cuisine. Brixen chefs are highly regarded and the traditional hospitality is celebrated.

The environs of Brixen: This beautiful region has provided inspiration to countless troubadours and artists. Albrecht Dürer, for instance, immortalised the city of Klausen (Chiuso), about 11 miles (18 km) south of Brixen – and accessible by train from Brixen – in his etching *The Good Fortune*.

A number of churches in the mountains surrounding Brixen house important art treasures. Three churches in the vicinity of **St Andrä**, a hamlet lying a short distance to the southeast of Brixen, are particularly worthy of a visit. The fresco cycle, depicting Christ's Passion as well as scenes from the legend of St John, painted by Master Leonhard of Brixen (1464), is housed in the **church of St John** in **Mellaun**. The carved altar, completed in 1482, is the work of Hans Klocker.

Meanwhile **St Nicholas's** in **Klerant** offers the most beautiful and complete examples of Master Leonhard's style of painting, including a remarkable rendering of an elephant (though it must be said that since the artist had no model on which to base his painting, the animal, entirely clothed in armour, resembles a horse with a trunk rather than a recognisable elephant). The altar here is also by Hans Klocker.

St John's in **Karnol** is Romanesque with a round apse and Gothic net vault dating from around 1500. This church, occupying a spur, is also richly decorated. The choir has Gothic frescoes (1500) painted by a Brixen artist, and the nave has a series of notable frescoes dating from the 16th and 17th centuries. The key to this church is obtained from the neighbouring farm.

The region surrounding Brixen is dotted with the remnants of innumerable castles and churches. The grey, crumbling masonry and bleached frescoes of many of them suggest infinite past splendour. Such ruins invariably nestle in lovely countryside, so visits are highly recommended. Indeed some of them have been painstakingly restored and turned into informal restaurants offering traditional South Tyrolean food and local wine. These are big hits among would-be modern-day troubadours, but if this sort of thing isn't to your taste then take a picnic.

On the other hand, more serious lovers of art and fine wine might be better off heading for the Neustift Monastery, founded in 1142 by Bishop Hartmann as an Augustinian canonical monastery. Although lying a mere 2 miles (3 km) from Brixen, it enjoys a blissfully peaceful location. The original Romanesque church was renovated in baroque style in 1742 and is the South Tyrol's most lovely church in this style. The Gothic frescoes in the cloisters are on a par with those of Brixen's cathedral cloisters. The paintings in the *pinakothek* and the codices in the library are also highly regarded.

THE EISACK VALLEY

Just beyond the town of Sterzing, the **Eisack Valley** (Isarco) narrows again and the road, railway and toll motorway squeeze through dark, wooded hills. In the vicinity of Brixen (Bressanone) the valley widens briefly, but south of here the mountains once again press closer, constricting the Eisack river and heavily travelled motorway like a tightly laced corset.

Motorists who stay on the broad main road along the valley basin miss the best sights, for to appreciate the essential beauty of the Eisack Valley it needs to be seen from above, from the quieter, narrower roads weaving along the mountainsides. These pass through out-of-the-way villages deeply rooted in tradition, where churches richly decorated with frescoes and carvings are waiting to be discovered by the independent tourist. Furthermore, from this height the dramatic beauty of the Dolomites is seen to best advantage. The spectacular peaks of the Geisler, the Schlern and Rosengarten Massifs form a stunning backdrop to the southern Eisack Valley.

Reifenstein, just south of Sterzing, is only one in the string of castles which grace this valley and have given it the name of "Valley of Castles". It is perched on a broad spur rising up out of a flat expanse which used to be a lake. With its ancient walls, drawbridge and castle gate, Reifenstein is the perfect springboard for a delve into the area's history. The crenellated parapet, replete with turrets and merlons, encircles an inner courtyard containing a well and cistern. In the living quarters, a maze of portals, passageways and galleries, you can see the bedrooms and a kitchen complete with an open hearth.

This late 15th-century castle, though well preserved, has been spared excessive restoration and gives a better idea of its period than any other castle in South Tyrol. The most interesting rooms are the arolla pine-panelled Gothic room, the green hall, which is decorated with green ornamental painting, and the so-called count's room, also panelled in arolla pine.

Just south of the castle, overlooking the road, is the late Gothic pilgrimage **church of Maria Trens**. It dates from 1498. The marble relief of a Madonna with child above the main portal was completed in 1510. Joseph Adam Mölk painted the frescoes. The marble altar in the chapel of grace, with its late Gothic Madonna figure in splendid baroque robes, is the work of Cristoforo Benedetti. The painting on the wall of the nave is of the procession of the miracle-working icon on Easter Monday of 1728.

The next castle along this route is **Welfenstein**, whose history dates back to the year 1271. The current structure, however, was built much later, in the late 19th century. Just past the castle is **Mauls** (Mules, 3,100 ft/945 metres). It was here that the **Mithras Stone**, today housed in Sterzing (*see page 132*), was found. The 13th-century **Staffler Guesthouse**, with its medieval vaults, is a pleasant place to pause for some refreshment.

The southern gateway to the upper Eisack Valley is guarded by the forbidding fortifications of **Franzensfeste** (Fortezza, 2,450 ft/747 metres). Built between 1833 and 1839, it was named after Austria's Emperor Franz I. The fortification served as a barracks as well as a portal to the friendly southern districts. The modern town of the same name is today little more than a shunting-station on the railway line connecting Italy with the north. The vineyards carpeting the countryside around South Tyrol's northernmost monastery, **Neustift**, are an indication of the strong southern influences to come.

Neustift Monastery/Novacella: This monastery was founded by Bishop Hartmann of Brixen, and the triple-nave basilica was built under Provost Conrad of Rodank. New frescoes were painted in 1370 when the Gothic arch and choir were constructed. The moat and curtain wall with towers and embrasures, construction of which began in 1476, endow the monastery with a defensive countenance. They were built at a time when central Europe lay in fear of a Turkish invasion. As it turned out, these walls were not even strong enough to withstand the onslaught of the rebellious peasants who stormed the fortification in the Peasants' War of 1525 with the intention of destroying the detested tax books.

The walls of the monastery church are Romanesque, but the interior is in magnificent late baroque style. The baroque renovation, carried out by Joseph Delai, was completed in 1738. The opulent stucco work is by Anton Gigl and the frescoes by Matthias Günther. The high altar is the work of Teodoro Benedetti.

At one time Neustift Monastery had early Gothic cloisters completely covered in frescoes, similar to those found in Brixen. The originals, however, were painted over in the 15th century, and in 1636 they were whitewashed. Consequently these cloisters do not provide visitors with anything like the wealth of frescoes found in the Brixen cloisters, but some of the original paintings have been exposed, which makes a comparison of the different styles interesting. Examples of the original frescoes are found in the first, second and sixth, as well as the 17th–19th arcades. In the third arcade, a 1490 painting of the *Parable of the Great Supper*, executed by Friedrich Pacher, is a vivid example of late Gothic art.

The most precious treasures of Neustift Monastery are found in the Romanesque **Victor Chapel**, the entire west wall of which is decorated with a monumental early 14th-century fresco. It depicts the journey of the three kings and their audience with King Herod. The **paintings gallery** houses further attractions, including ornamental painted panels, complete altar-pieces and statues. The **library**, completed in 1778 by Giuseppe Sartori, is said to be the most magnificent rococo room in all of South Tyrol. It houses a variety of medieval manuscripts, incunabula and early prints.

The **Klosterkeller**, the monastery's

View of the Eisack Valley and the Säben Monastery from Villanders.

wine cellar, is an excellent place to enjoy wine made on the premises as well as first-rate South Tyrolean ham. The neighbouring wineshop offers guided tours and sells the monastery wines by the bottle.

The tiny village of **Vahrn** (Varna, 2,260 ft/690 metres) lies to the west of Neustift, along the Schalderer brook. The **castle ruins of Salern**, luxuriant chestnut groves and the magnificent homes of the Eisack Valley nobility make it a very attractive village. Here again, the parish church is well worth a visit; it is decorated with a large and unusual fresco of the coronation of the Virgin Mary on its outside wall. The painting, rendered by the region's most prolific painter, Master Leonhard of Brixen, in 1478, includes an entire band of angels playing contemporary musical instruments.

Between Brixen and Bozen: In **Brixen** (Bressanone, 1840 ft/560 metres), the lines of hills flanking the River Eisack begin to grow much larger. Unfortunately, there is no through route along

Neustift Monastery nestles in vineyards.

the mountainside, but various small roads lead up into the mountains or into adjacent valleys, and a leisurely detour along one of these routes is an ideal way to escape the tolls and noise of the through motorway.

The first detour begins south of Brixen and leads up to **St Andrä** (St Andrea in Monte, 3,143 ft/958 m) and then almost to the peak of the 8,225-ft (2,507-metre) **Plose**. From this point, there is a spectacular view of the entire upper Eisack Valley and the Puster Valley as well as a lovely panorama of the Alps.

On the way back down the mountain, a fork to the east at the **Vallazza Guesthouse** leads to the **Würzjoch Pass** (Passo d'Erbe, 6,581 ft/2,006 metres). This route, which follows the northern face of the **Peitlerkofel** (Sass de Putia, 9,429 ft/2,874 metres) and leads down into the **Gader Valley** (Val Badia), is popularly known as the "Brixen Dolomite Road". The other possibility is to take the fork to the right beyond Halsl. This road leads to the **Villnöss Valley** (Val di Funes), directly below the northern·faces of the **Geisler Peaks** (the highest of which is 9,925 ft/3,025 metres). This valley is home to Reinhold Messner, world champion mountain climber and author of the opening chapter of this book.

St Peter, the main town of the Villnöss Valley, stretches loosely across the valley's meadows. At its centre is the huge parish church, reconstructed around 1800. Its free-standing domed steeple was not completed until 1897. The frescoes on the dome's interior are the work of Joseph Schöpf.

Much more interesting, however, are two other churches lying just off the main road. The first is **St Valentine in Pardell** which contains one of the valley's two triptych altar-pieces. Its shrine contains three sculptures, and the inner surfaces of the triptych wings are decorated with reliefs of saints. The paintings on the outer surfaces depict various scenes from the life of the church's patron saint. The altar-piece was created around 1500 in Hans Klocker's Brixen studio.

The other triptych altar-piece, in **St Jacob am Joch**, is even more beautiful than the one in St Valentine in Pardell. It is also embellished with sculptures. Statuettes decorate the pillars, and the paintings on the outer surfaces of the triptych are reminiscent of pictures of the Danube School. The altar-piece was created around 1517 in the Brixen School; Philip Diemer was the artist who painted the pictures.

Beyond the town of St Magdalena, in the area around the ancient **Ranui estate**, is the region's most beautiful countryside. The hunting estate, originally a much smaller farm, was commissioned in 1744 by Michael of Jenner. He also ordered the construction of the **chapel of St John** in the meadow. The decorative paintings on the outer walls of the chapel are in charming contrast to the dark forests and pale grey stone of the **Sass Rigais** (9,925 ft/3,025 metres) rising above.

A Renaissance treasure: The main centre of the mountain plateau stretching to the southwest is **Feldthurns** (Velturno), **Milk is transported on sledges.**

which can be reached directly from Brixen. The **Castle Velthurns**, situated along the road leading into the village, is unassuming from the outside, but, in fact, it is the most important Renaissance structure in the whole of South Tyrol. The castle was commissioned by Cardinal Christoph of Madruz in 1577 and completed under his nephew and successor as Bishop of Brixen, John Thomas Spaur.

Castle Velthurns served as the summer residence for the Brixen bishops from 1587 onwards. The relatively short construction period of only 10 years resulted in a rare uniformity of style. Its interior decorations are all in the style of the High Renaissance. Every room in the castle was conceived as a complete work of art, replete with handsome panelling, magnificent portals, coffered ceilings and paintings. The fine inlay work in the wooden panelling is particularly notable, and the frescoes, especially those decorating the rooms on the second floor, are outstanding. In accordance with the prevailing tastes of the Renaissance period, their subjects are allegorical.

The third floor served as the apartments of the prince-bishop. The four corner rooms here are representative of the magnificence of Velthurns Castle as a whole. The most spectacular room is the one in the southern corner, the "royal room", whose rich panelling and lovely coffered ceiling are considered masterpieces. The inlay, again exquisitely detailed, was designed by Hans Spineider of Meran, although his assistants carried out the actual work. Some 10,000 hours of labour went into the woodwork in this one room alone.

The first town south of Brixen in the Eisack Valley is **Klausen** (Chiusa), which lies at the foot of the venerable Säben (Sabiona) cliff. Formerly a customs point of the Brixen bishops who controlled the traffic along the Brenner route, Klausen was granted its charter in 1400. Just a few years later, massive walls were built linking the town to the nearby **Castle Branzoll**.

The parish church of Klausen, com-

In the remote regions, horses are still used on farms.

pleted in 1498, was constructed by Benedict Weibhauser of Brixen on the foundations of the original 6th-century church. The tympanum relief over the south portal belongs to the original church. The net rib vault is painted with figures of saints. The richly decorated organ loft in the western part was added in 1520.

The **Capuchin Monastery** has a particularly interesting history. Father Gabriel Pontifeser, born in Klausen, entered the Capuchin Order in Augsburg. From there he was sent to the court of Palatinate-Neuburg. When the court's princess, Maria Anna, married the Spanish king Charles II, Father Gabriel accompanied the young queen to Spain. Queen Maria Anna ordered the construction of a Capuchin monastery in honour of the monk in Klausen in 1697. A few years later she purchased the house of his birth, near the monastery, and commissioned a model of the Santa Casa (Holy House) of Loreto for the site. The treasury room of this chapel contains the **"Loreto treasure"**, paintings, sacral objects and robes belonging to the pious father.

The fortifications of Säben: The oldest church in Klausen is **St Sebastian**, a round church located in an orchard just outside town. Built around 1213 as a church of Our Saviour, it has one large and 12 smaller apses symbolising Christ and his apostles.

The town's most interesting sight, however, rises above the town, on the cliff 650 ft (200 metres) above the valley floor. This cliff housed an ancient settlement and is known as the **Säben Cliff**. Here, in the 4th century, the diocese of Säben was established, with a church and fortifications. This was the residence of the bishops until 970 when Bishop Albuin decided to move to more comfortable quarters in Brixen. Until then the cliff had been at the centre of a hard-fought battle between the bishops and the temporal rulers of Tyrol to control the region.

As late as 1460, the Säben fortifications were seized and occupied by Duke Sigmund's troops in his battle against Cardinal Nicholas Cusanus. In 1533, the compound was struck by lightning and reduced to a pile of rubble. In order to preserve the site's long history as a religious centre, a Benedictine monastery was built there in 1681 by Father Matthias Jenner of Klausen. This monastery still stands today.

The most interesting part of the **Säben Monastery** is the **church of the Holy Cross**, a single-nave construction dating from the 17th century and standing on the foundation of the original 6th-century bishop's church on the highest point of the Säben Cliff. A crucifixion scene, created at the end of the 15th century in Master Leonhard's studio, decorates the high altar. The most remarkable thing about the church is its interior. In 1679, the entire church, including the chancel, was painted in a linear perspective which creates a fascinating illusory effect. A *trompe l'oeil* of extensive pillared halls forms the background for painted biblical scenes. In fact, it is the work of an Italian painter of theatrical scenery. It is so perfectly executed that the visitor can never be sure

Left, native costume. **Right**, local beauty.

where the reality ends and the deception begins.

Self-sufficient villages: Just south of Klausen are several villages which merit a visit. On the west side of the Eisack is the picturesque **Villanders** (Villandro, 2,887 ft/880 metres) while on the east side are **Albions** (2,910 ft/887 metres) and **Lajen** (Laion, 3,609 ft/1,100 metres). The inhabitants of this region have always been self-sufficient. Due to the various climatic zones, they were able to grow almost all the crops they required, and, as in certain other regions of South Tyrol, mining took place around Villanders.

The church of St Nicholas in Albions is notable for its late Gothic carved altar-piece. South of Lajen are the ancient **Vogelweide Farms** which, some speculate, may have been the home of the famous troubadour Walther von der Vogelweide.

Waidbruck (Ponte Gardena), with its **Trostburg** fortress, is located at the entrance to the Grödner Valley (Val Gardena). The fortress, built around 1150 to protect the approach into the Grödner Valley and secure the route through the Eisack Valley, has a particularly formidable appearance. Ministers of the Brixen bishops occupied the fortress until 1220 when Meinhard II of Tyrol took over the building. In 1382, the Wolkenstein dynasty became the new owners, remaining so right up until 1967. Today's structure was begun in 1595.

Trostburg is unmatched by any other alpine castle in its wealth and range of architectural details. They date from various phases of construction. The most impressive room is the "Great Hall" on the top floor. It is probably the most unusual secular hall from the Renaissance period in South Tyrol. Completed in 1607, it was the work of Engelhard Dietrich of Wolkenstein, whose ambition was to match the magnificent Spanish Hall in the Ambras Castle. The latter was the model for Trostburg's artistically crafted coffered ceiling with its pattern of octagons and crosses. Intarsia in contrasting tones of wood, gilded rosettes and filigree fittings form the framework for the coats of arms of the Wolkenstein line and the families allied to it by marriage.

Holy waters: Just past Waidbruck, the road to Barbian forks off to the west. A turning right at the church with the leaning tower leads to **Bad Dreikirchen** ("spa of three churches") to the north of Barbian. Here, occupying an idyllic spot, are the three adjoining churches of St Nicholas, St Gertrude and St Magdalena. Their shared bathhouse dates from 1315; the churches are thought to have been founded as shrines, connected to the holy springs. Two altar-pieces from the Brixen School are found here, and St Gertrude's houses a series of early 15th-century frescoes.

A narrow road leads south from Barbian to the Ritten Plateau. This route affords not only a spectacular view of the Seiser Plateau and the Schlern Massif, but also the small hamlet of **Saubach** with its church of **Saints Ingenuin and Albuin**. Although tiny, this church contains three free-standing late Gothic altar-pieces.

Left, the steeples of Bad Dreikirchen above Barbian. Right, Klausen's old town is more interesting than it looks from the motorway.

THE EAST TYROLEAN VALLEYS

The expansive **Puster Valley** (Val Pusteria), running in an east-west direction, separates the Alps in the north from the Dolomites in the south. The valley basin is filled with vast moraine deposits through which the **River Rienz** (Rienza) has carved its path. Much of the Puster Valley is made up of steep wooded gorges from which it is impossible to see either the Dolomites or the Alps.

However, travellers who venture up into the surrounding hills or adjacent valleys will be treated to spectacular panoramas. The **Ahrn Valley** (Valle Aurina) in the north winds its way to the foot of the alpine glaciers, while in the south the road climbs through the **Gader Valley** (Val Badia) to the magnificent Dolomite passes. Finally, in the east, the **Höhlenstein Valley** and **Sexten Valley** lead directly to the heart of the Dolomite Sexten Range.

Mühlbach and Rodeneck: The ancient village of **Mühlbach** (Rio di Pusteria) is at the western end of the Puster Valley, on the right banks of the Rienz. In the Middle Ages it was an important trading post on the route between southern Germany and Venice. The ruins of a former border fortification along the **Mühlbach defile**, a short distance to the east of the village, serve as a reminder that this used to be the boundary between the counties of Tyrol and Görz. The Puster Valley remained an important trade route right up until recent times; the railway line, still in use today, was opened in 1871. And even now the valley is still an important thoroughfare. Recent plans to build a super highway to Venice through the valley have so far been thwarted by the protests of local residents.

The **parish church** in Mühlbach contains a number of frescoes by Friedrich Pacher (*circa* 1500). Those on the southern exterior wall date from the early 15th century. North of Mühlbach, **Meransen** (Maranza, 4,660 ft/1,420 me-

tres) is the centre of an extensive ski and hiking region.

South of Mühlbach is **Castle Rodeneck**, perched high on a cliff jutting out into the Rienz and guarding the entrance to the valley. This, South Tyrol's largest citadel, was originally built by Frederick I of Rodank, a powerful minister of the bishops of Brixen. Rodeneck passed into the hands of the Tyrolean princes, via the counts of Görz, and some time later came into the possession of the Austrian dukes. Veit of Wolkenstein, whose heirs still own the citadel today, received the castle as a present from Emperor Maximilian I on 22 July 1491.

The castle has an interesting **chapel**, which was dedicated in 1582. Its west wall is decorated with an impressive picture of the Last Judgement. The castle's owner at the time, all of his 17 children and the family coat-of-arms are also depicted here.

The living quarters of the original castle's main building houses one of the earliest examples (early 13th century) of paintings from a knight's castle. This unusual find came to light in the autumn of 1972. The cycle of paintings depicts 12 scenes from the saga of *Iwein* by Hartmann von Aue. The dramatic emotion which the Romanesque artist injected into these paintings is startling. The expressive faces of the figures, the animated battle scenes and realistic scenes of daily court life are superb.

Excursions from Vintl: The Pfunderer Valley stretches north from **Niedervintl**, whose baroque **parish church** contains some exceptionally beautiful frescoes by Josef Anton Zoller. From Vintl, the Puster Valley scenic route leads along the hillsides to Bruneck (Brunico). It is a very pretty road: small villages and isolated farmhouses nestle in lush green meadows; solitary churches keep watch from the hilltops. And every direction one looks there are the spectacular peaks of the Dolomites.

Near Terenten, the first village along this route, are two important Gothic altar-pieces. One is in the **church of St Margaret** in **Margen**, and the other is in the tiny **church of St Martin** in the hamlet of **Hofern**. The latter is particularly noted for the gilded ornamentation on its retable.

Beyond the rolling meadows, the barren peaks of the **Rieserferner Massif** (Vedrette di Ries) tower dramatically. Here, enjoying a captivating setting, lies the church of St Valentine near **Pfalzen**. The 1434 fresco on the church's exterior hints at the fine work awaiting the visitor inside, in particular the magnificent fresco cycle from the Pacher School (*circa* 1460).

The alternative route from Vintl follows the floor of the valley. This leads to the village of **St Sigmund** with a church of the same name. Completed in 1489, this is one of South Tyrol's most beautiful late Gothic churches. The exterior walls display two exquisite works of art: the first, between painted pillars beside the portal, is a Pietà in front of a cloud-filled landscape. The other is a huge painting of St Christopher on the south wall. In the background of this picture is an expansive landscape, with a farmhouse, castle, cliff and brook in which barely recognisable mermaids play musical instruments.

The church houses a real gem: the oldest Gothic altar-piece of South Tyrol still occupying its original setting. Constructed around 1430, it depicts a Madonna with Child between St Jacob and St Sigmund. Above the altar-piece is a filigree structure containing a Crucifixion scene. The altar is thought to have been executed in a Bruneck studio by a master craftsman from Styria or Carinthia in Austria.

A little further to the east, near **Kiens**, is a magnificent baroque castle surrounded by woods, the **Castle Ehrenburg** (Casteldarne). The two wings were added to the medieval core at a later date. The large interior courtyard, constructed in 1522, is lined on all three sides with two- and three-storey rounded arcades. The renovation of the east and north wings in baroque style was begun in 1732.

Suanapurc and the monastery: A visit to the **parish church** of Kiens is also recommended. This church, completed

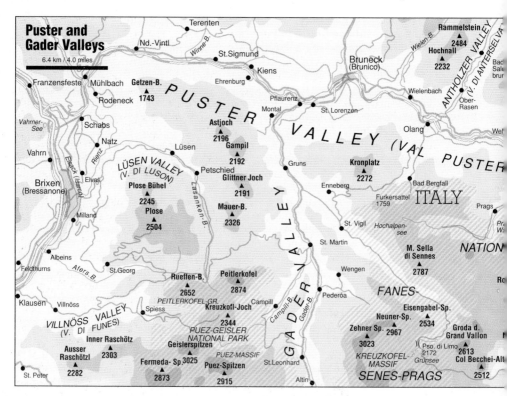

in 1701, was decorated with magnificently coloured frescoes by Josef Adam Mölk. These are framed in shell-shaped stucco decorations of the rococo period. Everything else in the church stems from the baroque era. The marble high altar was donated by Prince-Bishop Caspar Ignatius Count Künigl of Brixen in 1705. The *Corn Mother*, a miraculous image of a Madonna clad in ears of corn, dating from around 1400, still draws pilgrims.

The modest size of **Sonnenburg** belies its historical significance. Suanapurc, as the hamlet was once known, used to be the base of the counts of the Puster Valley. As early as 1020, Count Volkhold donated this castle and its extensive grounds as the site for a Benedictine monastery.

By the middle of the 15th century this monastery was so powerful that Cardinal Nicholas Cusanus of Brixen viewed it as a threat to his sovereignty and ordered its submission. The abbess at that time, Verena of Stuben, was not one to be subdued easily, however, and asked

Duke Sigmund of Tyrol to come to her aid. The dispute lasted 10 years, during which two bloody battles were fought. In April of 1460, the duke captured the cardinal and forced him to sign an agreement. The pope, hearing of this, had the duke instantly excommunicated. It was not until four years later that the emperor in Vienna intervened to settle the dispute.

The monastery now serves as a hotel. In 1975 one of the oldest crypts in Tyrol (1020) was discovered here. Fragments of frescoes, ornamentation and inscriptions lead experts to believe that the crypt was painted around 1200 in Romanesque-Byzantine style. The key to the crypt is kept at the reception desk of the hotel.

In the 12th century, a resthouse for crusaders, pilgrims and passing merchants was added to the monastery. All that remains of this complex today is the **church of St John** on a cliff just below the monastery's curtain wall. The monumental crucifix which dominates the interior of this church dates from the

Help for those without a map.

time of the church's original construction. The sculpture, over 6½ ft (2 metres) in height, was originally part of a Crucifixion group. The other two figures of the group are today housed in the Schnütgen Museum in Cologne. The church's altar dates from the 17th century, while the frescoes were painted in the 18th century.

On the eastern side of the entrance to the Rhaeto-Romanic Gader Valley is the old parochial village of **St Lorenzen**. Before Bruneck was founded, this village was the main town of the Puster Valley. The Romans maintained a post here (Sebatum) as a means of safeguarding the important transport route. The remains of their settlement lie on the north side of the Rienz.

Surviving from the original parish church of **St Laurentius**, built in the 13th century, are the north tower and the western end of the nave. The cross-vaults of the central nave were completed around 1380, the south tower around 1450. The church's most valuable treasure is the *Grape Madonna*, a work by Michael Pacher dating from 1460. The fact that this splendid work is just one isolated piece of the former high altar indicates how magnificent the whole must have been. Unfortunately the other figures and the shrine disappeared over the years, while the painted panels of the altar-piece are now in Vienna's Art Historical Museum and the Alte Pinakothek in Munich. Many of the houses in St Lorenzen have painted facades dating from the 17th and 18th centuries.

Just outside the town is the tiny **church of the Holy Cross** in **Fronwies**. Its onion-domed steeple was erected in 1732; the crucifix on the high altar dates from 1600.

Gader Valley to Val Badia: For the first 4½ miles (7 km), the scenery of the Gader Valley is less than inviting. The road winds along the valley floor flanked by dark, wooded slopes until it reaches the Vigil brook near the town of Zwischenwasser (Longega). At this point, it is best to leave the valley and follow the signs to **St Vigil in Enneberg**.

Spring blossoms and elegant living in the Puster Valley.

(Marebbe). The **parish church** here dates back to the early 12th century. Today's rococo structure was completed in 1782 by Giuseppe da Costa. Franz Singer from Götzens decorated the interior, and the lovely frescoes in the flat cupola are the work of Matthäus Günther of Augsburg.

The Rauh Valley runs in an almost straight line southeast of St Vigil. It is possible to travel by car as far as **Pederu,** which lies at an altitude of 5,079 ft (1,548 metres). But it is necessary to continue by jeep to reach the legendary Kleinfanes Plateau at 6,690 ft (2,040 metres). This mountain plateau, with an area of 4 sq. miles (10 sq. km), offers a wide range of attractions, from the picturesque **Green Lake** to the bubbling karst spring, from an "amphitheatre" of padded green limestone benches to the "rusty" peaks of the **Iron Forks** (Eisengabel).

From St Vigil it is possible to drive on to Enneberg and, a little further east, to take a cable car to the 7,454-ft (2,272-metre) high **Kronplatz**. This mountain, which is very popular with skiers, can also be reached by cable car from Bruneck. It offers an outstanding panoramic view of the central Puster Valley. Looking north, you can see the entire range of the Alps. To the south, the Dolomites dominate the landscape. From Kronplatz, one can follow the narrow road to the south which leads over the 5,804-ft (1,769-metre) high **Furkel Pass** and back down into the Puster Valley near **Olang**.

But let us first return to Zwischenwasser and from there back into the Gader Valley, where Ladin, a dialect of the Rhaeto-Romanic language is still spoken. Near St Martin is the road towards Brixen which leads over the 6,581-ft (2,006-metre) high Würzjoch Pass, the so-called "Brixen Dolomite Road". The hamlets of Campill and Untermoi along this road are traditional settlements of Rhaeto-Romanic farmers.

The rococo church in **St Leonhard** could easily be the twin sister of St Vigil in Enneberg. It was built in 1778 by Franz Singer of Götzens and decorated

The house near Toblach where Mahler composed his 9th and 10th symphonies.

with magnificent stucco. In the picture of *The Glory of St James*, the technique of *trompe l'oeil* painting is so masterfully accomplished that the horseback rider, surrounded by angels, actually seems to have reached the threshold of heaven.

The old pilgrimage **church of the Holy Cross** stands on a mountain above St Leonhard, at an altitude of 6,703 ft (2,043 metres). This church, which can also be reached by chair lift, dates from the 15th century. It stands directly under the west face of the Kreuzkofel group of mountains, the highest of which is Mt Zehner (9,918 ft /3,023 metres). From here the view of the Dolomites is spectacular; it stretches all the way to Mt Marmolada away to the south.

The Gader Valley divides near **Stern** (Villa). The **Cassia Valley** (Val di San Cassiano) forks off to the southeast and leads up to the 7,192-ft (2,192-metre) high Valparola Pass. From there, the road continues to the Falzarego Pass, meets up with the Great Dolomite Road and continues on down to Cortina

d'Ampezzo. The other fork, leading off to the southwest, leads into the **Abtei Valley** and the popular ski resort of **Corvara**, lying just below the towering massif of the Sass Songher (8,743 ft/ 2,665 metres).

The road directly south from Corvara presses on through the mountains to the Campolongo Pass and then back down to Arabba. An alternative route from Corvara leads in a westerly direction, winding over the Grödner Joch Pass to Wolkenstein in the upper Grödner Valley. Following either one of these last two roads, it is possible to tour the entire Sella group of mountains, whose highest peak is the Piz Boé (10,338 ft/3,151 metres). The route leads over the Sellajoch Pass and the Pordoijoch Pass.

In winter the trip around the Sella Massif can also be made on skis, at least with the help of cable cars and chair lifts. In summer, hikes and mountaineering expeditions of varying degrees of difficulty can be arranged. The Campolongo and Valparola Passes mark the border between the provinces of South Tyrol and Trentino.

Bruneck in the Puster Valley: The main town of the Puster Valley is **Bruneck** (Brunico, 2,815 ft/858 metres). It was founded by Bishop Bruno of Brixen in 1251 in order to secure his position against the counts of Görz. The system of fortifications, still visible today, was completed in the early 14th century. This consists of the castle and curtain wall and the main street, squeezed in between the banks of the Rienz and the castle hill. The St Ursula Gate and the Oberragen Gate, at either end of the main street, guard the entrances to this medieval complex.

Many of the houses' foundations date from the 13th century, although most of the buildings you see today were built in the 15th and 16th centuries. The neighbourhood of **Oberragen**, to the east of the fortifications and south of the Rienz, was built around the parish church in the late Middle Ages. **Ausserragen** grew up later on the north banks of the Rienz.

What better place to begin a stroll through the city than in the old **main street** (Stadtgasse). The **city apoth-** Rural idyll in the Ahrn Valley.

ecary is especially interesting. Here, in a vaulted room, frescoes of a fraternity with the coats-of-arms and mottoes of the members can still be seen. It was painted by Ulrich Springenklee in 1526. The sculptor Michael Pacher was born in house no. 29 around 1435. The outer side of the St Ursula Gate in the west is decorated with a series of frescoes by Hans of Bruneck.

Northwest of this gate is the baroque **church of St Ursula**, which was completed in 1427 and renovated in Gothic style in 1883. A 15th-century fresco depicting St Christopher is found in the choir. The most magnificent pieces in this church, however, are the three reliefs from the former altar-piece, created in the studio of the masters of St Sigmund. These were crafted between 1430 and 1440 and depict various aspects of the Nativity – the arrival of the Three Kings, the presentation of their respective gifts and their adoration of the baby Jesus. A fourth relief, depicting the death of Mary, is now on display in the Brixen Diocesan Museum.

The Oberragen Gate in the east also has a fresco decorating its outer wall, dating from 1389 and depicting a Crucifixion scene. At the centre of Oberragen is a pillar in honour of the Virgin Mary, dating from 1716, and the parish church, renovated in neo-Romanesque style in 1853.

The southern tip of the Bruneck city fortifications is formed by the bishop's castle. The original construction began in 1251, and the structure was expanded in 1330 and again in 1515. The main castle, with its great hall and keep, surrounds a small courtyard. The curtain wall, corner rondel and outer bailey indicate the importance attached to the defensive function of the castle. This was the summer residence of the bishops of Brixen for many centuries. Today, the bishops' rooms house a school, and during the summer months the complex is used to stage a variety of international events.

On the other side of the Rienz is the White Lamb (Weisse Lamm) Restaurant. The Tyrolean freedom fighter

Fields in the Prag Valley are still worked by hand.

Andreas Hofer was once a guest here; it is a convivial place in which to relax over a glass of red wine.

Just above the confluence of the Rivers Ahrn and Rienz, in Bruneck's Stegen district, lies the **parish church of St Nicholas**. Inside, the church's choir is decorated with paintings from 1410 by Hans of Bruneck depicting scenes from the legend of St Nicholas. In the nave is a Madonna painted by Simon of Taisten in 1481.

The district of **Dietenheim**, east of Bruneck, has numerous houses with late medieval facades. The Gothic **parish church**, dating mainly from the 15th century, contains Gothic frescoes. In the side chapel, Simon of Taisten painted a Gregorian mass, and below, a painting of the Roman emperor Trajan's liberation from hell. On the left wall of the choir, a 15th-century fresco has been exposed. It depicts the adoration by the Three Kings and the murder of the children of Bethlehem.

The former **residence of the courtier Mayr** has been converted to a folklore museum with open-air exhibits as well as the usual showcases. The representative main house, with its baroque house chapel, contains period furnishings. Several workshops can be seen in the large barn. Among the various outdoor exhibits are a grain mill, a saw mill and a baking oven.

The lower station of the cable car to Kronplatz is in nearby Reischach.

In Bruneck, the Tauferer Valley branches off to the north. Beyond Sand in Taufers (Campo Tures, 2,844 ft/867 metres), it becomes the Ahrn Valley (Valle Aurina) which stretches all the way up to the 10,000-ft (3,000-metre) peaks of the Ziller Valley Alps.

The Tauferer Valley to Sand: The Tauferer Valley (Val di Dures) begins as a wide trough. In **Gais** (2,759 ft/841 metres) a large **Romanesque basilica** was built in about 800. Parts of this are still standing. The **Castle Neuburg** dates form the 12th century. In **Uttenheim** (Villa Ottone), settled as early as 970, a baroque **parish church** still stands. Franz Anton Zeiller decorated the church in 1774 with elegant rococo frescoes.

The ruins of the 12th-century **Castle Uttenheim** lie in the woods overlooking the town.

Near **Mühlen** (Molini di Tures, 2,828 ft/862 metres), the Mühlwalder Valley converges with the Tauferer Valley. It is possible to drive through the valley as far as **Lake Neves**, a reservoir lying at an altitude of 6,089 ft (1,856 metres). From here, hiking paths branch out in all directions and there is a spectacular view across to the snow-capped Alps of the Ziller Valley.

Another route from Mühlen, to the northeast, leads into the Rain Valley (Val di Riva). This valley's major attraction is the Rain brook with its three **waterfalls**. The road comes to a dead end in **Rain** (5,233 ft/1,595 metres) at the foot of the glacier-covered Rieserferner Massif. This pleasant village is a popular departure point for taking hiking excursions into the surrounding mountains.

Near **Sand in Taufers** (Campo Tures, 2,844 ft/867 metres), the Great Moosnock (Palu) blocks the path of the wide valley, and the Ahrn cuts under a steep cliff occupied by the imposing **Castle Taufers**, a structure of unusual beauty. At one time this was the seat of the lords of Taufers, one of the Tyrol's most venerable aristocratic families, and at others in the hands of the Brixen bishops. In 1315, the counts of Tyrol purchased the castle. The Habsburgs repeatedly mortgaged the castle to the Brixen bishopric. Finally, in 1953, it was purchased by Hieronymus Gassner, the abbot of the Seitenstetten Monastery, who embarked on a programme of restoration.

Many of the furnishings given away in the past have now been repurchased or replaced. Today, visitors can tour the castle. The rooms are filled with paintings and sculptures as well as antique furniture, chandeliers and weapons. Of the 64 rooms, 24 boast magnificent panelling and artistically coffered ceilings. Among the most interesting rooms are the library, the weapons hall, the judicial room, the hall of knights and the **Romanesque chapel**, the latter a part of the original structure.

Right, on the border between Austria and Italy.

A DYING BREED

On one evening every year, sometime in May or June, the lights in an unusually large number of the farmhouses in St Peter in the Ahrn Valley are still burning well after midnight. The reason is that the ancient tradition of driving the cattle to the summer pastures is about to begin. Each spring for the past 1,000 years farmers of the Ahrn Valley have herded their cattle over the narrow mountain paths leading into the Ziller Valley and the province of Salzburg. Today, however, this rugged breed of farmers has dwindled to just one – Farmer Eller.

All those who have promised Farmer Eller their help in herding the cattle leave the warmth of their homes and assemble at his farm, ready for the adventure to start. Because many of these young men work in factories all week, the herding is scheduled for the weekend. In earlier times, dozens of farmers used to drive their herds to the private summer pastures.

The pastures lie at relatively low altitudes of between 3,300 and 5,200 ft (1,000 and 1,600 metres), but the passes to these pastures are covered with several feet of snow and the work is gruelling. Some of the helpers come equipped with picks and shovels. Their job is to cut a path for the cattle, hacking steps into the icy mountainside.

But before the trek begins, everyone is fed and a hearty picnic is packed for the journey. Feed for the cattle is also prepared. While the helpers are getting ready for the strenuous task ahead of them, Eller feeds and milks his herd. Fat and soot are rubbed into their udders to protect them from infection when they drag over the ice and snow. The calves will have already been herded up to a hut above the tree line on the evening before, for they are not strong enough to make the entire journey in one go. For the older animals, the climb is no problem. They have been practising on the steep mountainside for one hour each day for the previous three weeks.

Eller drives his herd over the 8,396-ft (2,559-metre) Mt Hundskehle. His reason for continuing to make the difficult trek is not because he is thrifty: "For a mere 2 million lire I could have the herd transported by truck," he says. He does it both to preserve a tradition and for the fun of it. He plans to continue making the journey for as long as he can persuade friends and neighbours to help him.

At 2am the first stage of the journey, up to the Sam, a mountain pasture, begins. The path here is not too steep so the cattle are in less danger of losing their footing. For his 30 cows, Eller needs 20 helpers. He recalls the time in 1980 when they needed 10 hours to cover a stretch normally covered in two. That was the year that a blizzard blew up and rescue teams had to be sent up from the valley to help.

The trickiest section is the path to the Hundskehl Pass. Crosses punctuate the path, marking the sites where man and beast have lost their lives. The snow is not very deep this year, a disadvantage since the cows can easily break through the surface and catch their hooves in the stones underneath.

But before the most difficult leg through the snow begins, it is time for refreshment. The picnic is unloaded and the men take a break.

The cattle, however, continue at a trot. The younger ones push past the older cows, trying to get ahead. At this point in the journey such jostling does not matter much. At narrower places further along the route, however, panic and pushing could lead to catastrophe. Every time an animal gets stuck, the helpers dig, swear a bit, pull, push and do whatever else is necessary to get the poor beast back on its way.

Seven hours later, the party reaches the icy summit. The men stand in a circle around the cross as Eller offers a prayer. The most difficult part of the journey is behind them and they reward themselves with a shot of hard liquor (the trek down the mountain is much easier; after an hour, they will be below the snow line).

These days Eller makes no promises of the extra kilogram of butter traditionally awarded to helpers, for today nobody participates in this endeavour for a reward. "Going over the mountain with the cows", as they call it, is an adventure, fun rather than toil. The men bid each other farewell and return home while the farmer and his son continue to the pasture alone.

This chapel is on the first floor of the older residential tower. It has a circular apse, a Romanesque crucifix dating from about 1200 and Gothic frescoes from 1482. The northern part of the former **knights' hall** contains a series of 26 portraits (painted on parchment between 1564 and 1567) of South Tyrolean families who were in some way connected with the castle.

By far the most beautiful of the rooms, however, is the **library** with its magnificent baroque coffered ceiling decorated with paintings of prophets. The exquisite tiled oven, decorated with motifs from the Turkish era, is one of the most beautiful in all of South Tyrol. The South Tyrolean Association of Castles (its current owner) has been responsible for the upkeep and maintenance of the castle since 1977.

The Ahrn Valley: Beyond Castle Taufers, the landscape has a wild rural beauty with scenery ranging from lush valley meadows to steep mountainside pastures and summer pastures high among the mountains. A journey by chair lift up to the **Michlreiser Plateau** at 6,560 ft (2,000 metres) provides the best views of this valley. The lower station of the lift is located about 2 miles (3 km) northwest of Sand.

From this plateau one can hike up to the 8,278-ft (2,523-metre) high **Speikboden** where a spectacular view unfolds, stretching from the Ziller Valley Alps all the way across to the sparkling crests of the Rieserferner peaks.

Just past the chair lift station, in **Luttach** (Lutago, 3,136 ft/956 metres), the road forks off to the left to Weissenbach. This resort, lying at an altitude of 4,364 ft (1,330 metres), is the ideal base for embarking on hiking expeditions into the southern regions of the Hochfeiler (11,515 ft/3,510 metres). The Neves Hut and Lake Neves can also be reached from here. The Gothic parish **church of St James**, completed in 1479, is worth a peek; it has a magnificent altar-piece dating from 1616.

Back on the main road and heading north, the route leads to **St Johann** with its pink baroque **parish church**. The

The baroque parish church in Toblach.

road passes through several small villages before reaching **Steinhaus**, the main town of the Ahrn Valley. This was once the transfer point for the copper ore mined in Prettau and other villages of the Ahrn Valley. The copper mining industry was first established in medieval times and benefited the town for centuries. Several lovely houses in Steinhaus serve as reminders of the town's former prosperity as a result of this valuable resource. The 15th-century **Faktor House**, for example, boasts a splendid stucco ceiling on the second floor and pictures of mining scenes dating from the late 17th century. The frescoes adorning the walls are from the Brixen School and date from approximately 1500.

St Jacob, St Peter, Kasern and **Prettau** (4,843 ft/1,476 metres) are the highest-lying settlements in this valley and South Tyrol's northernmost villages. The late Gothic **parish church** in Prettau dates from 1489. The frescoes of St Christopher, from around 1400, on the exterior walls show that masonry from an earlier church was utilised in the construction. One of the bells in the church dates from this period.

Antholzer Valley and Welsberg (Monguelfo): Continuing along the Rienz beyond Bruneck, the road reaches the peaceful holiday resort of **Olang** (Valdaora), on the south banks of the river. The houses at 22 and 28 Oberolang Street are decorated with frescoes dating from around 1500. This road continues south into the mountains to Furkel ridge (5,771 ft/1,759 metres) and the south face of Mt Kronplatz.

The **Antholzer Valley** (Val di Anterselva) branches off to the north opposite Olang. From this valley, one can reach the southern slopes of the Rieserferner range.

The road through the valley leads past the romantic **Lake Antholzer** and continues on over the 6,732-ft (2,052-metre) high Staller ridge and across the border to the Austrian village of Erlsbach in the upper Defereggen Valley. The border crossing, however, is open only during the day.

A traditional lime oven in the Tiers Valley.

The most interesting village in the Antholzer Valley is **Antholz-Mittertal**. The panelled walls of the "Apostle Room" in the **Bruggerwirt** restaurant are painted with a series of pictures depicting the 12 Apostles.

Beside the **Weger** restaurant is the **Weger Cellar**, at one time the village's purveyor of hard liquor (it was too much trouble to transport flagons of wine to this remote village). It is this fact which inspires the frescoes dating from 1696. Eight figures are depicted, each with a toast for the tippler. These range from the pope ("I absolve everyone") to a woman holding a glass ("I lead everyone astray") and a man holding a scythe ("I put up with everyone"). This cellar is locked, but the key can be obtained at the Weger restaurant.

A short distance beyond Antholz-Obertal, sheltering below the steep slopes of Mt Wildgall (10,735 ft/3,272 metres) and Mt Hochgall (11,280 ft/ 3,438 metres), is the enchanting Lake Antholzer. It lies at an altitude of 5,387 ft (1,642 metres).

Those who remain on the main road of the Puster Valley from Olang will arrive in **Welsberg** (Monguelfo) at an altitude of 3,280 ft (1,000 metres). The famous baroque artist, Paul Troger, was born in this town in 1698. His most notable works in South Tyrol are the frescoes in the cathedral of Brixen. In 1739, he painted three pictures, of St Margaret, St John of Nepomuk and the Adoration of the Magi, for the altar of the **parish church** in Welsberg.

More interesting from an architectural point of view, however, is the late Gothic **church of Our Dear Lady on the Rain**, constructed in the 16th century. The net vault, with its curving ribs, is particularly impressive. The altars, built around 1635, have pillared superstructures. The painting of *Mary with Child* dates from the 15th century.

The 16th-century **Castle Welsberg** peers over the village from a rocky promontory (3,714 ft /1,132 metres) in the woods .

Gsieser Valley and Prags Valley: The **Gsieser Valley** (Val di Casies) branches off to the north in Welsberg and leads

into the Defereggen Range, ending directly below Mt Hochkreuz (8,990 ft/ 2,740 metres). **Taisten**, at 3,947 ft (1,203 metres), with its magnificent view of the Sexten, Ampezzan and Prags ranges of the Dolomites, is the birthplace of Simon of Taisten, a follower of the Pacher School. Even more importantly, however, it is the site of two notable churches, which lie practically side by side. The one church houses magnificent Gothic frescoes and the other is an outstanding example of South Tyrolean rococo painting.

The Gothic frescoes are in the 12th-century **church of St George**. The late Gothic arches are from 1498, as is the huge St Christopher on the exterior and the Madonna in majesty on the north side of the apse. The latter were both painted by Simon of Taisten. The lower apse and the triumphal arch wall inside the church were painted in 1459 by Master Leonhard of Brixen. The most splendid of the treasures in the **parish church** is the fresco in the cupola of the transept. It depicts, in an expansive ba-

Left, the "Comici" route on the north face of the Grosse Zinne. **Right**, a wayside shrine.

roque hall of pillars, the wedding of Mary, attended by a crowd of figures. The richly decorated rococo pulpit is by Franz Singer. The tombs of the counts of Welsberg are in the Gothic Erasmus Chapel, which was completed in 1472. Frescoes by Simon of Taisten, dating from around 1500, are found in the cemetery chapel of St Jacob adjacent to the church.

Taisten is the site of one of South Tyrol's most beautiful Gothic wayside shrines, the **Tabernacle Shrine** in the centre of the village. Under a pointed shingled roof are four arched niches in which Master Leonhard of Brixen painted scenes of the Passion, various saints and the Early Fathers.

Just a few miles to the east of Welsberg, in a southerly direction, the **Prags Valley** (Val di Braies) branches off from the Puster Valley. This is a valley of meadow-covered slopes dotted with solitary farms. At the very end of the valley is the **Prags Wild Lake**, at an altitude of 4,898 ft (1,493 metres). Towering directly over the lake is the sombre northern face of Mt Seekofel (9,219 ft/2,810 metres).

By retracing the route, and taking the fork just beyond Schmieden, you can reach the Old Prags Valley and the spa of Old Prags, founded in 1490. The cold springs are said to possess healing qualities, especially efficacious in the cases of rheumatism or circulatory disorders. But the real charm of this valley unfolds along the drive to **Plätzwiese Meadow** (6,539 ft/1,993 metres). To the left, Mt Durrenstein (9,314 ft/2,839 metres) towers over the valley, while on the right, the queen of the Prags Dolomites, the Hohe Gaisl (10,299 ft/3,139 metres), dominates the horizon. The Hohe Gaisl was first conquered by man on 20 June 1870.

The Plätzwiese itself is a mixture of virgin forests, solitary larches and pines, and meadows carpeted with wild flowers. In early spring, these meadows are covered in a veil of white and pink crocuses. Travellers who are tempted to take the narrow path leading from Plätzwiese down to the Schluder brook, **Abandoned to nature.**

between Mt Strudelköpfen on the left (7,569 ft/2,307 metres) and Mt Knollköpfen on the right (7,231 ft/2,204 metres) should reconsider. It is very poorly maintained and is officially closed to the public.

From Toblach to the Drei Zinnen (Three Pinnacles): The historic town of **Toblach** (Dobbiaco, 3,954 ft/1,205 metres) dates from 828 when it was known as *Duplago*. This is the watershed where the Rienz flows south towards the Adriatic Sea and the River Drava east towards the Black Sea. It was here the vital medieval trade route between Augsburg and Venice, the *Strada d'Alemagna*, branched off to the south into the Höhlenstein Valley.

The **Castle Herbsten**, with its large oriels and lovely battlements, is just one of the many old aristocratic estates dating from those prosperous times. The rococo **parish church** was built by Rudolf Schraffl in 1782. The stucco work is by Franz Singer of Götzens, and the magnificent ceiling frescoes were painted by Franz Anton Zeiller. The celebrated Austrian composer Gustav

Mahler frequently came to stay in this region, and he composed his 9th and 10th symphonies here.

The summit of the 5,269-ft (1,606-metre) Mt Radsberg, accessible by chair lift, offers a spectacular panorama of the Höhlenstein Valley and the Sexten Dolomites. The old inn **Enziantres** in the Silvester Valley is renowned for its efficacious alpine herb liquors. The frescoes in the isolated church of **St Silvester**, located at 5,906 ft (1,800 metres), belong to the Brixen School and were painted in the second half of the 15th century.

The Höhlenstein Valley, which leads directly south, is the shortest route to the Three Pinnacles (Drei Zinnen, Tre Cime di Lavaredo), the Dolomites' most imposing peaks. The road leads past idyllic **Lake Toblach** and continues up to **Lake Dürren** at 4,613 ft (1,406 metres). Here you can catch the first glimpse of Monte Cristallo 10,551 ft/3,216 metres). The north faces of the Three Pinnacles tower above the ruins of the village of Höhlenstein, destroyed in World War I.

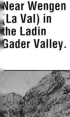

Near Wengen (La Val) in the Ladin Gader Valley.

These peaks are at their most spectacular just before sunset when the limestone begins to glow a deep pink in the rays of the evening sun.

Just beyond the San Angelo Pass is **Lake Misurina**. A toll road to the Auronzo Hut (7,612 ft/2,320 metres) branches off to the left shortly before the lake. This hut lies at the southern foot of the Three Pinnacles, the highest of which is the centre peak at 9,836 ft (2,998 metres).

The Innichen Monastery: The **cathedral** in **Innichen** (San Candido, 3,855 ft/1,175 metres) is Tyrol's most important Romanesque structure, although it was actually constructed at a time when Gothic structures were already being built elsewhere. The monastery here was founded by Duke Tassilo of Bavaria in 769 to assist in the Christian conversion of the Slavs. The original structure was replaced in 1170 by a triple-naved basilica with a semi-circular apse and a crypt. The transept with rib vaults, the octagonal cupola of the crossing, the tower, the side apses and the groin vaults in the nave were added in the second half of the 13th century. The three portals also stem from this era. The two reliefs on the pillars beside the entrance to the crypt date from the 12th century. The grape vines and the human figure were probably executed around 1170. The south portal, whose tympanum is decorated with a Majestas Domini and various gospel symbols, is from the original period of construction. The Tyrolean artist Michael Pacher painted the fresco on the southern exterior wall around 1480. It depicts the Holy Roman Emperor Otto I with St Candidus and St Corbinian.

Inside, frescoes dating from 1280 have been uncovered in the cupola of the crossing. They depict the six days of the Creation and the expulsion of Adam and Eve from the Garden of Eden. The second major attraction is the Crucifixion group above the modern high altar. The monumental wooden statues were carved in the Puster Valley between 1200–50, and were not, as legend has it, a gift from Tassilo. The statue of St

A popular trail in winter: the path to the Drei Zinnen mountains.

174

Corbinian, standing in the crypt, serves as a reminder that, until secularisation, Innichen was part of the diocese of Freising in Bavaria, whose patron saint is Corbinian.

The Sexten Valley to the border: In Innichen, the Sexten Valley (Val di Sesto) branches off to the southeast and meanders into the eastern ranges of the Sexten Dolomites. The main village is Sexten (Sesto, 4,321 ft/1,317 metres). Towering above the forests toward the south is the mammoth Dreischusterspitze (Cima Tre Scarperi) at 10,341 ft (3,152 metres).

The nearer one draws to Sexten, the more awe-inspiring this mountain becomes. Then, suddenly, as if appearing out of nowhere, the famous **Sexten Sundial**, with its five colossal peaks, looms into view. The peaks of these mighty giants reach 9,800 ft (3,000 metres). The beauty of the "sundial" can be admired from several different angles. Those with little experience in mountaineering would be well advised to drive from Moos, 1¼ miles (2 km)

beyond Sexten, to **Fischleinboden** (5,052 ft/1,540 metres). Here one can stroll through the mountainous landscape, totally enclosed by these five giants. The famous **Tschurtschenthaler Farm**, owned and operated by the same family for the past 500 years, is also found in Fischlein Valley.

There are two cable cars in the region. The one in Moos takes visitors up to the **Rotwand Meadow**, at an altitude of 6,316 ft (1,925 metres), from where experienced hikers can attempt the vertical "promenade" up to the 9,642-ft (2,939-metre) high "trapeze". The other is east of Innichen in Vierschach and goes up to the **Hahnspiel Hut**. From there, it is a one-hour hike up to the summit of **Mt Helm** (7,982 ft/2,433 metres). The view from both these points is stunning.

The Kreuzberg ridge, southeast of Sexten, is the boundary of South Tyrol. The Puster Valley continues on to the east of Innichen, but after just a few miles reaches the Austrian border and East Tyrol.

For many, this is a skiing paradise.

BOZEN

Tourists who don't want their romantic images of South Tyrol shattered are advised not to enter the city of Bozen (Bolzano) via any of the main routes from the north or the south. The front door to Bozen, from the south, is preceded by mile upon mile of depressing suburbs (in fact, it is virtually impossible to tell exactly where the town begins), and the route into town from the north is little better. Motorists might, at first, breathe a sigh of relief that after 18 miles (30 km) they have finally escaped the narrow Eisack Gorge, with its complex system of tunnels and bridges, but their sense of release is premature. They haven't yet reached the equally claustrophobic suburbs of Bozen.

Indeed the first indication of Bozen is the village of Rentsch am Sonnenhang, now in the clutches of the city's suburbs, beyond which lies an enormous shunting yard with a tortuous maze of tracks and broken-down trains. A short distance beyond this point the traffic congestion rapidly escalates to the point where everything comes to a complete standstill and drivers despair of ever reaching the centre of the town. In fact, they need not worry, for they already have: this is the city of Bozen.

No matter which of the major routes visitors take into town, whether by railway, along the motorway or via the old overland route, Bozen seems, on first impression, an unattractive place with more than its fair share of industrial ruins and ugly slums. It is inhospitable in other ways too – for example, its climate is icy cold in the winter months and unbearably hot in summer. Although there is much talk about preserving a green belt, in reality the urban sprawl is subject to few controls. A "development zone", "trade zone", "commercial zone" and now even an airport have all edged their way into the surrounding vineyards and orchards.

Bozen through the back door: But approached from the right angle even Bozen can appear beautiful. The most attractive approach to town is undoubtedly through the small back door, from the Sarn Valley, South Tyrol's most central and yet most remote valley, and the larch-filled meadows of Tschögglberg. From here one literally "drops" into the town.

Flanking this route are some of the region's most romantic castles: the 13th-century **Schloss Runkelstein** and **Schloss Ried** in the Talfer Gorge, **Rafenstein** towering high above, and some half a dozen others. The route follows the Talfer brook, from which Bozen gets its name as the Talfer city, until the neo-Gothic silhouette of the Germanic old town appears. Behind the old town, and just as impressive, rises the Rosengarten Massif (stunning at sunset) while, on the right, loom the bleak buildings of Italian rationalism. This is a fitting introduction to the essence of Bozen – contradiction: economic, cultural, architectural, human and climatic.

From Bozen to Bolzano: Bozen passed through a traumatic period in the Mid-

dle Ages, when it was a pawn in the battles between the Counts of Tyrol and the Bishops of Trent. But Bozen's many contradictions are rooted in its early 20th century history. Until 1921, it was a small town with some 25,000 inhabitants, the majority of whom were Germans. Goethe described Bozen during his travels through Italy in 1786 as the town "of many merchants' faces", a description apt right up until the beginning of this century. In fact, Bozen is still a commercial town – for example, it holds an annual trade fair – but both the image and the fair derive more from their past reputation than from their present significance.

In the 1920s Bozen experienced rapid growth thanks to the political events of the time. World War I had resulted in Italian sovereignty over South Tyrol and the government was anxious to Italianise its new German region. Bozen, as the capital of South Tyrol, was to be the linchpin in this operation. Factories were moved to Bozen and the administrative apparatus grew.

Economic factors took a back seat to political rationalism. Italians were given big incentives to move to Bozen; they were guaranteed job security and subsidised living quarters and promised lucrative retirement benefits. Mussolini supported the expansion of the town and changed its name from Bozen to Bolzano. At the outbreak of World War II it had 53,000 inhabitants, and by 1967 it had reached the status of an Italian metropolis, with a population of 100,000. For several years Bozen continued to grow, but in recent years the population has decreased and is now back to 100,000. Three-quarters of the residents are Italian and one quarter of German ethnic origin.

The ethnic duality is apparent at every turn in the city. On the one hand, for example, is the filigree Gothic spire and green and yellow mosaic roof of the **cathedral** presiding over the old town. It is 203 ft (62 metres) high and the centre of Catholic-based society. On the other hand, across the **Drusus Bridge** on the Talfer's western banks, in "New

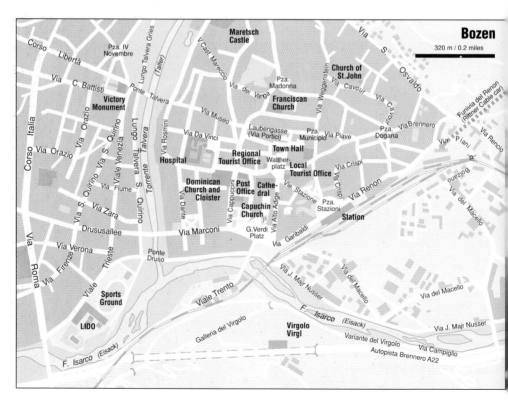

Bozen", is the **"Ex Gil"**, the one time building of Bozen's Fascist youth. This building is a radical expression of the power of the state, an outrage to alpine geniality. In the evening the clean sandstone of the Gothic cathedral is illuminated by floodlights while the dilapidated Ex Gil opens its doors as the town's only pornographic cinema.

Again and again, idealistic town planners design grand schemes for Bozen, incorporating the Fascist edifice in their plans. The latest scheme is to create a type of "Pompidou Centre" in the former Fascist building.

The old heart of Bozen is **Walther Square**, named after the famous troubadour, Walther von der Vogelweide, whose statue graces the square. Ever since this central monument was returned to its rightful place (under the Fascists it was removed to a park on the outskirts of the town) and traffic banned from the square, the area has been the focal meeting place of the town. It is dubbed the "grand hall of Bozen", "Bozen's drawing-room" or simply "the

Piazza". The pavement cafés which line the square are good places in which to watch Bozen life go by.

The Italian counterpart, across the river in New Bozen, is **Mazzini Square**. It is just as far to the west of the Talfer as Walther Square is to the east. The two squares, half a mile apart, are totally different from one another. Majestic 17th-century patrician houses frame Walther Square while Mazzini Square, named after the Irredentist Giuseppe Mazzini, is characterised by extreme austerity. Rationalism versus bourgeois *gemütlichkeit*.

From Walther Square to the Talfer Bridge: The route between the two squares also reflects Bozen's many contradictions. By walking north from Walther Square, across the old **Kornplatz** with its Gothic buildings, crossing over the **Silbergasse**, past splendid examples of Florentine Renaissance architecture (testifying to the city's former mercantile importance), you arrive at the **Laubengasse**, Bozen's main shopping street. The shops here are the most ex-

Bozen, the "gateway to the Dolomites".

clusive and expensive in upper Italy. While the atmosphere is delightful, the pavement is a bit too dilapidated for the street to merit the description grand. Nevertheless, what is called "the spirit of old Bozen" – the antithesis of the sprawling suburbs – can be found here. Even those who know Bozen only slightly are familiar with the Lauben-gasse. Modern shops set back under traditional arcades – sheltering shop-pers from both the sun and the rain – line what is now a pedestrian precinct.

To the east, through the narrow gaps between the Gothic houses, it is possi-ble to glimpse the Rosengarten Massif, albeit usually without the reddish glow seen in the tourist brochures. The *Alpenglühen* (alpine glow) occurs only on clear evenings.

Continuing west along the Lauben-gasse, you come to the **outdoor mar-ket**, a must for every tourist. This is a traditional food market where stalls sell fresh fruits and vegetables, wonderful cheeses, roasted chestnuts and other delicious and aromatic morsels. On 11

September 1786, Goethe visited the market and noted: "On the square sat women, selling fruit in round flat bas-kets, over four feet in diameter. Peaches lay next to one another in the baskets to prevent bruising. And the same was true of the pears."

By continuing straight across the marketplace and walking down **Mu-seum Street**, you come to the **Talfer Bridge**, the subject of much contro-versy. Town planners are in favour of replacing this turn-of-the-century bridge, a remnant of the era when Bozen was still part of the Habsburg Empire, with a more modern structure which could better handle the ever-increasing flow of traffic, a scheme which has infuriated environmentalists and pres-ervationists. These interests have won the battle for the time being and the bridge remains in place. Below the bridge is the **Talfer Green**, a park stretching along the banks of the river – a popular recreational area for Bozen residents, especially on warm summer days and evenings.

At the Bozen market.

From the Talfer Bridge to Mazzini Square:
On the other side of the bridge lies another source of contention, the **Victory Monument**, a triumphal arch bearing all the insignias of Italian Fascism (as well as grafitti denigrating the German "natives"). South Tyrolean politicians are constantly arguing over what should be done with this monument. Sometimes they demand its removal, and sometimes they want to transform it into something totally different. The Italian army parades in front of the monument, and war veterans like to pose for photographs here.

Each Armed Forces Day (4 November) Bozen's mayor lays a wreath at the monument, an action that invariably leads the deputy mayor, an ethnic German, to issue a protest. Numerous attempts by rebels to blow up the monument have failed.

On this side of the river, the atmosphere is entirely different. Cyclopean structures from the 1930s dominate the scene. The weekly Saturday market is a big draw for visitors,who believe (wrongly) that the goods on offer here are cheaper than those available in the old town.

Just as Bozen's Germanic culture is reflected in the Gothic arcades in the Laubengasse, the Italian culture is apparent in the Lauben (arcades) along **Freiheit (Liberty) Street**. These are tall, austere and right-angled.

This street crosses Mazzini Square and continues on to the leafy suburb of **Gries** with its huge baroque **Benedictine Monastery**. A little further to the north is the old Gothic **parish church** containing a richly carved and painted altarpiece by Michael Pacher. Behind the church are the elegant promenades. Although the climate of Bozen is extreme – it is often Italy's coldest town in the winter and its hottest during the summer months – until the turn of the century, Gries was a thriving health resort almost on a par with Meran.

Town and country: In no other town of South Tyrol is the contrast between the very poor and the very wealthy as evident as in Bozen. Government sources

Someone to talk to.

always use statistics that show South Tyrol as a wealthy area. When asked how the wealth is distributed, however, the government usually prefers to evade the question.

Bozen comprises on the one hand middle-class employees from the new satellite neighbourhoods on the town's southwest outskirts, and on the other hand a new class of South Tyrolean civil servants. The municipal government, with its elaborate bureaucracy, has no real power. As is always true in politics, this lies with those who control the pursestrings, in this case the government of the province of South Tyrol.

The provincial government, however, does not favour the town of Bozen. The newest generation of top-level bureaucrats tends to avoid Bozen like the plague. They have built a housing area for themselves in **Haslach**, just to the south of the town, but whenever they can afford it, they move out into the surrounding countryside, for their affinity lies with the villages rather than the provincial capital. The South Tyrolean People's Party, the strongest of the political parties, has a hard time finding candidates for the Bozen municipal government.

From Bozen, it is easy and quick to ascend the surrounding mountains. The cable car leading up to **Mt Kohlerer**, to the southeast of the town, was the first passenger cable car of any size.

First in food and fashion: Bozen's cuisine profits greatly from the various cultural influences at work in the town. Local specialities and Italian dishes are found in most restaurants. Hotel Greif in Walther Square is among the city's most celebrated restaurants.

The cultural mix of the various ethnic groups has also had a beneficial effect on fashion. The German and the Italian ladies of Bozen's middle and upper classes are extremely fashionable and have plenty of choice when it comes to shopping.

What is lacking in Bozen, however, are the cultural occasions which warrant elegant clothes. Despite its considerable size, Bozen has no decent theatre. The Italian middle classes, probably the more elegant of the two ethnic groups, used to frequent a basement theatre on the outskirts of town, but this wasn't a very sophisticated venue (for one thing, the audience was forced to spend the intermissions huddled in a dimly-lit hallway) and it was not at all the place where people might go to see and be seen. This building has since burned down and those in search of cultural sustenance are now relegated to a shabby cinema.

Such a blatant lack of amenities leads to social frustration, which is evident in the political calamities of the town. Nobody can offer a solution to these problems, not even the Catholic church, for this too is divided. The German religious leaders, along with the bishop (also a German but responsible for all sectors of the population), attempt to make the best of all these difficulties. The Italians lean toward the type of theology of liberation that is practised by priests in Latin America, and are thus displeased with this state of affairs. The result is Bozen.

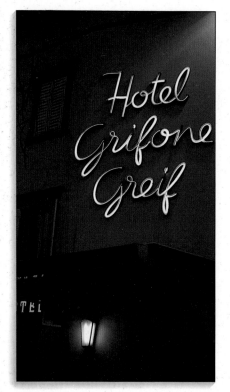

Left, the Greif Hotel at Walther Square. Right, view of Bozen towards the south.

186

When the evening sun hangs low on the horizon, the jagged peaks of the Rosengarten Massif are bathed in a luminous red glow. It is a spectacular sight which can be glimpsed from various vantage points in Bozen. It inspires many of the town's visitors to leave the bustling and often smog-filled Eisack Valley and head up into the surrounding mountains where a well-developed network of hiking paths lead through alpine meadows dotted with larches and alongside mountain brooks and idyllic farms. Up here the air is bright and clean, the countryside is relatively unspoiled and the panoramic views are superb.

Ritten's past: This area is steeped in a rich history. Archaeological digs at Ritten, a spur of the Rittner Horn (Corno di Renon, 7,408 ft/2,258 metres) have uncovered the remains of over 50 fortresses. In the days of the Roman Empire, the main trading route led over the Ritten Plateau (the difficult and dangerous gorges of the Eisack Valley made construction of a more direct route impractical) and, later, the German emperors passed along this route on their way to their coronations in Rome. Even today many people refer to the modern road as the Roman Way. Remains of the original road, which was paved with stone slabs, can be seen near the village of St Justina.

The **Kommende Estate** in **Lengmoos**, today the scene of the Ritten Summer Cultural Festival, once served as a hospice for Teutonic knights.

The Ritten (Renon) Plateau has long been a popular summer destination. It prides itself on being South Tyrol's oldest and most congenial mountain resort. Illustrations dating from the 16th century depict it as a place of relaxation, with men playing billiards outdoors and families strolling through the lanes and meadows. Much of its attraction is due to the agreeable climate; while Bozen, lying in the shade of the mountains, is besieged by icy cold conditions in winter, the Ritten Plateau remains mild. On

clear days, sunlight on the Ritten raises temperatures considerably above those in the valley. Consequently the regions around **Oberbozen** (Suprabolzano) and **Maria Himmelfahrt** are popular places for wealthy Bozen families to build their summer residences.

Oberbozen and **Klobenstein** (Collalbo) are the region's most important towns. They are connected to one another by a **rack railway** which has been in operation since 1907 (though it came close to being closed down in the 1960s). Until 1966, the railway ran all the way from the centre of Bozen, but today it operates along only a 7-mile (12-km) stretch through meadows and woodland. The journey provides magnificent views of the Dolomites. On a clear day, it is possible to see right across the Geisler Peaks, the Grödner Joch Pass, the Sella Massif, Mt Langkofel and Plattkofel, the Schlern Massif, Rosengarten and Latemar.

The rack railway is the best way to travel through the Ritten region. Indeed Ritten was not opened to automobile

traffic until 1965. Visitors can leave their cars in the valley and take the cable car (just east of the main train station) up from Bozen. From here proceed on foot or take the rack railway. For the more ambitious, there are three hiking paths (nos. 2, 3 and 6) leading up from the Oswald Promenade in Bozen. The hike takes about 3 hours.

Path no. 6 leads past the **earth pyramids**. These pyramids, up to 98 ft (30 metres) in height and conical in shape, look like giant towers of sand, with a slab of stone perched precariously on each peak. This strange phenomenon has been caused by a slow process of erosion. What was formerly a mountain has been washed away until the only parts remaining are those lying under a stone slab. If a pyramid loses its slab it is also eroded.

The Ritten of today conforms to the stereotypical image that most tourists have of South Tyrol. It is especially popular with older visitors, though during the winter months it offers a wide variety of sporting activities and is very popular among the young. There are two cross-country ski trails, in **Pemmern** and **Klobenstein**, as well as a number of skating rinks. The ski region of **Tre Vie** is especially popular; from here five ski lifts lead up to Mt Rittner Horn.

It is possible to reach the alkaline-saline springs of **Bad Dreikirchen** by travelling across the Ritten Plateau and through **Barbian**. The village's three churches, built virtually one on top of the another, are its star attractions. According to local sources, they occupy a site of pre-Christian worship dedicated to the Germanic gods of the springs. Because motorised traffic is not permitted in the village, Bad Dreikirchen has managed to preserve much of its original character. Paths nos. 8 and 8A from Barbian also wind up here.

Hiking on the Salten: Across from the Ritten Plateau rises **Mt Salten**, nicknamed Tschögglberg. It is a spur of the Sarn Valley Alps and forms a kind of buttress between the Eisack and Etsch Valleys. It spans **Mölten** (Meltina, 3,898 ft/1,188 metres) and **Jenesien** (S.

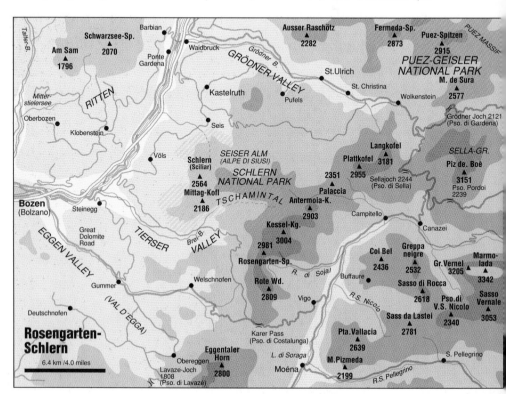

Genesio, 3,573 ft/1,089 metres) and is covered by an extensive network of hiking trails. One of these is the European Hiking Trail No. 5. The best times to explore this region are either in spring when the abundant wild flowers are in full bloom or in autumn when the larch-filled woods are a mass of rich colours. The region was only recently opened to traffic and so the steep and narrow roads are not yet plagued by interminable lines of vehicles. Even though it is now possible to drive from Hafling and Mölten to Jenesien, this mountain is still mainly the preserve of hikers. It is also one of the few remaining regions in South Tyrol whose main source of income is still derived from agriculture and forestry rather than tourism.

Jenesien is connected by cable car to Bozen, and the mountain station of the cable car from **Vilpian** in the Etsch Valley is about a one-hour hike from Mölten. The 15th-century **parish church of the Assumption** in Mölten contains remains of frescoes from the 16th and 17th centuries. From Mölten, a hiking path leads to the small **church of St Jacob** near Lafenn. The core of this building is Romanesque. **Lafenn** itself comprises little more than the church, a farm and a guesthouse (open only six months of the year).

The return hike leads past the **Tschaufer Guesthouse**, built in 1335, and **Verschneid** (Frassineto). The entire route should take about four hours. Those who wish to avoid the crowded and noisy road between Meran and Bozen, and who have plenty of time on their hands, could make the journey on foot, following the European Hiking Path No. 5. Here, as from the Ritten region, there is a magnificent panorama of the Dolomites.

Schlern Recreational Park: Mighty and impressive, checked only by the jagged edges of the Santner Peaks, **Mt Schlern** (Sciliar, 8,412 ft/2,564 metres) stands like a fortress at the western edge of the Dolomites, high over the Eisack Valley. Unlike many other mountains of the Dolomites, such as the Latemar or the Rosengarten, this compact massif of

he nostalgic itten railway.

impervious rock strata has not been the victim of erosion. At the foot of this mountain is Europe's largest expanse of mountain pastureland, a plateau known as the **Seiser Alm** (Alpi di Siusi), comprising almost 20 sq. miles (50 sq. km) of meadows.

These sweeping meadows backed by Mt Langkofel and Mt Plattkofel, along with the neighbouring Schlern National Park and the surrounding villages, make the Seiser Alm one of the most popular tourist destinations in South Tyrol. During the 1970s the Seiser Alm was developed as a major centre for hikers and skiers. Ski lifts and a vast car park were built and unattractive hotel buildings and souvenir stands sprouted up all over the place.

This rapid bout of construction did nothing to enhance the landscape. Those looking for the quieter hiking trails will not find them here (in view of the number of tourists who make their way across the plateau day after day it is amazing that agriculture still manages to function at all). Nevertheless, the Seiser Alm has retained a certain charm, one which is best appreciated in the less crowded early morning and evening hours.

From the village of Kastelruth (Castelrotto), a path leads up to **Mt Puflatsch** (7,139 ft/2,176 metres), across the Seiser Alm to the ruins of **Hauenstein** and back to Kastelruth. Altogether this hike takes about six hours. The most important villages at the foot of Mt Schlern are **Völs am Schlern** (Fie allo Sciliar), **Seis** (Siusi) and **Kastelruth**. The **church of St Michael** in the hamlet of that name, with its splendid Romanesque tower and 15th-century frescoes, and the chapel in **Castle Kastelruth** are both worth a quick peek inside. If your visit to Kastelruth happens to coincide with Corpus Christi it is well worth hanging about. The annual procession which happens on this day is a very colourful occasion, when participants don traditional Tyrolean costumes. The women decorate their hair with garlands of wild flowers and the men sport fancy plumes.

Völs, like Kastelruth, has a well pre-

A village on the Salten.

194

served town centre. Travellers looking for a hotel which is a bit out of the ordinary should try to book into the romantic **Hotel Turm**. The building is said to date from the time when a member of the Roman aristocratic family Colonna fell out with the pope and subsequently moved north to the mountains. He selected a cliff on which to build a tower, which, over the course of the next several centuries, served various functions, ranging from a prison to an inn. Extensions were added at various times, and for the past four generations the building has operated as a hotel under the Pramstrahler family. Son Stefan is the chef *par excellence* and father Karl has amassed a collection of over 2,000 works of contemporary art, most of which hang in the rooms and hallways of the hotel. Many of the artists are frequent guests at the hotel. But the most important art treasure in Völs is the 1489 triptych in the **parish church of the Assumption**.

Völs is also famous for its **hay baths**, a somewhat prickly therapy based on the centuries-old tradition practised by peasants of the area of lying down in the freshly-mown grass of the meadows to cure assorted aches and pains. Today, patrons of the baths do not go out to the mountain pastures but are packed in hay in the modern baths of Völs. The healing essences of the herbs and flowers from the mountain meadows are supposed to be absorbed by the skin and inhaled through the lungs. The cure is said to be good for a wide variety of ailments – with the exception, of course, of hay fever.

The Schlern region can be reached from the Eisack Valley either via the extremely steep road up from **Tisens** (Tisana) or from **Blumau** (Prato all Isarco) just before Bozen. The latter road is only slightly less steep. From autumn onwards, when it is not uncommon for snowstorms to blow up or for the roads to ice over suddenly, tyre chains are essential for either route. There is also a connecting road from the Schlern region leading over a pass to St Ulrich in the Grödner Valley.

The Seiser Alm is a popular region for hikers and strollers.

THE ROSENGARTEN

On a clear day in Bozen, the Rosengarten, with its jagged tooth-like peaks, looks close enough to reach out and touch. The massive mountain, with its dramatic contours, provides a scenic backdrop for this smog-choked city. It imparts a fairy-tale aspect to what is otherwise a solidly industrialised pocket of South Tyrol. Thus it is no surprise that the **Rosengarten** (Gruppo del Catinaccio, 9,780 ft/2,981 metres) is one of the region's top attractions.

Routes and observation points: The easiest way to reach the Rosengarten region is through the **Eggen Valley** which merges with the Eisack Valley just a few miles to the north of Bozen. From **Kardaun** (Cardano), a town directly under the towering trusses of the Brenner motorway, the serpentine road winds through the **Eggen Valley Gorge**, a ravine so narrow that the road barely squeezes through. After 7½ miles (12 km), the road forks. The route to the left leads to **Welschnofen** and the great **Dolomite Road**. The right fork ascends to **Eggen** (S. Nicola di Ega, 3,675 ft/ 1,120 metres) and **Obereggen** (5,020 ft/ 1,530 metres) at the foot of the deeply-fissured **Mt Latemar** (9,173 ft/2,796 metres). A cable car leads up to a station at 6,890 ft (2,100 metres) from where numerous hiking paths lead to such lovely spots as the **Mairl-Alm** and **Ganischger Alm**, mountain pastures dotted with huts.

A small road just before Eggen leads through sparsely settled territory to the village of **Deutschnofen** (Nova Ponente, 4,452 ft/1,357 metres). Deutschnofen was settled by Germans while Welschnofen was settled by the Rhaeto-Romanics. Deutschnofen offers, in addition to a spectacular panorama of the Latemar Massif, the full range of summer and winter sports.

Just a few miles from town is the **church of Maria Weissenstein** (Pietralba), a pilgrimage church with a disproportionately large stairway. This is one of South Tyrol's most important places of pilgrimage. Along the side aisles are countless votive plaques relating the various misfortunes suffered by the population.

Welschnofen (Nova Levante, 3,878 ft/1,182 metres) is the main point of departure for expeditions into the Rosengarten Massif. Numerous hiking paths lead into this enchanting region which is dotted with stately farms. The **Frommer Alm** (5,840 ft/1,780 metres) and the **Kölner Hut** (7,339 ft/2,237 metres), both lying at the foot of the mountain, can be reached by foot or by cable car.

Continuing along the snaking road, motorists reach **Lake Karer** (Carezza), in which the peaks of the Latemar are reflected. This picturesque mountain lake is a favourite spot for visitors. Anyone who wants to enjoy the true serenity of the lake should try to arrive in the early morning hours to avoid the crowds.

A few miles past the lake is the **Grand Hotel Carezza**, complete with tennis courts, a golf course, ski lifts and all the other facilities deemed necessary to at-

tract tourists. Then suddenly, rising out of the blue, the magnificent panorama of the Rosengarten appears.

Latemar limestone and Dolomite stone: According to legend, King Laurin, a mythical mountain king who resided deep inside the mountain of Welschnofen, built a splendid rose garden which was his pride and joy. Then, one day, his enemies attacked his kingdom and, forced into submission, King Laurin placed a spell on his splendid garden, turning it into stone and declaring that the garden would never bloom again, either by day or night. But the king forgot just one thing, namely the twilight hours. And so it is that when the sun sinks in the west, casting its last magical rays on the Rosengarten, the mountain is transformed by a magnificent rose-coloured blush.

The **Karer Pass** (Passo di Costalunga, 5,751 ft/1,753 metres) marks the border between the provinces of South Tyrol and Belluno. This border runs along the mountain tops, across the Sella Ridge, along the foot of Mt Plattkofel and over the Rosengarten and Latemar peaks. Geologically, the mountains on either side of the Karer Pass are extremely different from one another. Mt Latemar is composed of latemar sandstone and the Rosengarten of pure dolomite stone, a double carbonate of lime and magnesia. The Dolomite mountains get their name from the French mineralogist Déodat Guy Gratet de Dolomieu (1750–1801) who was the first to discover their geological properties – limestone mixed with magnesium – on a trip through this region in 1788.

Continuing across the pass, the road winds down into the **Fassa Valley** and to **Canazei**. From here the route ascends to the Sellajoch Pass where it rejoins South Tyrolean soil. An alternative route, which is equally picturesque, is the great Dolomite Road, which runs east from Canazei to **Cortina d'Ampezzo**, the **Cristallo Massif** and the **Drei Zinnen**.

Gherdeina, the Grödner Valley: Of all the many valleys in South Tyrol, the Grödner Valley is surely the most well known.

The Langkofel as seen from Sellajoch Pass.

Nobody knows whether the valley owes its fame more to the carvers of wooden religious figures, the rugged Langkofel Gap, the impressive Sella Massif or the romanticism of the Rhaeto-Romanic mountain dwellers, known in South Tyrol as the Ladins. Even those who are familiar with none of the above will probably have seen the valley's snow-covered slopes on television when ski races are broadcast.

Refuge for the Ladins: Nobody really knows when or how the valley was settled. Based on the evidence of archaeological finds dating from the Mesolithic Age, it is assumed that this valley was settled relatively early on. Because no trade route ran through here, it remained largely unaffected by the activities going on in other parts of the empire. The upper Grödner Valley became a safe refuge for the Ladins as they were pushed further and further into the mountains. Today, despite the movement toward European unification, minorities all over Europe are clinging to their culture, language and traditions.

The Ladins are no exception. But the days when terrorists were busy dynamiting monuments and power lines in South Tyrol in an effort to gain independence are over.

But the problem of accommodating all three of South Tyrol's very different ethnic groups, the Germans, the Italians and the Ladins, is still acute. The Ladins are found mainly in the area around the Sella Massif, where about 20,000–25,000 still live, as well as in the Fassa Valley, Gröden, Buchenstein, and the Gader and Fanes Valleys. Their dialect of Rhaeto-Romanic is one of the world's oldest languages. It is based on Latin and exhibits traces of Catalonian, Provençal and French. Through centuries of struggle, this small ethnic group has managed to preserve its own identity, even though the Ladin are divided among themselves on the question of national sympathies, with positions ranging all the way from pure indifference to demands for an autonomous Ladin province.

Citizens in the **Abtei Valley**, a sub-

Hikers are rarely short of company on the more popular trails.

ordinate valley of the neighbouring Gader Valley, have established the **Pic Museo Ladin**, the first folk museum for the Ladins. The museum is located inside the community centre of **St Kasian**.

One can reach the upper **Grödner Valley** (Val Gardena – Ladinish: Gherdeina) via either one of two beautiful passes: the **Grödner Joch Pass** (6,959 ft/2,121 metres) leading from the Gader Valley, or the **Sellajoch Pass** (7,362 ft/2,244 metres) from the Fassa Valley. It is impossible to say which of these routes is more spectacular. If time permits, independent motorists should try to travel both.

The contemporary political structure of the Grödner Valley dates back to the Middle Ages when the valley was under three different jurisdictions. Today the valley is still divided into three communities, almost exactly as it was in earlier times: Wolkenstein (Selva Gardena), St Christina (S. Cristina) and St Ulrich (Ortisei). All three of these towns have latched on to the booming tourist industry. The Grödner Valley has South

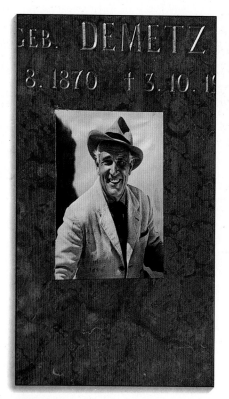

Tyrol's most well developed infrastructure for tourists, with ski lifts, hiking and cross country ski trails, bars, restaurants, hotels and the usual surfeit of souvenir shops.

By entering the valley over the Sellajoch or Grödnerjoch Pass, you arrive first in **Wolkenstein** (5,128 ft/1,563 metres). It was here that the famed writer and poet Oswald von Wolkenstein spent many years of his life. Most visitors, however, come not out of a burning interest in the history or culture of the region but rather to enjoy its marvellous scenic qualities. From here one has a spectacular view of the mighty **Sella Massif** (10,338 ft/3,151 metres), a seemingly insurmountable wall dominating the entire region like a giant stone fortress.

Jagged edge: Those who approach the Grödner Valley over the Sellajoch Pass will be treated to a view of **Mt Marmolada** (10,965 ft/3,342 metres), the region's highest mountain. But the scenic highlight along this route is **Mt Langkofel** (Sassolungo, 10,436 ft/3,181 metres) with its ferociously jagged peaks. This mountain is considered to be the essence of the Dolomites. In the summer months as well as during the winter, Mt Langkofel presents a backdrop of dramatic, some say unparalleled, beauty.

Further west through the valley from Wolkenstein lies the town of **St Christina** (4,683 ft/1,428 metres). Here sport enthusiasts will find a wide variety of activities on offer, ranging from paragliding to mountain biking and hiking in summer to snowboarding, cross country and downhill skiing in the winter. Cable cars from St Christina carry visitors up to the peak of **Col Raiser** (6,972 ft/2,125 metres) or **Ciampinoi** (7,480 ft/2,280 metres).

The next town after St Christina is **St Ulrich**, the largest of the valley's three communities and the last village in the valley. This is the birthplace of the 20th century's most famous son of the region, Luis Trenker, mountain man and film star.

Here, too, you will find **Dolomiti Superski**, Italy's largest ski area.

Left, South Tyrol's most famous native son, Luis Trenker. Right, celebrating Oswald von Wolkenstein.

A POET AND A SOLDIER

"Be off with you!" shouted Michael
von Wolkenstein,
"Run for your lives!" echoed Oswald
von Wolkenstein,
"Hark!" said Leinhart von Wolkenstein,
"Just see how they flee from Greifenstein."

This poem may have lost something in translation but in its original German and for the people of South Tyrol it has lost none of the drama which inspired its author Oswald von Wolkenstein, 500 years ago. It refers to the brave defence of Castle Greifenstein by the Wolkenstein brothers, who were allied to their lord. They made a daring escape, stormed the camp of Duke Frederick of Tyrol and routed the enemy.

Oswald von Wolkenstein was born sometime between 1375 and 1378 in Castle Schöneck in the Puster Valley. He grew up in Castle Trostburg above Waidbruck and later acquired Castle Wolkenstein in Gröden. He was captured by loyal followers of Duke Frederick in Castle Forst near Meran and finally settled down in the remote Castle Hauenstein on the Seiser Alm at the foot of the Schlern Massif:

On a hill, smooth and
small
With dense woods all
around
A world of mountains
high and valleys deep
And stones, shrubs,
sticks and snow abound.

Oswald was a travelling man, a minstrel, for half of his life. His verses celebrated his various military campaigns, adventures and tournaments in Prussia, Russia, Lithuania, Sweden, Denmark, Brabant, Flanders, France, England, Scotland, Turkey, Byzantium, Greece, Aragon, Castile, Granada, Navarre, Portugal, León and Provence. He courted the favour of beautiful queens and was always the centre of festive celebrations, known for his "raving antics, singing, whistling, drumming and picking the strings".

In the service of King Sigismund, Oswald appeared at the Council of Constance in 1414, where debates, intrigues and the burning of heretics were interspersed with tournaments and celebrations. It was a high point in Oswald's career, particularly since it coincided with the time when Frederick of Tyrol fell out of royal favour. Oswald's dream of becoming a knight seemed about to be fulfilled.

For many years Oswald, the second eldest son, had been battling for sole ownership of Hauenstein, for a knight was not a genuine knight without his own castle. His armour was of the finest; it included expensive imports from Milan, English helmets, Hungarian shields and clubs and Turkish weapons. In addition to his 50 crossbows and handguns, Oswald had the most modern cannons.

The poems he wrote after winning Castle Hauenstein suggest that he finally gained peace after a lifetime of restlessness:

How the pain in my heart has gone
Since the snows did melt on the Seiser Alm.
Now birds both great and
small in song
In the woods of
Hauenstein.

Oswald von Wolkenstein was the archetypal knight of the Middle Ages. He made a pilgrimage to Jerusalem and donated large sums to the cathedral in Brixen (there is a memorial to him in the adjacent cemetery).

He was also generous to the Neustift Monastery, where he obtained board and nursing care in his later years. But he retained his shrewdness. Wary of being exploited by the monks, he wrote out a contract in which he specified that he should take his meals "from the bowl of the provost" (certain to contain only the best) and secured the right to be buried in the monastery.

Oswald died in 1445. He is remembered as the most important German lyricist of the late Middle Ages. He lived at a time of revolutionary change. Although he held fast to the principles of feudalism and papal authority, his poetic works show his thinking was broader, anticipating the coming age of humanism. Oswald is not the "last minstrel", as romantics like to claim. Rather he was the first to free himself from the forms dictated by medieval literature. His songs, strongly autobiographical, seem as fresh today as they were 500 years ago.

His memory also survives in the sagas of the Dolomite's Ladin inhabitants. In these he was known as *Man de fyèr*, Ironhand, the singing prophet of a promised paradise.

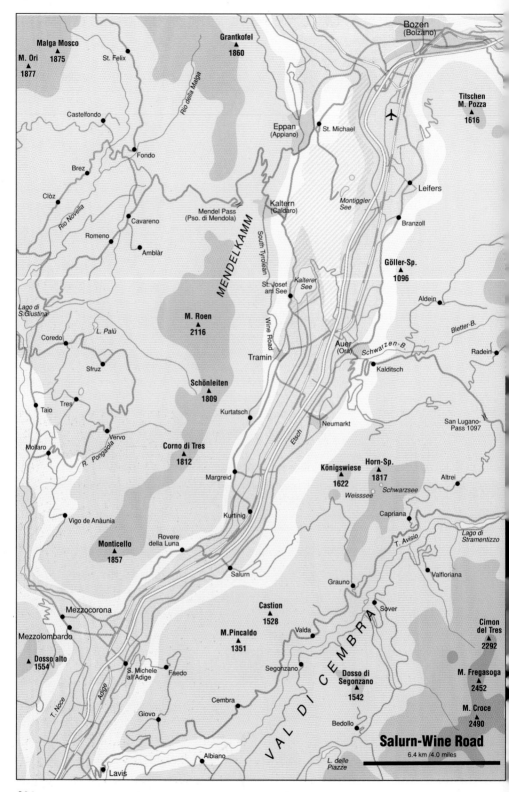

Salurn-Wine Road

6.4 km /4.0 miles

THE WINE ROAD AND THE LOWLANDS

The numerous brochures advertising the Überetsch-South Tyrolean Lowlands (Unterland), the Wine Road and the Trudner Horn Nature Reserve, tend to place this region at the very top of the superlative ladder: "the sunny south of South Tyrol" is the description currently favoured by tourist offices.

In fact, these enticing slogans are not always as vacuous as they sound; the claims made are firmly based on statistics. More days of sunshine and fewer cloudy days are registered in South Tyrol's Lowlands than in any other alpine region between Bavaria and the Po plains. The number of cold and foggy days can be counted on the fingers of one hand. Spring is known here as "little summer" and autumn is invariably described as "golden".

Sun and tranquillity: The wide variety of Mediterranean, even subtropical, vegetation is the most obvious evidence of the region's mild climate: majestic Mediterranean cypress trees, palms, pines, olive trees, magnolias, Judas trees, bamboo and dark laurels all flourish here. The blossoms of the almond and peach trees announce the arrival of spring, and sweet figs are harvested twice annually. Bright orange persimmons and pomegranates grow easily, and the sweet aromas of rosemary, lavender and jasmine scent the air.

Southern South Tyrol stretches 25 miles (40 km) from Bozen along the Etsch to the Salurner Klause (a defile). The plains of the Etsch are almost exclusively devoted to orchards while the hilly regions are covered with vineyards. Towering above, speckled with meadows surrounding mountain villages, are the forests of the Trudner Horn Nature Reserve in the east and the Mendel mountain range in the west. The lovely terraced landscape of Überetsch lies at the base.

Because in former times the River Etsch frequently overflowed its banks and flooded the valley, the villages were built at the foot of the slopes or on raised levees. The towns on the west bank of the river were linked by the South Tyrolean Wine Road , those on the east by the old Brenner road.

The character of the region's town centres is surprisingly urbane. Instead of exhibiting a dreary lineality like some towns in South Tyrol, they are marked by an astonishing diversity of architecture: buildings that jut out to the front and rear, arched gateways, exterior stairways, oriels, retaining walls, loggias and courtyards, all of which blend and complement one another perfectly, are just some of the architecural features commonly found.

Close contact with Roman neighbours has had a marked influence on the local dialect. Distinguished by a gentle open pronunciation and deep tones, it has a distinctly melodic quality. This dialect is said to reflect the good-natured, sunny disposition of the region's inhabitants – people who are, for example, never averse to a jolly round in a wine cellar.

The "Wine Road": "On the opposite banks of the Etsch we saw extremely

fertile mountains with numerous castles and villages. The wine grows exceptionally well there and the other fruits are wonderfully sweet" (Felix Faber, 1483).This pilgrim, on his way to Jerusalem over 500 years ago, was so enchanted by the beauty of the Überetsch landscape that he took a long detour from his planned route in order to sample the region further. He was thus the Wine Road's first documented tourist. According to the journal that he kept on his travels he was richly rewarded by the detour, seeing it as an excursion into a "paradise on earth", complementing his spiritual pilgrimage.

Like the string of a pearl necklace, the South Tyrolean Wine Road connects the villages of Eppan, Kaltern, Tramin, Kurtatsch, Margreid, Kurtinig and Salurn, all celebrated for their excellent wine. Undulating up hill and down dale, the road seems to imitate the gentle rhythm of life in this part of South Tyrol. To enjoy the area fully, it is strongly recommended that motorists set a gentle pace, stopping to savour the landscape and its main product at regular intervals.

Vineyards dominate the landscape. They seem to cover the hills, slopes, mounds and valleys like a frilly and closely fitting undergarment. The trellises, running horizontally, trace the landscape's contours: on the steep slopes they form an elaborate stairway; in the hollows they curve like rows of seats in an amphitheatre; on the hills they lie like ripples in sand dunes and on the plains they resemble tiny oscillations in a peaceful bay.

The approach to Eppan (Appiano, 1,476 ft/450 metres) is guarded by **Castle Sigmundskron**, fortified by the Tyrolean duke Sigmund the Wealthy in 1480 as the largest fortress in South Tyrol. Sigmund, known for his magnificent court (hence his nickname), kept a string of splendid residences. The walls of Castle Sigmundskron are 16 ft (5 metres) thick in parts.

Eppan's main village is the bustling **St Michael**, 5½ miles (9 km) from Bozen. To the east (Berg, Pigenó), lie many **Lake Kalterer.**

magnificent aristocratic residences. From 1550 to 1650, it was the fashion among the Tyrolean nobility to own a feudal country residence built in the style of the Italian Renaissance *palazzi*. These generally had arched gateways decorated with coats-of-arms, exterior staircases, loggias, double-arched windows with fancy wrought-iron decoration, oriels and pinnacles.

The interior comprised a vaulted central hall with Renaissance panelling, majolica-tiled stoves, frescoes and stucco. It came to be known as the "Überetscher style".

Above Pigenó, **Castle Englar**, with its steep gables, displays late Gothic influences. The magnificent **Castle Gandegg** is characteristic of a Renaissance palace. Further up, past the double-steepled **Gleif church**, the **Castle Moos/Schulthaus** offers visitors a peek into Tyrolean life in the 19th century. (The season for all Überetsch-Unterland castles and museums that are open to the public runs from April until the beginning of November.)

This castle-filled region provides plenty of opportunities to sleep like a king. At Englar and Aichberg, for example, visitors are guests of the aristocratic Khuen-Belasi family. Utter luxury is available at castles Freudenstein and Korb while the castles of Warth, Wickenburg and Paschbach offer irresistibly romantic rooms.

Nowadays, it is not only aristocrats who long for a home in the country, so the vineyards are dotted with hundreds of holiday homes and guesthouses.

The streets and architecture of **St Pauls** are typical of many of the villages along the Wine Road. It is dominated by the mighty triple-naved **Dom auf dem Lande** (Cathedral in the Countryside), begun in 1461 in late Gothic style with decorative stone masonry but not completed until 1647. Its patrons, the village's prosperous vintners, did not want to be thought of as yokels and insisted that a "modern" baroque onion dome was placed on top of the Gothic steeple.

In a northerly direction, across the terraced vineyards of Missian, is the

The vineyards are the pride of the lowlands.

Eppan Castle Triangle. From Castle Korb it is possible to climb up to **Boymont**. Although this has been a ruin for over 500 years, the former magnificence of this once mighty fortress is easy to visualise.

Castle Hocheppan, on the other hand, is austere and well-fortified, reflecting the bellicose nature of the Eppan counts. In the battle for sovereignty over the "Land on the Etsch" in the 13th century, the Eppan dynasty was defeated by the Tyrolean counts. If things had turned out differently, the province (and also this guidebook) might have been known as "South Eppan". The Romanesque frescoes of the Foolish Virgins in the apse of the chapel look as fresh as when they were first painted 800 years ago. A dignified-looking Mary reigns in the choir of angels. *The Dumpling Eater* in the manger fresco is said to be the oldest depiction of this famous Tyrolean dish.

In April the region celebrates the *Bauernkuchl* (rural cuisine), and the restaurants serve typical local dishes. Be sure to sample the *polenta*. Up until just a few decades ago, this dish was the "daily bread" of the people of Überetsch and the lowlands.

Kaltern on the wine lake: The village of **Girlan** (Cornaiano), which can also be reached directly from Sigmundskron/Frangart, is surrounded by extensive vineyards. It is possible to sample the local wines, such as Pfefferer and Jungferl, at Schreckbichl. The fact that neither of these, nor many other wines, are included in the official list of European Community wines places them among the endangered wine labels of Europe.

The Montiggl Forest, with its two small lakes, is a pocket of undeveloped land within the heavily settled Etsch Valley. The sunny Frühling (spring) Valley stretches from Montiggl to Lake Kalterer. Here, spring is heralded by vast carpets of snowdrops, primroses and violets, which draw hordes of hikers to the valley. Alpine roses bloom between the chestnut trees at an elevation of 1,600 ft (500 metres) along the Mendel Pass road, above Gands.

The typical blue apron…

Passing through the hamlet of Unterplanitzing (above which, crouching in the vineyards, is Oberplanitzing), the road reaches **Kaltern** (Caldaro, 1,476 ft/450 metres). The question about whether to call this town Kaltern "on the lake" or "on the Wine Road" was disputed long and hard by the tourist industry and the vintners. The obvious compromise, "on the wine lake", was never considered, perhaps because it was too reminiscent of the vast quantities of Kaltern wine which flooded the European market for decades.

In fact, much of this came from the Po Valley or southern Italy (or even Spain) and "diluted" the reputation of the true Kaltern wine. With the introduction of the controlled certification of origination (DOC), this miraculous deluge came to a halt.

The large wine cellar cooperatives are located next door to one another at the entrance to town. As in all the villages along the Wine Road, wine-tasting and guided tours are available.

The four districts of Kaltern are Kaltern-Markt, Mitterdorf, St Nikolaus and St Anton. The main square, occupying the village centre, boasts a wonderful mix of patrician houses, fountains, pubs, the town hall and the parish church, richly decorated with stucco and baroque paintings (1792) and sporting a Gothic steeple (1500).

Close by is the South Tyrol Wine Museum which traces the development of the wine industry through the centuries. Displays show the various stages of the vintner's art, from the point at which the grape is picked to when it is bottled. The *Saltner*, the vinter's equivalent of a scarecrow, is there in all his fearsome glory, looking much like an African medicine man.

When you have had enough to drink you can dine like royalty in the beautiful Renaissance residence of Castle Ringberg (on the road to the lake).

Gothic frescoes decorate the churches of **Mitterdorf**, St Nikolaus and St Anton. A cable car from St Anton takes visitors up to the Mendel Pass (4,472 ft/1,363 metres). From here as well as from

... is worn by both young and old.

nearby **Penegal** there is a magnificent panorama.

Ancient beech forests and modern resort facilities line the way to the Gothic **Altenburger church** (3 miles/5 km). Beyond the church and down the hill, lies Lake Kaltern. Well constructed walkways through the wild and romantic Rastenbach Gorge leads directly to the lake's shores. Occupying a jutting cliff are the ruins of the early Christian **church of St Peter** (5th century) with a baptismal font carved into the cliff. Some theories claim it occupies a pagan site of human sacrifice.

The most lovely part of the Wine Road is between Kaltern and Magreid. Here, the traffic is much thinner and the numerous tractors creeping along the road force motorists to slow down and enjoy the scenery. The Wine Road, lined on both sides by vineyards, runs along the hillside.

Lake Kalterer (Lago di Caldaro), one of the warmest lakes in the Alps, is a popular place for bathing, surfing and sailing from May through to the begin-

ning of October. The lidos are found on the northwest shores near St Josef and in the northeast. On the southern shores, environmental groups have so far been successful in preventing the draining of an extensive swamp and wetlands region in order to make orchards and bathing beaches. This area is a paradise for a wide variety of waterfowl and the most important resting place for migratory birds in South Tyrol.

Gewürztraminer and Schnoppviecher: The road gradually ascends to the town of **Tramin** (Termeno, 906 ft/276 metres). By law, every family in Tramin enjoys a guaranteed right to its own wine cellar, a privilege that has existed since 1214, the year that the Traminers began building their fortress. Whether this was because the people viewed a daily ration of wine as one of life's staple needs or whether it was because they feared the foot soldiers might steal their wine is uncertain.

Until the 19th century, the Traminer wine was the most famous and most expensive of the Etsch Valley wines. Old books tell how the wine was recommended to wine lovers for its flavour, to the ill for its healing powers and to tired lovers for its aphrodisiac qualities (it was said to bring "the proper heat into the blood").

It is no wonder, then, that the controlled certificate of origination had already been introduced for this wine 500 years ago, and its production was closely watched by official supervisors. "Just past Tramin my thoughts remain", sang the minstrel Oswald von Wolkenstein in 1418 as he sampled the sour wine of the Lake Constance region. Today the Gewürztraminer grape is found in practically all the wine-producing countries in the four continents. Every year at the beginning of May, Gewürztraminer wines from all over the world return to their birthplace for a wine-tasting competition. The Traminer distilleries of Roner and Psenner produce fruit and wine brandies.

Tramin's venerable farmhouses, fine patrician residences, traditional wine shops and craftsmen's homes testify to the prosperity of former times, a pros-

Left and right, in the medieval centre of **Neumarkt.**

perity founded firmly on the export of wine. The mighty Gothic church steeple (272 ft/83 metres) is Tyrol's highest stone building.

Tramin also boasts many art treasures. The churches of St Valentine at the cemetery and St Mauritius in Söll house magnificent Gothic frescoes of the Bozen School (*circa* 1400). The hilltop **church of St James** on **Kastelaz** contains unique art treasures. Its apse is decorated by a vivid depiction of vice and passion (1220): grotesque human-jackal figures, counts of darkness, water-nymphs, dolphin riders, a centaur, a merman, seals, a winged siren and a unicorn tumble across water. Witnessing the scene are Christ and the Apostles. The lovely Gothic frescoes are especially impressive, in particular the 16-ft (5-metre) tall Goliath and the 2-ft (65-cm) David.

Today's Tramin is the centre of tourist activity in the lowlands. Below the town hall, the small village museum gives visitors an idea of how man lived and worked here in former times.

On Shrove Tuesday in uneven years, the town holds the *Egetmann Parade*. Figures with heads of dragons and other beasties represent a fertility cult of the pagan past. According to myth, the parade's "old women's mill" turns old ladies into attractive young girls. Despite modern day emancipation, tradition still holds that only men (600 of them in all) are allowed to participate in the parade.

Passing through steep terraces of vines, the road continues to **Kurtatsch** (Cortaccia, 1,093 ft/333 metres), whose wonderful location has earned it the less than pithy slogan "grape-wreathed sentry of the lowlands". Isolated villas, clutches of farmhouses and the hillside hamlets of Penon and Graun dot the countryside. The landscape changes from vine-covered slopes to thickly forested hills. Here, in the southern regions of the lowlands, tourism plays a more minor role. Even in the main tourist season things are relatively quiet and it is never difficult to find a room in one of the small guesthouses, inns or farms.

The lauben (arcades) provide shade in summer and shelter from the elements in winter.

Fruit and wine production are still the main source of income.

South Tyrol's most complete private collection of old farming implements is found not in a museum but on a working farm, **Beim Schweiggl**. Because the farmer must move his tractor and spraying machines in order to get to his antique treasures, guided tours are only possible by appointment. These can be made through the local tourist office.

The Romanesque church tower, unchanged for the past 700 years, is visible from a distance. At one time the simple image of the Virgin Mary on the right-hand altar of the church drew countless pilgrims: it is said that, from 1733 to 1738, the figure shed continuous tears and the numerous votive plaques testify to the miraculous answering of prayers. The elegant lifestyle once enjoyed by the aristocratic vintners is recreated in the panelled Renaissance room of the **Guesthouse of the Rose** near the car park in the centre of the town.

Even in the Middle Ages the people of this region would flee the worst heat of summer, making their way up to the wooded plateau of **Fennberg** (3,608 ft/ 1,100 metres). On the way, at the milestone marking 13 km, a group of Californian giant sequoias grow.

On weekends, the inhabitants of Fennberg gather in front of the guesthouse to play boccia or cards. The reflection in the lake of the Romanesque-Gothic hilltop church is especially charming. It is said that the iron chain surrounding the church grows by one link every year and that when the chain wraps around the church three times, the end of the world is nigh.

In the ruins of a number of Roman houses in Kurtatsch carbonised remains of grape vines were found, further proof of the area's long wine-making tradition. Products of the modern day vintners, whose grape vines grow at elevations of 650–3,300 ft (200–1,000 metres), can be sampled at the **wine co-operative** (directly on the Wine Road), or in the pub of **Castle Turmhof** in **Entiklar**. This castle also houses folk art drawings depicting a wide variety of

animals and human figures in a mythological setting of ponds, cascades and grottoes. Guided tours are held on Tuesday and Friday mornings.

Shortly before **Margreid** (Magré, 791 ft/241 metres), on the right, is the "dripping rainstone", a strangely shaped rock. According to local legend, a magic spell was once cast upon a castle here, turning it, its princess and her treasures into stone.

Probably no other town of this size in South Tyrol has such a sophisticated air as Margreid – a sharp contrast to the wild backdrop of the Dolomite cliffs of Mt Fennberg (for those not bothered by dizzying heights, the path to the mountain's summit begins 2 miles/3 km south of town). Along the narrow streets leading off its main square, architects from further south constructed Renaissance and baroque buildings on German Gothic foundations. The Renaissance church, built in 1618, is unusually light and expansive, with decorative stucco, Palladian motifs, frescoes and splendid marble altars.

The tractors and other farm machinery lying behind doorways decorated with coats-of-arms testify to the gradual replacement of the aristocracy by generations of farmers. In the autumn, trucks clog the streets outside the wine cellars and the aroma of young fermenting wine wafts through the town. This is the perfect time for a stroll through the village. One of its star attractions is an ancient grapevine in the Grafengasse. Planted here in 1601, as documented on the marble corbel, this grapevine has been harvested by a dozen generations. German Sanin (Wein Street 6, Tel: 0471-817768) is the place to purchase organically grown wine.

The countryside along the road to **Kurtinig** (Cortina all'Adige, 696 ft/ 212 metres), produces delicious white wine grapes. This southernmost, mainly German-speaking, community is the only village in the midst of the Etsch plains. The **Maierhof** farm in Harpf Street is a a fine example of the farmhouses once characteristic of this region: the vine-covered farmhouse is

A Tyrolean hat with unusual decorative feathers.

216

constructed over a vaulted cellar. Behind the pinnacle-decorated courtyard gate lie the farm buildings and barns. The road continuing to Salurn (3 miles/5 km) is lined with orchards.

Along the Brenner Road: The Salurn defile marks the border with the province of Trentino. The population of **Salurn** (Salorno, 735 ft/224 metres) is mainly of Italian origin. As an hour or two spent in any of the local bars will testify, the natives switch back and forth from Trentino to the Tyrolean dialect, often speaking a mixture of both known as *Mischiót*.

The pinnacle tower of the **parish church** in Salurn dates from the Gothic period while the church itself, with its richly ornamented facade, completed in 1640, is an example of the classical Renaissance style. The baroque cemetery chapel, on the other hand, is airy and whimsical. Many noble palazzi with exquisite arched gates, coats-of-arms, arched windows and oval oculi were constructed here in the 17th century. The chronicle of the catastrophes of the Etsch floods decorates the facade of one of these palaces (at the beginning of Noldin Street).

Battistiplatz and **Andreasplatz** are good examples of successful communal architecture. The streets are cleverly arranged into a neat, compact space. Before the area was turned over to motorised traffic, the lively theatre of village life was conducted around the village fountain: markets, festivals and funerals, political battles and reconciliations, assignations and farewells. The **Torbogen** (arched gate) **Festival** at Pentecost is an attempt to recreate the atmosphere of such times.

The traffic over the Brenner route brought early prosperity to Salurn. The Elector of Heidelberg employed the famed dwarf Perkéo here in 1720. Student drinking songs still praise his talents: "Although he is tiny in stature, his thirst is gigantic." Another famous guest of Salurn was Albrecht Dürer, who passed through here in 1494 when a flood forced him to make a detour from his planned route.

From the Salurn waterfalls, one can hike up to the Saúc-Saddle (3,281 ft/ 1,000 metres). The unusual beech arbours hereabouts were formerly used to trap birds. Although birds are no longer feature on the menus of **Rifugio Saúc**, visitors can still enjoy hearty Trentino specialities. From its perch on a cliff, the fortress **Haderburg** guards the old Brenner route. A papal legate was attacked and kidnapped here in 1158 by the Salurn knights.

A narrow road meanders through vineyards, orchards and chestnut groves to **Buchholz**, the home of the sparkling Haderburg champagne (tel: 0471-889097) and on past **Crozzolhof**, where organically-grown Burgundy wine is produced (tel: 0471-889084). It continues up to the village of **Gfrill** (4,357 ft/ 1,328 metres), an ancient summer resort which nestles amidst the cool forests of the nature reserve.

To the north of **Laag**, 650 ft (200 metres) before the turn off to Margreid, an ancient church is found on the left side of the Brenner route. The frieze of the church's apse is decorated with

A farmer from the Lowlands.

lovely Romanesque sculptures. To the right above the electrical power plant, solitary and remote amidst the woods and preserved in its original form, is the medieval wayside hospice of **St Florian**, a former refuge for the region's many pilgrims and wanderers.

Neumarkt (Egna, 702 ft/214 metres) was established in 1189 as a trading post. It was granted a unique privilege: all goods being transported through Neumarkt had to be taken to the large building at the lower end of the arcades where duty was levied. Additionally, the right to transport the goods further was granted only to Neumarkt residents. Thanks to these laws town tradesmen were kept in employment.

For centuries, the traffic between Germany and Italy flowed through this town, and the arcades (still extant and well worth a closer look) protected craftsmen, merchants, publicans and their customers from sun and rain. The houses are narrow and deep. The covered atrium between living quarters and commercial rooms served as passage-way, staircase, living and working space all at once. Cast a glance at the staircase of the building at Lauben 22.

Neumarkt was the last town in South Tyrol to play host to the captured freedom fighter Andreas Hofer. From here he was taken to meet his death sentence in Mantua.

With the introduction of the railway in 1859, Neumarkt reverted to being a quiet little village with cows and oxen trotting through the arcades. It was not until it was named as county seat of the lowlands that it was awakened from its slumber. The historical centre has been carefully restored. The "Open Air Theatre Festival of the South Tyrolean Lowlands" takes place during the first half of August.

At the end of the arcades (which, incidentally, are transformed into a huge outdoor festival hall during the arcade festival held each September), is the **church of St Nicholas** with its Gothic masonry and frescoes. The **Museum for Common Culture** (Andreas-Hofer-Lauben No. 24) provides an insight into **Southern climes.**

typical 19th-century lifestyles. Wine and food buffs will probably want to stop at **Johnson & Dipoli** which offers an international selection of wines and first-rate cuisine.

The suburb of **Vill** contains the triple-nave **church of Our Dear Lady**, which is well worth a quick peek inside. With its magnificent net rib vaults, this church is one of Tyrol's loveliest late Gothic buildings. According to Roman road maps, Vill was the location of the rest station Endidae on the Via Claudia Augusta.

The impressive ruins of **Castle Caldiff** stand at the edge of the gently terraced hills of **Mazon**, a town known by wine connoisseurs as the centre of pinot noir. A short detour across the hillside terraces of **Montan** (Montagna, 1,640 ft/500 metres), dominated by **Castle Enn** (privately owned), rewards the effort. The Gothic church houses a lovely sandstone chancel. Continuing on through the vineyards (top quality wines can be purchased at the Vineyard Ordenthal, tel: 0471-812280), the road

The world-famous vinotheke Johnson & Dipoli in Neumarkt.

reaches the idyllic village of **Pinzon** whose late Gothic carved altar by Hans Klocker is one of the most beautiful in South Tyrol. Here and there along this route one comes across viaducts and tunnels of the former Fleims Valley railway (1917–63).

Spend time in Arcadia: Painters of the Romantic Age referred to the hills of **Castelfeder** as the Arcadia of Tyrol. Between the barren porphyry knolls, worn smooth by the glaciers of the last Ice Age, are wonderful cosy hollows, prairie grass, grazing cattle, wildly flourishing shrubbery, marshy pools, ancient oaks and an incredible variety of Mediterranean flora.

In prehistoric times, the lowlands' largest "city" was located here, and the women of the region used to slide down one of the smooth cliffs on their stomachs in an ancient fertility rite. The remains of Byzantine and Lombardian walls as well as a medieval fortress can be seen on the hilltop. Today the Castelfeder is a nature preserve.

The pass route into the Fleims Valley

leads to the three mountain villages of the lowlands. These villages, which have been popular summer resorts for centuries, today attract cross-country as well as downhill skiers.

The farms of Aldein (Aldino, 4,019 ft/1,225 metres) are scattered like little principalities along the mountain ridge. Dark forests carpet the landscape right up to the foot of Mts Weisshorn and Schwarzhorn (8,330 ft/2,539 metres). Between Aldein and Radein lies the Bletterbach Gorge, 2,300 ft (700 metres) deep. Here the exposed vari-coloured sedimentary rocks provide an insight into the geological structure of the Dolomite range.

From Kaltenbrunn (Fontanefredde), it is possible to proceed to **Radein** (5,105 ft/1,556 metres), one of the highest villages in the region. Names of the many famous guests who visited Radein at the turn of the century are found in the guest book of the Zirmerhof inn.

Truden (Trodena, 3,698 ft/1,127 metres), 2 miles (3 km) from Kaltenbrunn, and **Altrei** (Anterivo, 3,967 ft/ 1,209 metres), 4 miles (7 km) from San Lugano Pass, nestle in the midst of the **Trudner Horn Nature Reserve**. This park, filled with forests and larch meadows, is a paradise for nature lovers. In the villages here time seems to have come to a standstill. Firewood is piled high in front of the wooden houses, cows low contentedly in ancient stables, chickens pick their way over manure heaps, ancient farming implements that would be museum objects in other regions are still in use and, on the village outskirts, the meadows are filled with wild flowers. The larch groves around Altrei turn a magnificent golden-yellow in autumn.

The Fleims Valley Road, known as the gateway to the Dolomites, begins in **Auer** (Ora, 794 ft/242 metres), the tourism centre of the lowlands. It holds several festivals relating to local food and wine, including a South Tyrolean cooking competition (mid-April), the Apple Festival (late May) and the lowlands Wine Tasting Week (late October) during which wine seminars are offered. The **Schwarzenbach Recrea-** tional **Park** is a big attraction for sports enthusiasts, who should have no trouble managing the 530 cliffside steps of the "Cat Ladder".

The orchards of the lowlands and Überetsch are criss-crossed by a well-developed network of minor roads that are very popular with cyclists. For those who arrive without a bicycle, shops in Eppan, Kaltern, Tramin, Kurtatsch, Neumarkt, Auer and Leifers all offer bikes for hire.

As the floor of the **church of St Peter** is 16½ ft (5 metres) below ground level, in former times the building was susceptible to bad flooding. The church contains a Gothic cross rib vault, a baroque high altar and the oldest organ in South Tyrol (1601). A cemetery for those who died in World War I is located beside the church.

Until construction of the railway (1859), **Branzoll** (Bronzolo, 781 ft/238 metres) was the last stop for vessels plying the Etsch. Log rafts left here for Venice and ships with wares from the Orient landed here. In the inns of the village one can still hear the native dialect of *Bronzolót*. The **porphyry quarries** on the mountainside still supply road paving material for half the roads in central Europe.

In the shadow of Mt Mitterberg to the west crouch groups of houses belonging to the town of **Pfatten** (Vadena). From here, a road leads over the Kreith Saddle directly to Lake Kalterer. In the course of just a century **Leifers** (Laives, 837 ft/ 255 metres), only 6 miles (10 km) from Bozen and populated mainly by Italians, has developed from a small farming village to the fourth largest town in South Tyrol.

The old pilgrimage route to Maria Weissenstein (4,987 ft/1,520 metres), Tyrol's largest place of pilgrimage, is still in use. In a matter of only a few minutes one can travel from the centre of Leifers, invariably clogged with traffic, to the wildly romantic Branden Valley from where the Leiferer Ridge Path leads along the mountaintop to **Seit** (2,854 ft/870 metres). From here there is a panoramic view over Bozen and the entire lowlands.

An avenue of apple trees.

BURGGRAFENAMT

This short stretch of valley linking South Tyrol's two largest cities is richer in history than any other region in the province. This area, between the cornerstones of Burggrafenamt, **Castle Hocheppan** west of Bozen and **Castle Tyrol** north of Meran, was the arena of the many battles for sovereignty over the region.

Lords of the castle: In the 12th and 13th centuries, ministers of the Trent bishops ruled in both castles. In Castle Hocheppan the job was given to the counts of Eppan and in Castle Tyrol to the counts of Vinschgau. Both constructed mighty fortresses and attempted, over the course of several generations, to eliminate the other. To do this they stopped at nothing. In 1158, the Eppan brothers, Henry II and Frederick II, even attacked their own feudal lord, Bishop Adelpret of Trent.

Nevertheless, the counts of Vinsch-

gau, who had in the meantime changed their title to the counts of Tyrol, eventually proved victorious. In 1259 they managed to force Bishop Egno of Trent (himself an Eppan count) to relinquish his castle to them. Over the course of the following 36 years, Meinhard II of Tyrol successfully crushed the power of the Trent and Brixen bishops and expanded Castle Tyrol into a formidable and princely residence.

The core of **Castle Hocheppan** was probably constructed in just one decade, from 1200 to 1210. The walls, built of evenly laid, smoothly cut, reddish porphyry blocks, indicate that it was built at one stroke. The central element of the building is the well-preserved main tower. On the west side, the castle was joined to a palace which was built directly against the cliff and crowned by dovetail parapets. The outbuildings were built on the east flank of the ring wall. Next to the tower there was an enclosed courtyard that was entered through a gate. This could be closed off whenever enemies approached. Upon taking over the fortress, the Tyroleans initially maintained it for defence purposes, but from the 16th century it was allowed to deteriorate.

The jewel of the castle is its chapel, consecrated in 1131. Inside, the three walls as well as the three semi-circular apses are covered with extraordinary frescoes painted between 1207 and 1210. Above the three apses, in a painting which extends to the side walls, Christ reigns as judge with the 12 Apostles in attendance. The vault of the central apse is dedicated to Mary with the Christ child and angels. Below, to the left and right of the window are the Wise and Foolish Virgins. On the walls of the nave, the life of Jesus Christ is depicted in two rows of paintings.

On the altar wall with the three apses, the monumental austerity of the Byzantine-influenced High Romanesque style is clearly evident, but the nave's walls are distinguished by their naturalistic and even distinctly Tyrolean details. The most beautiful example of this is *The Dumpling Eater,* the first depiction of the Tyrolean dumpling.

receding ages: ading his afling to asture. Left, rapes in erlan.

Burggrafenamt
6.4 km / 4.0 miles

Oswald and Margarethe: Another fortress, **Castle Greifenstein**, situated across the valley near **Siebeneich** (Settequerce), was built about 200 years after Castle Hocheppan. Although now a ruin, at one time it was the military headquarters of the Starkenberg counts. It was from here that they directed the insurrections of the "Elephant Alliance", a group of aristocrats who joined forces against the duke Frederick with the Empty Pockets.

Although the duke laid siege to the castle on two occasions, he was unable to conquer it. During the first siege, the famous poet Oswald von Wolkenstein defended the castle with the help of his two brothers. Staging a courageous sortie, they managed to force the enemy to retreat. The second siege lasted almost two years. The fortress managed to hold fast; but in 1426, after the Elephant Alliance fell apart, the castle was turned over to Frederick. After the 16th century, it fell into ruin.

Another ruined castle lies a few miles to the north, above **Terlan** (Terlano).

Castle Neuhaus was built in 1220 by the count of Tyrol. It was destroyed by the bishop of Trent about 50 years later, but by 1320 it had been rebuilt. This castle has been a ruin since the end of the 17th century. Its more familiar name is **Maultasch**; it is not clear whether this name is derived from the Tyrolean princess Margarethe Maultasch or from the narrow pass above the castle (*malatasca* means mousetrap).

Around Terlan the rolling hills of the vineyards spread out in all directions. "Terlaner" is a green burgundy-like grape whose roots, experts claim, reach all the way down to the veins of silver running between the rock strata (silver was mined in this community well into the 18th century). Wine has been produced here since the time of the Romans and the wine called Torilan dates back to the year 923.

The **parish church** has existed at least since 1204; the current building, with its Gothic choir, was begun around 1385 and the Gothic steeple was added to the church in 1500. Inside the church, whose

The first snows.

roof is covered in colourfully glazed tiles, there is a series of outstanding frescoes; the choir, nave and side aisle are all decorated with works of the Bozen School. The oldest frescoes are found in the choir, which is almost entirely dedicated to the Virgin Mary, although the Apostles and 14 saints are also featured. The dome depicts Christ with halo as well as symbols of the Evangelists. Most of the scenes have architectonic backgrounds and were painted by an anonymous Bozen master artist around 1390. The sandstone sculpture depicting the crowning of Mary, thought to have been executed in about 1318 in a Veronese studio, is an art treasure in its own right.

Mölten, Andrian, Nals: From Terlan, the drive up to the small village of **Mölten** (Meltina), located at 3,740 ft (1,140 metres) on the south slopes of Mt Salten, is well worthwhile. This settlement evolved around the Lombardian castle Maletum, destroyed by the Franks in 590. However, the first settlements in this sunny hillside region between the Etsch and the Sarn Valley date back to prehistoric times.

The **parish church** of Mölten was built in the 12th century, but it was not until the end of the 15th century that the lancet arch window and star-vault were added to the nave. It was at this time, too, that the height of the steeple was extended. The original fresco decorations were unfortunately almost completely destroyed after a number of further additions were made in the 17th century and neo-Gothic renovations were carried out in the 19th century. The neo-Gothic altars were constructed about 1860, but contain sculptures which are much older.

The European Hiking Path No. 5 runs along the ridge of Mt Salten above Mölten, leading up to Meran 2000 and then right across to St Leonhard in Passeier.

Directly across from Terlan, in **Andrian** (Andriano), the visitor is confronted with further evidence of the region's bellicose history – the **Festenstein ruins**. Located on a steep cliff

More than half a million tonnes of apples a year are harvested here.

above the Höllenbach hollow, the castle was originally built by members of the Eppan family in the early 13th century. From 1305 onwards, it was owned by Henry von Vestenstein. The castle was so cleverly sited that entrance was possible only via a single drawbridge. Andrian itself was a station for the Romans (*castrum Andriani*).

Its **parish church** dates back to 1235 and was renovated in the late Gothic period. During renovation and reconstruction, lasting until 1854, much of the original building was destroyed. The church's late-Gothic choir became the sacristy (frescoes dating from 1520 have been uncovered). The neo-Gothic high altar was built in 1904 but contains much older statues: St Sebastian and Mary with child date from the end of the 15th century, St Barbara, St Catherine and St Anne were probably created in the early 16th century.

Nals (Nalles), the next village to the north, also provides ample evidence of the region's battle-torn history. **Castle Payrsberg**, today a ruin, was built at the beginning of the 13th century. All that remains of this once mighty castle is its imposing tower.

What is today known as **Castle Schwanburg** dates from 1286, when it was known as the "Nag's House". In the 14th century it passed into the hands of the lords of Boymont-Payrsberg. The castle's interior contains murals and furnishings from the time of construction as well as various coats-of-arms. The castle's small **chapel**, which is dedicated to St Catherine, contains an altar dating from 1671.

The **parish church** of Nals (1209) once belonged to the Abbey of St Afra in Augsburg. The free-standing tower with its round arch door and the round arch windows also date from this time. The dome was added between 1810 and 1814 when the present-day church was built. The entire interior furnishings, with the exception of the organ, date from the time of construction.

Prissian, Grissian and Tisens: Even the small village of **Prissian** could not get along without a castle. Built in the late

The Falkner path above Meran; in the background is Dorf Tyrol.

13th century, the rectangular **Castle Fahlburg** was originally called *Vall*. It was owned by the counts of Zobel until 1597 when it came into possession of the counts of Brandis. Shortly after 1600 they constructed the current building, in the Renaissance style and with a forecourt and corner towers. The interior houses a wealth of furnishings and decorations from the 17th century, including ceiling paintings done on canvas, handsome panelling, coffered ceilings and tiled stoves.

The tiny hamlet of **Grissian**, lying about 650 ft (200 metres) above Prissian, has a particularly fine church, the small **church of St James**, founded by Rudolf von Marling and consecrated by the bishop of Brixen in 1142. Visitors are greeted by a Gothic fresco on the exterior wall above the portal. This picture, painted about 1400, depicts Christ in majesty accompanied by the 12 Apostles. Inside the church, the triumphal arch and the apse are decorated with Romanesque frescoes dating from about 1200. The apse depicts Christ as judge with Mary and John and the symbols of the Evangelists.

On the left side of the triumphal arch, the hand of God blesses the sacrifice brought by Abel. On the right side, the clenched fist threatens Cain, who is turning away. Above, Abraham and Isaac approach the place of sacrifice. What is special about this scene is that the background depicts a natural landscape of snow-capped mountains – similar to the Dolomite landscape – rather than the usual stylised background. This mountain landscape is the first depiction of the region's native environment and, with its three-dimensional effect, it marks a totally new stage of development in Romanesque painting.

The small village of **Tisens** to the west of the Etsch was originally a Lombardian fortification, mentioned in the *Vita Langobardorum* of Paulus Diaconus as Castle Tesana. The **parish church** of Tisens existed as long ago as 1194. The lower portion of the tower, which can still be seen today, dates from the original Romanesque structure. In 1670 the round

arch windows and the dome were added. The nave was renovated in late Gothic style in 1529 when the lancet arch main portal was added. The choir, with its lancet arch tracery windows, was added at the same time. The nine glass paintings in the three choir windows also date from the time of the late Gothic renovation. Aside from the finely drawn Bible scenes with their many figures, the windows depict the coats-of-arms of the donors.

The most beautiful views hereabouts are to be gained from the top of the hill occupied by the tiny **church of St Hippolytus**. This hilltop was the site of a settlement in prehistoric times and during the Stone Age there was a fortress here. From here one has a view across 20 villages and some 40 castles and fortresses.

The last stop before Meran is the large town of **Lana** in the heart of Burggrafenamt, nestling picturesquely in lovely rolling orchards. This town was settled as early as prehistoric times. The fortress ruins, semi-preserved castles

A friendly policeman.

and stately residences are testimony to the numerous battles fought in the area as well as to its wealth.

Especially impressive evidence of the area's former prosperity is found in the **parish church of the Assumption** (Maria Himmelfahrt) in **Niederlana**. The church was first documented in 1276 and was consecrated in its present late Gothic form in 1492. Inside the church is South Tyrol's largest late Gothic winged altar-piece. Some 46.3 ft (14.1 metres) high, it fills the entire choir all the way up to the net vaults and represents a first-class monumental work of art. This altar-piece, the work of Hans Schnatterpeck from southern Germany, was commissioned by the citizens of Lana in 1503. Schnatterpeck was given eight years to complete the work and the agreed fee was 1,600 gilders – at the time equivalent to the value of about three large orchards. He and his assistant, Bernhard Härpfer, as well as the artist Hans Schäufelein adhered to the terms of their contract and completed their masterpiece in 1511.

The fact that this altar-piece survived the baroque era intact is due solely to the legal interpretation of the original contract: at the end of the 18th century the church's priest, a certain Father Lippis, decided that the altar-piece was too old-fashioned and should be dismantled. The citizens of Lana quickly informed him that the altar-piece had been commissioned and paid for by the parishioners and was thus their property and not that of the Church. If the priest was not able to like the altar-piece, they said, then he could pack his bags and leave. The altar-piece thus remained.

First impressions of the altar are dominated by the incredible amount of sculptural detail. In the central panel and carved mounting alone there are 33 figures. Additionally, reliefs decorate the side panels. The central panel is divided into two pictorial zones: below is the throne of grace with Peter and Paul, and above is the coronation of Mary between the St Anne with Mary and the child Jesus and St Catherine. The hollow groove of the altar-piece's frame contains 10 elegantly executed statuettes of the Wise and Foolish Virgins. The inner surfaces of the panels are decorated with reliefs of the Proclamation, the Birth of Christ, the Circumcision and the Adoration of the Magi. The outer surfaces are painted with scenes of Christ with Pontius Pilate, the Mount of Olives and the bearing of the cross. The richly-ornamented mounting contains Christ in Judgement, trumpeting angels, the Man of Sorrows and various saints.

The **chapel of St Margaret** is also interesting in its own way. This small church with its three round apses dating from the Romanesque era was turned over to the Teutonic Order by Emperor Frederick II in 1215. In the 17th century it was completely renovated and in 1896 it was again reworked in accordance with contemporary tastes. Thus for a long time the Romanesque frescoes decorating the triumphal arch and the three apses, dating from the early 13th century, were painted over. Portions have once again been exposed, and work from 1215 is easily recognised.

Left, the fertile Etsch Valley is exploited to the full. **Right**, apple blossom in spring.

THE APPLE BASKET OF SOUTH TYROL

South Tyrol's most famous product is wine, and dairy farming is its most widespread agricultural activity, but it is the apple orchards which earn the largest income, even though the region's 20 million apple trees occupy only 2 percent of the land. The ideal growing conditions of South Tyrol make it Europe's largest apple-producing region. The orchards stretch from Salurn to deep into the Vinschgau, running over 60 miles (100 km) along the River Etsch.

At the end of April, when the apple trees are in full bloom, the landscape looks as though it has been visited by spring snow. Anyone who rises at the crack of dawn after a chilly night will be rewarded by a truly glorious sight. The first rays of the early morning sun illuminate the soft pink of blossoms shimmering through shells of ice. Each individual blossom is contained by an icy case formed by the frost during the night. Incredibly, adequate warmth is set free during this freezing process to prevent damage to the blossoms.

A hike through these orchards in autumn is no less spectacular. Then the branches of the trees strain under the weight of the ripe apples. The orchards are transformed into hives of activity as temporary workers from Europe, Africa and Pakistan, or globetrotters from Australia and America join in the harvest.

In spite of this, the apple orchards have had little success as a tourist attraction. When local tourist offices from Lana to Eppan made a valiant attempt in the 1960s to lure tourists to the region with a "South Tyrolean Apple Road", they quickly discovered that it did not have the same allure as the so-called Wine Road, launched at the same time. The Wine Museum had been in existence for 35 years before Lana's Fruit Museum finally opened its doors in 1990. Auer holds a South Tyrolean Apple Week, but its popularity lags far behind that of the various wine-tasting weeks offered in other villages. Tourism officials have not even attempted to organise an Apple Festival.

And yet, up until a few decades ago, the range of fruits in South Tyrol was far more varied than that of its wines. The 100 or more different apple and pear varieties had such tempting names as Tasty, Rosemary, Champagne, Triumph, Kalterer, Kaiser and Good Louise. But dealers and customers alike gradually grew to demand only those products which were standard in taste, size and colour, the so-called universal varieties such as Golden Delicious, Red Delicious, Jonathan, and Granny Smith. Thus the local apple farmers were left with no choice but to axe all the lovely old trees which did not produce these popular varieties.

Today, the motto is "uniform rank and file" – from the orchards to the shop shelves. Up to 4,000 dwarf apple bushes per hectare (about 2½ acres) stand in tight espalier rows. The methods of preserving harvested apples has also changed. At the turn of the century, South Tyrolean fruit was still individually wrapped in tissue paper, packed in special padded crates and sent to such far away destinations as the court of the Russian czar. Today, 700,000 tons of apples piled in huge containers roll into warehouses where they are stored under "controlled conditions", ensuring that they remain fresh and crisp well into the following summer.

Inevitably the extent and ecologically unfriendly practices of modern apple farming have caused a host of environmental problems. Meadows, fields, grape vines, moorlands and pastures have fallen victim to the apple monoculture. Chemicals were introduced to take over the functions of the natural pest predators.

Recently, however, farmers have started to realise the dangers of such methods and have reverted to natural forms of plant protection and reduced the use of chemicals. They are even beginning to replant hedges in the hopes that the necessary insects will resettle. And apple lovers who place more value on the taste of an apple than on its appearance will be glad to know that, with a bit of searching, they can still sample some of the local varieties threatened with extinction. Local farmers markets or natural food shops are usually good sources (see addresses for Organic Fruit Growers in Travel Tips section).

MERAN AND ENVIRONS

The city of **Meran** (Merano, 1,063 ft/ 324 metres) nestles in a wide basin. Five valleys converge here from all sides, making the city their hub. Two large rivers also merge here: the glacier green **Passer** and the **Etsch**, which flows through the whole South Tyrol.

This region has been known as "Burggrafenamt" for as long as anyone can recall. Contrary to popular misconceptions, the name has nothing to do with the area's extraordinary wealth of castles and fortresses (the word *burggrafen* meaning castle lords); instead it dates back to the Middle Ages when a particular type of administrative structure was established under which the judicial, public notice and tax authorities of the region were governed by the lords of Castle Tyrol.

Capital and spa: Two periods of history in particular have left their mark on the landscape of this region, the heart of Tyrol. The first was during the Middle Ages, from about 1265 to 1363, when Meran became the capital of Tyrol. The influence of this period on the architecture is still evident in Meran's old town. The last ruler of Tyrol, Princess Margarethe Maultasch, was forced to relinquish " the principality of Tyrol, the land and the region along the Etsch and in the Inn Valley, along with Castle Tyrol, all the other castles and all the residents" to the Habsburg ruler, Rudolf IV, on 29 September 1363, after the death of her husband and son.

With this, the capital of the region became Innsbruck and the mint was moved to Hall in the Inn Valley, marking the end of Meran's importance. The former capital quickly declined into a sleepy little country town.

It was not until 500 years later that Meran was woken from its slumber, when it was discovered by the tourist industry and the city once again attained significance. The year 1836 marks the official birth of Meran as a resort. In 1855, the spa administration was officially recognised by the government in Vienna and received permission to issue spa regulations. It was one of the first spas to be established.

In 1874, the first spa house was constructed and a large number of inns and hotels, including several grand establishments, were built to accommodate the increasing number of guests, who came from all over the world. Elisabeth, empress of Austria, came in 1870 for the first of many therapeutic visits. Meran soon ranked among Europe's largest and most well equipped spa resorts. The English novelist and poet George Meredith, writing to his friend Frederick A. Maxse in 1861, enthused: "Meran is southern in heat and luxury of growth of all kinds of fruits."

Old town and arcades: The historic quarters of Meran, in particular those occupying the right-hand banks of the Passer, are very well-preserved. The town's most important sights are the parish church of St Nicholas, with its mighty steeple, the arcades, the royal castle and the old district of Stainach. Three of the four original city gates are

still standing: the **Bozen Gate** on the southern side of town, the **Passeirer Gate** to the north and the **Vinschger Gate** to the west.

The **parish church of St Nicholas** was consecrated on 10 November 1465, after an extremely long period of construction. Its imposing size serves as a reminder of the Tyrolean capital's glory. Its most notable features include the Gothic portals, the magnificent triple-naved interior, paintings by the Tyrolean artist Martin Knoller and the lovely stained-glass windows. Directly behind the church is the **chapel of St Barbara**, built in Gothic style and containing a lovely Pietà as well as 15th-century frescoes. It adjoins Meran's oldest district, **Stainach**, whose narrow streets are lined with interesting buildings, many of which are currently undergoing restoration.

To the west of the church square (Pfarrplatz) are the **Meran arcades**, the main shopping street, whose traditional buildings house modern shops and restaurants. The southern part is called **Wasserlauben** (water arcades) and the northern part **Berglauben** (mountain arcades). Some of the houses on the street have picturesque old courtyards and staircases open to the public.

About halfway down the arcades, at the point where the path up to **Tappeiner Way** begins, the **Landesfürstliche Castle** (castle of the counts) lies behind the city hall. From about 1450 onwards this castle was gradually converted into a city palace, probably because Castle Tyrol, quite a distance outside the city, was too uncomfortable for modern tastes. The castle contains furniture, weapons, lovely wood panelling, tiled stoves and paintings.

The city's districts: Meran consists of four communities which were joined into one administrative unit after World War I: Meran, Gratsch, Untermais and Obermais. In **Untermais**, on the left banks of the Passer, across from the main post office, is Meran's most harmonious church, the **church of the Holy Ghost**. Built by the German architect Stefan of Burghausen, it was conse-

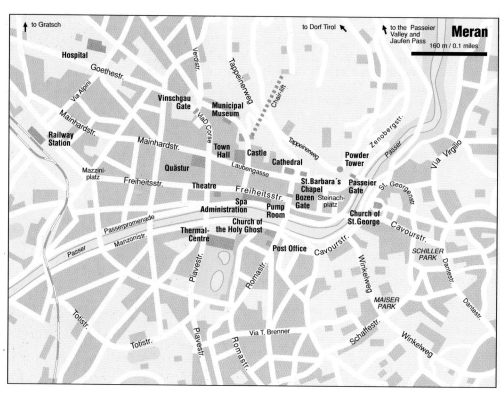

crated in 1431. Unfortunately the grand Gothic portal has suffered somewhat from the effects of traffic pollution. The interior, decorated with magnificent works of art, is rather dark despite the many windows, which adds to its mystic atmosphere.

From here, Rom Street leads into the centre of Untermais and the **parish church** and the **church of Our Lady of Comfort**. The latter, dating from 1520, has recently received attention from art historians on account of its well-preserved frescoes.

Meran, and especially **Obermais** boasts numerous castles, many of which occupy extensive parks. Most of these are private homes and not open to the public. Some, however, such as the castles of Labers, Rundegg, Fragsburg, Rametz and others, serve as hotels or restaurants. A museum and botanical garden are planned for Castle Trautsmannsdorf.

The many castles and fortresses in the surrounding countryside also date from the time when Meran was the centre of Tyrol. Again several of these are purely private residences while others have been converted to museums open to the public.

Spa in the park: Meran offers much more than medieval architecture, however; the lovely promenades and walkways, for instance, were constructed during the city's development as a spa. One of the most important buildings of the spa era is the **spa house**, on the right banks of the Passer in the centre of town. The older portion of this building, constructed in neoclassical style, dates from 1874.

The huge **spa hall**, directly next to the Spa House, was opened in 1914 and is considered the most beautiful as well as the largest Art Nouveau building in the entire alpine region. Much time and money has been invested in its renovation, and its original character has been carefully preserved. As a concert hall, it has excellent acoustics. It is the venue for many cultural and festival events, the most notable of which is the "International Meran Music Week Festival".

Some of the mountains and valleys around Meran.

The ceiling paintings are the work of two Viennese Art Nouveau artists, Jettmar and Rothaug.

The **Meran City Theatre** is located to the west of the spa house. This is a lovely building, with an architectural style lying somewhere between neoclassical and Art Nouveau. It was built by the Munich architect Dülfner. It, too, has been renovated in strict accordance with its original style. The **Wandelhalle**, with its landscape frescoes by the Meran artist Lenhart, is also an interesting stop for visitors.

One of the special appeals of this town, however, is its wonderful network of walkways and promenades. The **Tappeiner Way**, running along the slopes of the Küchel hill, is one of the most popular promenades. Mediterranean plants grace its borders and it boasts some superb views. Equally delightful is the path leading up to Tappeiner Way, the **Gilf Promenade**, which is lined with exotic flora and provides a beautiful view down to the rushing Passer river. The **Kur Promenade** itself leads along the Passer from the spa house to the railway bridge. On the left bank of the river, in the summer park, is a statue of Meran's most famous 19th-century guest – Elisabeth, the beautiful empress of Austria.

Across from the spa house, to the south of the spa and conference centre, is a huge park equipped with thermal and other therapeutic baths. There are still plenty of hotels dating from Meran's heyday as a spa resort, including many in the neoclassical style. There are plenty of examples of Art Nouveau, though some of these are no longer used as hotels. A walk through the villa and hotel district of Obermais is a pleasant way to spend time, not only because of the splendid architecture but also because of the parks which give Meran its southern flair.

The international **race track**, the largest and most attractive racecourse in the Alps, is in Untermais. It specialises in steeple chasing. The "Great Prize of Meran", linked to a national lottery and held annually in September, has the

Exchanges on the Passer promenade.

highest stakes of any steeple chasing in continental Europe.

Castles and fortresses: Above Meran, on the slopes of the Mutspitze near the town of Dorf Tyrol, is the ancestral **Castle Tyrol**, eulogised by writers for centuries. The Innsbruck historian Franz-Heinz von Hye noted in his speech at the celebration of the castle's 850th anniversary in the summer of 1990: "Castle Tyrol is no everyday castle. Even among the comparable so-called ancestral castles such as Habsburg, Zollern or Staufen, all cradles of great dynasties, it occupies a special position. For, even today, an entire state bears its name. One must search far and wide to find a similar example."

Castle Tyrol is built on one of the loveliest pieces of property in all of the southern alpine region and offers a magnificent panorama. In recent years it has been fully restored and **concerts** – recommended for their wonderfully romantic setting – are held here during the summer months. It houses an exhibition of Tyrolean history as well as an archaeological museum.

The **chapel portals** of the castle, whose frescoes depict an interesting mixture of Christian and pagan symbolism, are also impressive. The interior of the chapel is dominated by a large Crucifixion group from the first half of the 14th century. Above the door to the great hall, the first **Tyrolean eagle**, dating from the period between 1271 and 1286, is perched. Today Castle Tyrol is accessible only by foot, either from **Castle Thurnstein** via St Peter or from **Dorf Tyrol**. Nevertheless, a stop at Castle Tyrol is an absolute must for all visitors.

Between Castle Tyrol and Castle Thurnstein – the latter now doing sterling service as an esteemed and popular restaurant – lies the venerable **chapel of St Peter** above **Gratsch**, documented in the history books as long ago as 1178. Inside, ancient stucco and frescoes, discovered only recently, have been renovated. The Romanesque fresco of the Apostle Paul in the southern transept is thought to date from 1080.

Down the hill from Castle Tyrol is **Brunnenburg**, a castle which was rebuilt in 1904 by a German. In more recent times this castle was purchased by the Rachewitz family who have endeavoured to keep it in mint condition. The modernist poet Ezra Pound (1885–1972) spent the last few years of his life here and it is his grandson who now runs the **agricultural museum** housed within its walls.

East of Dorf Tyrol, along the Passeier Valley, is **Riffian**, the most important place of pilgrimage in the county of Burggrafenamt. The monumental church here houses the famous sculpture of Our Lady of Sorrows (*circa* 1420). Also noteworthy is the **cemetery chapel** beside the pilgrimage church, constructed around 1400. All of the interior walls of this chapel were painted by the master artist Wenzelaus.

The busy resort of **Schenna** (Scena) is perched on a hill across from Riffian. This town is dominated by Castle Schenna and the Kirchhügel. The latter is a hill where the parish church, the architecturally important **church of St**

Sunbathing in front of the Meran spa house.

Martin and the neo-Gothic **mausoleum** of the archdukes of Austria or, as the case may be, the counts of Meran, are located. It is here that Archduke John, who was awarded the aristocratic title of "Count of Meran", lies buried with his family.

Castle Schenna, which still belongs to the Meran family, descendants of Archduke John, is open to the public as a museum. Among the many splendid room are a number of great halls, most of which are furnished with historical pieces and paintings.

The small **church of St George** lies just above the village of Schenna. It is an unusual circular building, constructed around the year 1200. Gothic frescoes from about 1400, many of which are very well preserved, decorate the church's walls. The handsome winged altar-piece – some of its statues have unfortunately been stolen – was created by one of Hans Schnatterpeck's assistants in about 1510. *St Kummernus on the Cross* is interesting from a folk-art point of view.

Villages and hiking paths: Straggling above Schenna is the village of **Hafling** (Avelengo), the home of the famous Hafling breed of horses. The village can be reached either via a well-constructed road heading up from the valley or with the help of the cable car which runs to **Meran 2000**. The region surrounding Hafling is a popular hiking area in summer, and a favourite wintersports venue for Meran's residents and guests during winter. The landscape here is dominated by **Mt Ifinger** with its 8,468 ft (2,581 metres).

Lying to the west of Meran, at the bottom of Töll, is the important fruit- and wine-producing village of **Algund** (Lagundo). In 1977, a new church designed by the architect Willy Gutweniger was consecrated. It is one of only a handful of noteworthy modern buildings in Burggrafenamt. Its interior, rich in symbolism, and its unusual 230-ft (70-metre) high bell tower make a visit worthwhile.

Algund lies directly at the foot of the Texel Massif, a group of mountains reaching heights of almost 10,000 ft (3,000 metres). This massif shelters the Meran Basin from the north, a major reason for Meran's temperate climate. In addition, the massif's glaciers serve to balance the extreme summer temperatures that would otherwise prevail, resulting in pleasantly mild summer nights in Meran.

Algund is also the site of the Forst Brewery, South Tyrol's largest and one of the most important beer producers in Italy. The family tree of the owners, the Fuchs family, includes the names of numerous brewers from that famous beer region on the other side of the Alps: Bavaria.

Via **Marling**, the road leads directly to **Tscherms** where **Castle Lebenberg** stands amidst rolling vineyards. This castle is also open to the public. In addition to housing a wealth of artworks and ornaments from the 16th and 17th centuries, it contains furnishings from the rococo period.

From Tscherms the road continues to **Lana**. Aside from being an important fruit-growing/processing town, Lana relies heavily on tourism. The old **parish church of the Assumption** in **Niederlana** contains important art treasures.

The path along the mountainsides, leading around the entire Meran Basin at an elevation of about 650 ft (200 metres), also deserves mention. This path, known as a **waalweg**, leads alongside the water channels (*waal*) once used to irrigate the orchards. On the whole, the orchards are now irrigated by other means, but these paths still exist and offer wonderful opportunities for a leisurely hike.

The **Algund Waalweg** leads from the end of the Tappeiner Way in Gratsch all the way to Töll. There one must cross over the highway in order to reach the **Marling Waalweg**. This, in turn, leads through Tscherms and continues down into Unterlana. These paths are especially beautiful in spring, when the apple blossom is out, and in autumn when the foliage is at its best. The many inns offering food and drink for weary wanderers along the way make them even more appealing.

MARGARETHE MAULTASCH

Was she horribly ugly, or was she indescribably beautiful? Was she a depraved nymphomaniac or was she the very model of female moral virtue? No other figure in the history of the South Tyrol evokes as much speculation as Margarethe Maultasch; and few South Tryrolean personalities – apart from Andreas Hofer – have been the subject of so many stories, from anecdotes to complete historical novels. The most famous work about her is *The Ugly Duchess* by the Munich-born writer Lion Feuchtwanger. It was first published in Britain in 1927 and achieved resounding success.

Margarethe was born in 1318. Her grandfather Meinhard II, who secured and extended the "land on the Etsch and in the mountains", is considered to be the creator of Tyrol. When her father Henry succeeded to the throne his priority was to secure an heir and thus prevent the inheritance from crumbling. His three marriages produced only two daughters, one of whom was of poor health. The other was Margarethe.

When Henry died in 1335, Margarethe duly took up the reins of power. The country had been brought to the brink of ruin by the wasteful excesses of her father, but Tyrol's strategic position between northern Europe and Italy still made it important in the eyes of the great European powers. Certainly, the marriage between the 12-year-old Margarethe and the nine-year-old John of Luxembourg, son of King John "the blind" of Bohemia, who died in the saddle at the Battle of Crècy, and brother of the later Holy Roman Emperor Charles IV, had nothing to do with love. Through this expedient marriage, arranged five years before Henry's death, the House of Luxembourg succeeded in breaking the supremacy of the competing Bavarian Wittelsbachs and the Austrian Habsburgs in the alpine area.

But this situation was only temporary, for the marriage was not a happy one and the local nobility had little sympathy for Margarethe's husband, who summoned ever more officials and advisers to the Tyrol. He attempted to limit Margarethe's influence and preferred hunting to directing the affairs of state. In 1341 he returned from hunting to find all the doors and gates closed. The disenchanted Margarethe had locked him out and he was forced out of the country.

But Margarethe, now 23 years old and ruler of her country, did not stay single for long. Both she and her country remained highly sought after. Even before the exit of her first husband, influential Tyrolean nobles had entered into negotiations with the Wittelsbach emperor Ludwig "the Bavarian" whose eldest son, Margrave Ludwig of Brandenburg, was of marriageable age. In the eyes of the church, however, Margarethe was still married. All attempts to convince the papal authorities that her marriage was invalid as it had been arranged when she was only a child and hadn't even been consummated failed. But this didn't deter Ludwig. He ignored Rome and proceeded with the wedding preparations. Margarethe gave her full consent.

But things began to go badly wrong for the couple when the Bavarian Bishop of Freising died after being thrown from his horse on his way to bless the marriage. Pope John, whose relationship with the Wittelsbachs and Ludwig was less than amicable, excommunicated the young couple. He also punished Tyrol: from then on all religious ceremonies were banned in Tyrol, children could not be baptised and the dying could not be administered the last rites. The locusts, floods, earthquakes, fires and outbreaks of the plague that visited the land of Tyrol during the time of Margarethe's rule were interpreted by the people as the "wrath of God".

Her life continued to be dogged by ill-fate: two daughters died very young, her second husband died of a heart attack in 1361 and her sickly 20-year-old son died two years later in a hunting accident. Margarethe finally gave up, bequeathed Tyrol to the Austrian Archduke Rudolf IV and went into exile in Vienna, where she died in 1369.

Although Margarethe used to be portrayed as an evil character, today she is more often seen as a helpless pawn caught in dynastic struggles, of which she was a victim rather than the perpetrator.

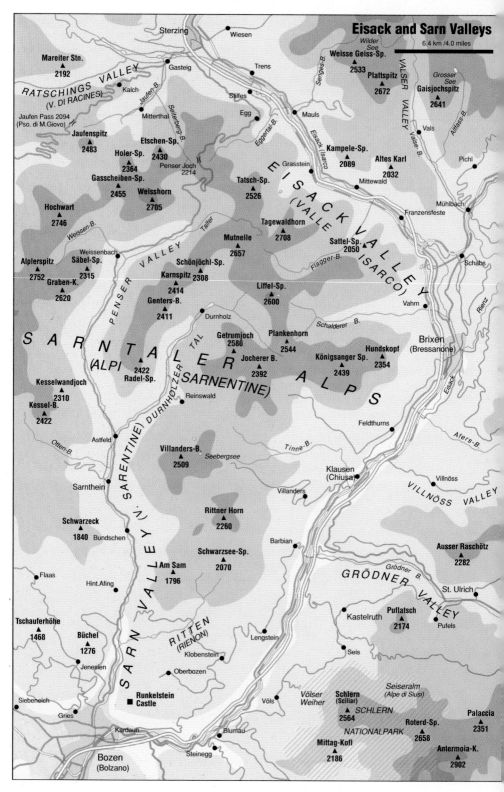

Eisack and Sarn Valleys

6.4 km /4.0 miles

Sterzing
Wiesen

Mareiter Stn.
▲ 2192

RATSCHINGS VALLEY
(V. DI RACINES)

Gasteig
Trens

Wilder See

Weisse Geiss-Sp.
▲ 2533

Plattspitz
▲ 2672

Grosser See

Gaisjochspitz
▲ 2641

Kalch
Jaufen-B.
Stilfes

VALSER VALLEY

Vals
Pichl

Jaufen Pass 2094
(Pso. di M.Giovo)

Mitterthal

Seitenberg-B.

Egg

Mauls

Eisack (Isarco)

Jaufenspitz
▲ 2483

Etschen-Sp.
▲ 2430

Holer-Sp.
▲ 2364

Penser Joch
2214

Kampele-Sp.
▲ 2089

Altes Karl
▲ 2032

Mittewald

Franzensfeste

Mühlbach

Grasstein

Gasscheiben-Sp.
▲ 2455

Weisshorn
▲ 2705

Tatsch-Sp.
▲ 2526

E I S A C K V A L L E Y
(V A L L E

Sattel-Sp.
2050

Schabs

Hochwart
▲ 2746

Weissen-B.

Taller

Tagewaldhorn
▲ 2708

(V A L L E
I S A R C O)

Flagger-B.

Alplerspitz
▲ 2752

Säbel-Sp.
▲ 2315

Weissenbach

Mutnelle
▲ 2657

Schönjöchl-Sp.
▲

Karnspitz ▲ 2308
▲ 2414

Liffel-Sp.
▲ 2600

Vahrn

Rienz

Graben-K.
▲ 2620

PENSER VALLEY

Genters-B.
▲ 2411

Durnholz

Schalderer B.

Brixen
(Bressanone)

S A R N T A L E R
(ALPI

Getrumjoch
▲ 2580

Plankenhorn
▲ 2544

Jocherer B.
▲ 2392

Königsanger Sp.
▲ 2439

Hundskopf
▲ 2354

A L P S

DURNHOLZER TAL

▲ 2422
Radel-Sp.

SARNENTINE)

Eisack

Kesselwandjoch
▲ 2310

Reinswald

Kessel-B.
▲ 2422

Feldthurns

Astfeld

Otten-B.

SARNENTINE)

DURNHOLZER

Villanders-B.
▲ 2509

Seebergsee

Tinne-B.

Klausen
(Chiusa)

Villnöss

VILLNÖSS VALLEY

Sarnthein

(N.

Villanders

Schwarzeck
▲ 1840

Bundschen

Rittner Horn
▲ 2260

Barbian

Ausser Raschötz
▲ 2282

S A R N   V A L L E Y

SARNENTINE

Schwarzsee-Sp.
▲ 2070

GRÖDNER

Grödner B.

Flaas

Hint.Afing

Am Sam
▲ 1796

St. Ulrich

VALLEY

Tschauferhöhe
▲ 1468

Büchel
▲ 1276

RITTEN
(RIENON)

Lengstein

Kastelruth

Seis

Puflatsch
▲ 2174

Pufels

Jenesien

Klobenstein

Siebeneich

Oberbozen

Gries

■ Runkelstein
Castle

Kardaun

Völs

Völser Weiher

Schlern
(Sciliar)

Seiseralm
(Alpe di Siusi)

Bozen
(Bolzano)

Steinegg

Blumau

▲ SCHLERN
2564

NATIONALPARK

Mittag-Kofl
▲ 2186

Roterd-Sp.
▲ 2658

Palaccia
▲ 2351

Antermoia-K.
▲ 2902

244

THE SARN VALLEY

The Sarn Valley, one of South Tyrol's largest valleys, runs north from Bozen all the way to the **Penser Joch Pass** (7,264 ft/2,214 metres). Crossing over the pass, the road leads down into Sterzing (Vipiteno) and the Eisack Valley. Within the Sarn Valley there are two other valleys – the **Durnholzer** and the **Penser** – and the entire region is encircled by the **Sarn Valley Alps** (Alpi Sarentini).

The **River Talfer**, which flows south to Bozen, springs from these mountains, near the valley's northernmost village of Asten (Laste). Although the Sarn Valley Alps, including Mt Hirzer (Punta Cervina, 8,786 ft/2,678 metres) and Mt Tagewaldhorn (Corno di Tramin, 8,885 ft/2,708 metres), reach enormous heights, they lack the spectacular jagged contours of the Dolomites. The expansive, high-lying pastures as well as the lovely dwarf-pine-covered slopes make this region a favourite place for cross-country ski expeditions. The climate of this region, unlike that of Meran or the lowlands further to the south, is more alpine, guaranteeing snow well into spring.

History and inhabitants: The first settlers in this valley are believed to have been the Baiuvari (Bavarians) from the north, although archaeological finds at Penser Joch Pass and the ancient sites at Auener Joch point to either the existence of settlements or at least the passage of migrants as far back as the Bronze Age. The existence of numerous buildings and farms is documented from the 13th century. This valley enjoyed relative prosperity at an unusually early period, as shown by the number of 12th- and 13th-century churches richly decorated with frescoes. What's more, the town of Sarnthein had quite early in its history a highly-paid priest.

The inhabitants of the Sarn Valley have a reputation for eccentricity. Due to the isolation of the valley, they developed an independence which they have maintained to this day. The wearing of the **Sarn national costume**, often decorated with the famous peacock quill embroidery, is just one sign of their individuality. Another sign, as the locals are quick and proud to point out, is the fact that most of the farms are still intact and functioning, in spite of the many drawbacks to farming in these parts. Although the valley's raw climate and remote location make the growing season short and transportation of goods and supplies difficult, farmers have resisted the temptation to leave the land and seek jobs in the city.

Compared with other regions in South Tyrol, the landscape here has remained almost virgin. The Sarn Valley has been spared the worst aspects of tourism, and hotels, chair lifts and cable cars are minimal.

Through the Talfer Gorge: The Sarn Valley road leads north from the Bozen triumphal arch and out through the suburbs. It passes the station of the **Jenesien Cable Car** (Funivia S. Genesio) which takes visitors up to the village of **Salten** (Salto), situated at 3,573 ft (1,089 metres), at the foot of the Salten Massif. This massif, the most southern ridge of the Sarn Valley Alps, is covered with meadows. Each spring, the moment the weather turns warm, these explode in a magnificent array of wild flowers, making it a favourite haunt for hikers.

By following the **Talfer** (Talveria), you come to **Castle Rendelstein** across from the cable car station. A bit further on, on the right bank of the river, the silhouette of the 13th-century **Castle Runkelstein** (Castello Roncolo), which would make the perfect backdrop for a Disney film, leaps into view. The castle, turned over to the city of Bozen by the Austrian Emperor Franz Joseph, houses a number of Gothic frescoes. From March to November, it is possible to take a guided tour of the castle followed by modern-day victuals in the wood-panelled restaurant.

Leaving the castle and continuing north through the narrow Talfer Gorge, the road presses close to the steeply towering cliffs and passes through a series of 19 tunnels, many of which are unlit. In between ducking in and out of tunnels the road provides brief but exciting glimpses of the rushing Talfer river far below.

Between tunnels 2 and 8, the ruins of the small **Castle Fingeler** and the steep face of **Mt Hanniskofel** with its tiny church can be seen on the opposite bank. It was from here, at the beginning of this century, that the young son of a Bozen aristocrat plunged to his death, heartbroken over his thwarted love for a simple baker's daughter.

There are few buildings along this route: Moarhäusel, Halbweg and Zum Touristen, all inns, are the exceptions. Shortly after Zum Touristen, a steep road leading up to the **Ritten** (Renon) region branches off to the right. If the weather is clear, it is well worth taking a short detour up this road to see the view. From here there is a spectacular panorama of the lower Sarn Valley, extending all the way to the village of Sarnthein and the surrounding mountains of Mt Öttach (7,011 ft/2,137 metres) and Mt Mittag (7,946 ft/2,422 metres).

Back on the main road and continuing north the route crosses the **Tanz Brook** (Rio Danza) to the tiny hamlet of **Bundschen** (Ponticino), meaning "small brook". Just before Bundschen, a small road forks off to the right, leading back to Tanz brook and then on to **Nördlerhof**. Near here are two old mines, evidence of a Sarn Valley industry dating from prehistoric times.

Sarnthein in the Sarn Valley: Suddenly the road reaches an expansive valley filled with meadows and high-lying mountain pastures. **Sarnthein** (Sarentino, 3,173 ft/967 metres) is the valley's largest and most important town. It also has the distinction of being South Tyrol's most far-flung community, covering over 116 square miles (300 sq. km) in all. Despite its remote location, Sarnthein became prosperous early in its history and, in the 14th century, was already able to pay its priest the considerable salary of 60 ducats. From 1443 to 1445, the priest of Sarnthein was Enea Silvio de Piccolomini. In fact, this priest never set foot in the town and in 1458

Gathering hay is not so easy on slopes such as these.

Piccolomini resigned from his post when he was elected Pope, taking the name Pius II.

The **church of St Cyprian**, in the eastern part of town, is a real jewel. Its oldest frescoes date from 1395; the vast differences in quality point to the fact that they were executed by more than one artist. One of South Tyrol's oldest inns is also found here. It is the **Guesthouse zum Hirschen**, founded in 1494. The lovely vaulted ceiling in the entrance and the historic 16th-century ceiling beams lend the inn plenty of character. Over the Talfer Bridge lies the centre of Sarnthein. The parish church, first documented in 1211, has undergone numerous renovations and so little of the original edifice remains. The town itself is a peaceful mountain village with relatively little traffic.

Fortress Reinegg, reigning over Sarnthein to the east, was the scene of an important aristocratic wedding in 1263. The aristocratic residence **Kränzelstein** (1362), with its residential tower, dominates the eastern end of the town, directly next to the bypass road. It is said that a similar tower existed in Nordheim, but the exact location has never been discovered. Other such towers, dating from the 13th century, are scattered throughout the valley. In most cases they are incorporated into farms. The Stofnerhof farm in **Steet**, east of Sarnthein, is just one example.

Traditions and superstitions: Two traditional festivals in the Sarn Valley deserve special mention. The first is the annual **Sarner Kirchtag** (church festival) held at the beginning of September. On the first day of the festival a colourful parade takes place which draws participants not only from the Sarn Valley but also from Austria and Germany. The brightly coloured national costumes and the music of the marching bands make it a very popular event. In the evening, the bands play dance music. The next day, South Tyrol's largest animal market is held. Bartering is still common and deals are still sealed with a handshake.

The other big attractions of the region

nderst, the ast farm in the Durnholzer Valley.

fall in September and October: the **Sarner Speciality Weeks**, organised by the **Bad Schörgau** and **Bad Rungg** restaurants. This is the time and place to enjoy the best of typical Sarn cooking in an elegant setting (though prices are similarly upmarket).

Anyone interested in the ancient tradition of *Federkielsticken* (peacock quill embroidery), a craft verging on extinction, can see it being done in Sarnthein. Peacock quills are split into long thread-like strands and used to embroider leather. The holes through which the strands are sewn must be close enough to create an attractive design but far enough apart to ensure that the leather does not rip – an exceedingly delicate operation. Embroidered leather goods ranging from handbags, shoes and book-covers to small items such as key rings and wallets can be purchased in the shops of Alois Thaler (Kranzelsteinweg) or Johann Thaler (Rohrerstrasse).

A road leads up to the **Sarner Ski Hut**, perched at 5,315 ft (1,620 metres) on the eastern slopes of Mt Karkofel. Those who prefer to hike can reach the hut in approximately 1½–2 hours. This cosy mountain hut makes a good starting point for further hikes all around the western ridge of the Sarn Valley Alps, especially to the comfortable **Auener Alm** hut (about a 1-hour hike on well-worn paths) or all the way to Meran 2000 and then on to Meran. The path leads across the Auenjoch, following the ridge across Mt Schwarze Wand (6,512 ft/1,985 metres), Mt Kreuzjoch (6,844 ft/2,086 metres) and Mt Maiser Rast (6,650 ft/2,027) to the Kirchsteig cable car.

By following the path to the left at Auenjoch, toward **Mt Hohe Reisch** (6,572 ft/2,003 metres), you can reach the Stoanernen Mandl (petrified men) which play an important role in the region's history. These piles of stones were first documented in 1540 during the Sarnthein witch trials. To this day, it is still not clear whether their function was merely to mark the path for travellers or if they had a connection with ancient pagan rites.

It seems that the people of the Sarn Valley were obsessed with all kinds of superstitions during the Middle Ages. Among the many curious stories documented in the town chronicles is one concerning a large Anabaptist movement which spread throughout the Sarn Valley in 1540 during the Peasant Revolts. Eventually supporters of the movement were forced to leave their homes and farms behind and flee for their lives to Moravia. Those who failed to escape the persecutors were hung on the gallows that were stationed between Sarnthein and Nordheim. There is also the fascinating account of Barbara Pächerlin, a humble peasant living in the village of Windlahn, who was burned at the stake as a witch in 1540 after having been accused and tried for "contorting" young boys, exercising her powers over the community's milk and conjuring up bouts of bad weather.

The great horseshoe expedition: The Sarn Valley Alps enclose the northern end of the valley like a horseshoe. Whereas the Salten and Ritten ridges to the south are popular summer resorts

Two official languages wherever you go.

because of their easy hiking paths, the **great horseshoe expedition** demands physical stamina.

The first day's tour on the horseshoe expedition takes about 5 to 6 hours and leads from Sarnthein over Mt Schartbiwak (7,808 ft/2,380 metres) to the refuge on **Rittner Horn** (7,415 ft/ 2,260 metres). On the second day, the usual course is to hike back to Gasteiger Saddle (6,745 ft/2,056 metres) and across Mt Jocherer to **Heiligkreuz Hut** (7,556 ft/2,303 metres) in about 5 hours. On the third day hikers head for the **Flaggerscharten Hut** (8,140 ft/2,481 metres) which can be reached in about 6 hours via the Tellerjoch (8,268 ft/2,520 metres). On the four day they cross over Mt Astenberg (7,635 ft/2,327 metres) to the inn at **Penser Joch** (6 hours). The fifth day's hike leads across the Sarn Weisshorn (8,875 ft/2,705 metres) to the village of **Rabenstein** in the valley. Those who feel they have already walked far enough can take a bus from here; otherwise, the hike continues to the **Kesselwand Refuge** (7,546 ft/2,300 metres; 6 hours). The last day's tour leads across Auenjoch and returns to Sarnthein.

The villages of Sarnthein, Nordheim (Villa, 3,278 ft/999 metres) and Astfeld (Campolasta, 3,350/1,1021 metres) have expanded so much that they are practically one. Nordheim's **church of St Nicholas** on the right side of the main street was first documented in 1367. In the last century, a German anthropologist visiting this church noted: "A deck of cards was found in a small sack hanging beside the entrance. Every card contained a pious text and a deed of atonement. When a peasant had committed a sin, he drew a card and performed his penitence."

The Durnholzer Valley: Beyond Astfeld, the **Gentersberg Range** divides the Sarn Valley into the **Penser** and the **Durnholzer Valleys.** The latter is a sparsely settled impasse. Isolated farms pepper the land next to the Durnholzer brook, and a small group of houses clusters where the road crosses the brook. In this narrow but fertile valley the main

The patriarch.

source of income is from breeding horses. The **Reiterhof Berger** is just one of the many farms which breed the famous **Hafling**. It is said that this resistant breed of horses first developed in the Sarn Valley.

About halfway along the valley, a steep road branches off to the right to **Reinswald** (S.Martino, 4,895 ft/1,492 metres). This town is the only one in South Tyrol which has its own parish guesthouse, run by the priest and his housekeeper. This is also the only noteworthy ski resort in the Sarn Valley, boasting a double chair lift and two T-bars. The slopes are not exactly world class, but are ideal for families with children, beginners and for those who like to avoid crowds. There are a couple of smaller hotels here as well as accommodation to be had in a number of private homes.

The highlight of a drive – or a hike – through the Durnholzer Valley is **Lake Durnholz** (Lago Valdurna, 5,144 ft/1,568 metres) at the very end of the valley. With its deep blue water and reedbeds at the northern end, this lake is one of the most beautiful stretches of water in South Tyrol. Unfortunately, the more well-known it becomes, the more it is spoiled by cars. Environmental damage to the lake has escalated in recent years. In an attempt to curb these problems, a large car park has been built at the entrance to the town. From here it is only a short walk to the lake. A stroll around Lake Durnholz takes only an hour – unless, of course, one is detained by a visit to the fisherman's restaurant (recommended) or by watching the many fishermen at work.

Also worth a stop is the **church of St Nicholas**, which dates back to between 1000 and 1300. The church's interior is covered with well-executed frescoes painted about 1430 (most probably by Master Conrad von Erlin of Ulm). They offer a lovely contrast to the church's rather austere exterior and remote location. The cemetery, too, always gorgeously decorated with flowers, merits a closer look.

Early Sunday mass in the Durnholz

Left, on the way to Sunday mass. Right, flag bearer at the Sarn church dedication festival.

church, followed by a visit to the parish guesthouse located just next door for some liquid refreshment and dinner, is a real experience. Practically everyone in the congregation dresses in national costume. The pork roast, by the way, is divine in itself.

The Penser Valley: The main valley extending north from Astfeld is the **Penser Valley**. Following the Talfer, the road hugs the left side of the Gentersberg Ridge. Here, as in the Durnholzer Valley, settlements are scarce. There are only four proper villages: **Muls** (Mules, 4,101 ft/1,250 metres), **Weissenbach** (Riobianco, 4,380 ft/1,335 metres), **Pens** (Pennes, 4,783 ft/1,458 metres) and **Asten** (Laste, 5,095 ft/1,553 metres). Along the way, about 500 ft (150 metres) up the hillside on the left, is the tiny settlement of **Aberstückl** (Sonvigo).

Near Muls, on the left, is an abandoned mine where zinc and silver were formerly mined. Pens, 2½ miles (4 km) further on, is the last stop made by buses during the winter months. The Penser Joch Pass is normally closed from the beginning of October.

The road to Penser Joch has relatively few bends. After passing through the pastures of the **Astenalm**, it arrives in the mountainous region of **Penser Joch** (Passo di Pennes, 7,264 ft/2,214 metres). On dark cloudy days this drive can be spooky. On fine days, however, there are spectacular views of Mt Hohe Scheiben (8,409 ft/2,563 metres), Mt Mutnelle (8,727 ft/2,660 metres) and Mt Tagewaldhorn (8,885 ft/2,708 metres) and, more distantly, the Ziller Valley Alps to the north and the Stubaier Glacier off to the left.

The route through the Sarn Valley from Bozen to Sterzing (and thus on to Brenner) has little historical importance, but due to the lovely scenery and its many cultural attractions it offers a good alternative to the crowded toll motorway. From Bozen to Penser Joch the distance is about 31 miles (50 km), and from Penser Joch down to Sterzing in the Eisack Valley and on to the Brenner Pass is a further 30 miles (48 km).

The *Reggel*, a tobacco pipe typical of the Sarn Valley.

THE PASSEIER VALLEY

For the Tyroleans the Passeier Valley is strongly associated with the name of Andreas Hofer, a Passeier Valley innkeeper and horse trader who rose to fame as Tyrol's freedom fighter in the early 19th century.

Reminders of the folk hero are everywhere in the valley. The first are found in **Schenna** (Scena), a village with a population of 2,500 at the valley's entrance: the new Gothic mausoleum of reddish granite, where the Austrian Archduke John (1782-1859) and his wife, Anna Plochl (1804-85), a humble postmaster's daughter, are buried, and Castle Schenna, the venerable fortress towering over the rooftops of the modern tourist village.

The lord of Castle Schenna: Without the aid of the archduke, who was a great supporter of the Tyrolean rebellion, it is doubtful that Andreas Hofer would have dared to spearhead the popular revolu-

tion against the powerful Bavarian-French alliance in 1809. Even though the revolution was doomed to failure, the fearless archduke harnessed himself to the Tyrolean revolt as a matter of principle. The Court in Vienna, under Francis I, the archduke's own brother, quickly distanced itself from the movement, accusing the archduke of making plans to establish an independent Rhaeto-Alpine principality out of Tyrol and Grisons.

The archduke enjoyed immense popularity among the Tyrolean people, partly on account of his unconventional marriage to a commoner. Worried about his radical plans and his extreme popularity, the Viennese Court issued a decree banishing John from the Tyrol, an edict that remained in effect until 1833. He spent this period of exile in Vienna, but the moment that the ban was lifted he returned to his beloved Tyrol. It was significant that he chose to settle in the town of Schenna, in Andreas Hofer's native valley. He purchased Castle Schenna in 1844.

The gentle-mannered and scholarly archduke, who preferred to read about history and politics rather than become directly involved in them, emerged from his self-proclaimed "exile" in Castle Schenna for the last time in 1848 when the German National Assembly, meeting in Frankfurt's church of St Paul, named him as imperial administrator, a euphonious and impressive title for an office with neither power nor influence. The wise archduke relinquished the office within the year. Discouraged by the political quibbling, John retired to pursue his own interests until his death 10 years later.

These interests included active support of agriculture, folk art and scholarship in Tyrol and Styria, as well as the renovation of Castle Schenna. He lived in exactly the manner he claimed to prefer in an entry written in his diary a few decades before, when he was living in exile: "If the truth be known, I, although an archduke, would live as the common folk do, wearing the traditional clothing, respecting the customs, loving the country and its citizens, en-

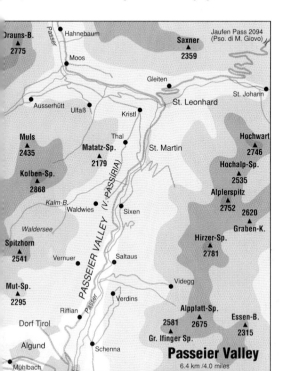

Jaufen Pass 2094 (Pso. di M. Giovo)

Passeier Valley

6.4 km /4.0 miles

Left margin (partially cut off):
...eceding ...ges: the ...ung River ...sser in the ...per reaches the Passeier ...lley. **Left,** ...ew of the ...wer Passeier ...alley.

suring their happiness and simply being like them in all they do."

At his death, the archduke bequeathed the castle to his heirs, the counts of Meran, who remain its owners to this day. They frequently visit Castle Schenna from their home in Styria in Austria.

Castle Schenna is still furnished in the way the archduke left it. A portrait of him as German imperial administrator, painted in 1848, hangs in the bedroom-cum-study. The inscription, written by John himself, reveals his political aspirations: "No Austria, no Prussia – a united and free Germany". This was written at a time when Austria and Prussia were being formed as new imperial states.

In a large corner room on the second floor of the castle hang portraits of the archduke and his family. The handsome-looking John is accompanied by his gently smiling wife Anna, his junior by 22 years. Her maiden name was Plochl but she assumed the title Countess of Meran upon her marriage. For John's sake she relinquished all claims of inheritance for herself and her children. The room also contains a portrait of their only son, Francis, Count of Meran, who ordered the construction of the new Gothic mausoleum beside Schenna's parish church in honour of his parents.

Also in this room, which was used by the archduke as a receiving room and parlour, is a portrait of Andreas Hofer, the only portrait of him painted during his lifetime. Jacob Placifus Altmutter painted the 42-year-old freedom fighter in the autumn of 1809 when Hofer was supreme commander of Tyrol and at the pinnacle of his power. It depicts a peasant with a bushy red beard, proudly wearing the golden chain of honour awarded him by the emperor.

Also here is a picture of Sandhof, the house near St Leonhard in which Andreas Hofer was born, and a picture of his capture in the snow-covered Pfandler Alm pasture in the Passeier Valley in January of 1810. The two men thus remain closely linked long after

Castle Schenna near Meran at the entrance to the Passeier Valley.

their deaths. Although they were born into stations worlds apart, both fought for their ideal of a free and independent Tyrol. They both risked much for this shared goal: Andreas Hofer his life, Archduke John a glorious political and military career.

The castle's origins: Castle Schenna was built around 1350 by Petermann of Schenna, the Count of Tyrol, on the hill overlooking the Meran Basin. After Petermann's death, it passed to his son-in-law, a member of the powerful Starkenberg family. The Starkenbergs, who owned various castles all over Tyrol (in addition to Schenna, they owned the castles of Goyen, Forst, Naturns, Juval, Greifenstein and Ulten) made no secret of their dislike for the rulers in Castle Tyrol.

The Starkenbergs were among the leaders in the alliance of the aristocracy against the Tyrolean ruler, Frederick with the Empty Pockets. But Frederick's revenge was swift: the moment that Ulrich von Starkenberg crossed over the Alps to fight in the war against the

Hussites, he attacked Castle Schenna. Ulrich's wife, Ursula Truchsess von Waldburg, with the help of many loyal followers, valiantly defended the castle for a time. But in the end she was forced to surrender. The castle later passed into the Tyrolean aristocratic family of the Lichtensteins. After changing owners several more times, it finally came into the possession of Archduke John in the 19th century.

Another notable building in Schenna is the **church of St George**, an original Romanesque circular structure which is thought to have been built in the first half of the 13th century. Some 150 years later – it is impossible to give exact dates – the interior, constructed around a central pillar, was decorated with frescoes. The dome is decorated by a Last Judgement and the Wise and Foolish Virgins, which, according to the gospel of St Matthew, symbolise the damned and the blessed.

The church's wall-paintings tell the legend of St George, in particular formal and brilliantly coloured "courtly"

The capture of Andreas Hofer.

depictions of the brutal torture undergone by the saint. The artist, who may have been an itinerant Italian painter or perhaps even a local man, was clearly influenced by the Italian works in Bozen's Dominican church. There is enormous attention to detail in the frescoes: George is thrown into the dungeon and pushed over the edge of rocky cliffs, he is tormented in a barrel with glowing hot nails, bound to a wheel, tied to two wild horses and, finally, beheaded. The pictures virtually represent a handbook of medieval torture methods. However, their grim subject matter is counterbalanced by the painting's urbane Gothic buildings, the background's strong resemblance to the Dolomites and the naive depiction of the plants and trees.

The St George Chapel has a Gothic triptych (unfortunately it has been plundered) and a "St Kummernus", an interesting wooden statue of a crowned bearded man wrapped in long robes and nailed to a cross, looking much like Jesus Christ. In fact, this is a saint who was revered in many European countries, particularly during the High Middle Ages. The saint was, in fact, a woman, the Christian daughter of the Portuguese king. In order to avoid marriage to a non-Christian, she prayed to God that a beard would grow on her face which would repel her suitor. After her prayers were answered, the bearded princess was rejected by her fiancé, renounced by her father and, in the end, crucified. Or so the story goes.

Passeier as transit region: An important transportation route led through the Passeier Valley. In 1342, the son of the Wittelsbach emperor, Ludwig of Brandenburg, travelled over the Jaufen Pass and through the Passeier Valley to Meran in order to meet his future wife, Margarethe Maultasch (though she, at the time, was still married to another man; *see page 241*). In addition to soldiers and emperors, it was common for pilgrims to journey through the region. Indeed, a pilgrim is depicted next to the west entrance of the church of St George in Schenna. He is dressed in simple pilgrim clothing, and bears the obligatory pilgrim staff and several cockle shells which place him under the protection of St James of Compostela, the patron saint of pilgrims.

Many travelling artists also passed through Tyrol. They were frequently recommended to one lord by another, and in this way they built up a vast network of connections. They travelled thoughout Europe and even further afield, moving from one commission to the next. One of these travelling artists was Wenceslas of Bohemia, whose work decorates the **cemetery chapel** of **Riffian** (Riffiano), a popular place of pilgrimage. He signed his name on a banderol in the chapel as "Magister Venclaus". Art historians have identified the painter of the 1415 mural as being the Bohemian court artist.

At that time, Wencelas was in the service of the sovereigns of Trent, in whose castle, Buon Consiglio, he painted the pictures of the months in the Eagle Tower. In Riffian he painted Old and New Testament scenes, including the worship of the golden calf, the manna falling from heaven, the feast of Pentecost, the bearing of the Cross, the adoration of the Magi, the discovery of the Cross and the Exodus to Egypt. These paintings offer interesting examples of "international Gothic", a style exported from upper Italy and Burgundy to Bohemia where it was enriched and embellished and then exported to the southern regions of Germany.

The Riffian **parish church** attracts even more visitors than the lovely murals of the cemetery chapel. This baroque building, with its high compact steeple, is also a place of pilgrimage. The late Gothic church, celebrated for its supposedly miraculous Gothic Pietà (*circa* 1420) on the high altar, was renovated in magnificent baroque style in the 17th century by members of the Delai family. This family, Italians who had settled in Bozen, were widely acclaimed as architects.

North of Riffian farms dot the slopes on both sides of the River Passer. Many occupy commanding sites and have a distinctly defensive architecture. Good examples near the hamlet of **Saltaus** are

ANDREAS HOFER

"Farewell cruel world. Death comes so easily to me that no tears will fall. Written at 5am, and at 9 o'clock I will leave this world to meet my God. Mantua, 20 February 1810. Your beloved Andreas Hofer from Sand in Passeier."

These are the final words of Andreas Hofer's parting letter, written just a few hours before his execution in Mantua. He went bravely to his death. Refusing to be blindfolded, he glared directly into the eyes of the French firing squad. When the officer in charge, in a state of shock, floundered, Hofer himself shouted the command, "Fire!"

Andreas Hofer was born at Sandhof in the Passeier Valley on 22 November 1767. When he was three years old, his mother died and at the age of seven he lost his father. At 22 he married Anna Ladurner of Algund who bore him eight children. As an innkeeper in Passeier and as a horse trader and wine dealer throughout Tyrol, Hofer came into contact with many different people. He made numerous friends and won great respect among his fellow countrymen. At the age of 23 he was selected to represent the Passeier region in the Tyrolean Parliament in Innsbruck. This legislature was critical of the enlightened anti-clerical reforms of the Emperor Joseph II and supported Tyrolean independence.

In the years following, Hofer joined forces with a rifle company against the encroaching French troops. His real mission, however, began in 1805. The Treaty of Bratislava separated Tyrol from Austria, granting it to Bavaria which was allied with the French. According to paragraph eight of the treaty, Tyrol was to retain its former rights but come under the rule of the Bavarians.

But in the Bavarian constitution, issued in 1808, these former rights were abolished. Financial reforms were instituted, taxes increased, the Tyrolean constitution and the privileges of the Tyrolean aristocracy were abolished, the youth of Tyrol were conscripted, religious festivals were restricted or banned and the name Tyrol was deleted from the map. The Tyroleans were outraged.

When Archduke John, a brother of the Austrian emperor, Francis I, called upon the Tyroleans to revolt against Bavaria in 1809, promising them military support, they assumed that the word of the emperor's brother had the same weight as the word of the emperor himself. With the cry "It is time!" the Tyroleans rose up in April 1809.

During the first victorious battle against the Bavarian and French occupying forces in Innsbruck, Andreas Hofer was in command of the Passeier company. In the second battle, at Berg-Isel near Innsbruck, he led all the Tyrolean rebels. In the third Berg-Isel battle in August of 1809, the Tyroleans won with no outside assistance.

Andreas Hofer arrived at the palace in Innsbruck as supreme commander of Tyrol. This bearded man in *lederhosen* and green jacket, the innkeeper of Sand and loyal commander of the Tyrolean freedom fighters, entered the stucco-and-gold embellished residence of the Habsburgs with a childlike trust. He ended his triumphant speech to the jubilant masses with the words, "I promised you, and you've seen the results, God bless you."

One of his first actions was to issue new rules of morality. He forbade deep décolleté and coquettish curls in women; he attributed all his good fortune to God and the Virgin Mary; and he emphasised that he was not speaking as the Sand innkeeper but rather in the name of the emperor and Archduke John.

But on 14 October the emperor signed a treaty with Napoleon, relinquishing Tyrol to Bavaria and Italy. To begin with Hofer refused to believe it, on the basis that just a few months before the emperor had promised never to accept such a treaty, but eventually he was forced to face reality.

He scoffed at the Bavarian offer of amnesty for all Tyroleans who agreed to lay down their weapons. Although aware of the hopelessness of the situation, Hofer, urged on by the Capuchin priest Joachim Haspinger and other fanatics, fought on and signed a senseless call to battle. He was forced to flee and went into hiding at the Pfandler Alm in Passeier. There he was betrayed and taken to Mantua for trial. The hero of the Tyroleans was a man who ultimately failed.

the farms of Obersaltaus, Weingart and Saltaus. The latter has been transformed into an imitation castle. Further into the valley is the Erbion farm. Near the village of **St Martin**, on the east banks of the Passer, is the new Buchenegg farm, and on the western slopes is the lovely renovated Kalm farm with its five-storey medieval residential tower.

Other interesting farms are the Baumkirch farm which has been converted into a holiday home, the Gereut farm with its Romanesque door and window portals, renovated in the 19th century, and Steinhaus which dominates St Martin. These old farms, along with Camian and Happerg near St Leonhard, are known as **Schildhofs** (shield farms), something between a farm and an estate. They are mentioned in many of the region's legends.

The owners of the valley's 11 shield farms still like to dress up with spears and shields inscribed in Gothic type, the last vestiges of the many privileges their ancestors once enjoyed. These signified, from the 14th century onwards,

that the Passeier shield farmers were on a par with the aristocracy. They were allowed to bear weapons in court and in church and enjoyed, along with all nobles, full hunting and fishing privileges. The main advantage enjoyed by the shield farmers, however, was that they were not expected to pay any taxes, though in return they were compelled to assist the sovereign whenever he went to war – at that time a fairly regular occurrence. In the long term, this generally turned out to be rather more costly for the shield farmers than if they had paid regular taxes. Military expenditures even in the Middle Ages amounted to a fortune.

Home of a hero: The villages of St Martin (San Martino in Passiria) and St Leonhard (San Leonardo in Passiria) are spick-and-span resorts with many modern buildings in the typical alpine style found in so many tourist villages throughout the Alps. Located about halfway between the two is **Sandhof**, a well-managed and popular inn (their speciality is a delicious smoked ham)

During the summer months, mos of the hillsid pastures have to be irrigated.

which was the birthplace of Andreas Hofer on 22 November 1767. This white-washed house is built in typical Passeier style with a protruding oriel.

Other tributes to Hofer can be found in the graveside chapel, built by Hofer's grandfather in 1698, and in the Roman-esque Heart of Jesus chapel, dedicated in 1899, with its depictions of historic events.

St Martin is noted for the pious paintings depicted on the facades of some of its houses. Although these pic-tures are classified as primitive art, they do not appear as naive as examples found elsewhere in Tyrol. They are found on the tower house, on *Hochwies*, on the "high house" and on the so-called "art-ist's house". The latter, one of St Mar-tin's loveliest buildings, was the home of the 18th-century school of art respon-sible for these works (examples of such paintings are found far beyond the Passeier Valley).

The school's patron was Michael Winnebacher, the scholarly pastor of Moos, and the teacher was Nicholas Auer, who had studied in Munich and Augsburg and imported their ideas into his native valley. Other notable artists from this school, which lasted into the 19th century, were Johann Evangelist Holzer of Vinschgau (who painted a great many frescoes in southern Ger-many), the painter Josef Haller and the sculptor Anton Ferner whose master-piece is the high altar in the **parish church** of St Martin.

The village of **St Leonhard** lies at the junction of two ancient well-travelled routes which have been in use since prehistoric times. One of them leads over the Jaufen Pass into the Eisack Valley and the other over the Timmelsjoch Pass into the Ötz Valley in Austria. A hospice for pilgrims was built here 1,000 years ago.

The traffic which passed over these routes was controlled from the medi-eval Jaufenburg Fortress above St Leonhard. A painting of this simple fortress, providing interesting historic and architectural details, is found in the late Gothic **church of the Holy Cross**

Milk churns along the way.

in St Leonhard. Cycles of frescoes from the first half of the 16th century were brought to light in this church only a few years ago.

The hamlet of **Glaiten**, located along the Jaufen road just above St Leonhard, is notable for its small, hillside church of St Hippolytus which contains Gothic frescoes, dating from 1380, depicting the legend of Hippolytus, the Last Judgement and the coronation of Mary. This cycle, the oldest found to date in the Passeier Valley, is characterised by Giottoesque-Italian influences.

Like the fresco of St Christopher decorating the exterior wall, painted at about the same time, it is yet further proof that many travellers passed through here during the Middle Ages, bringing a wealth of cultural innovations into this seemingly remote region. Before the construction of the road through the Eisack Gorge in the 15th century this route over the Jaufen Pass and through the Passeier Valley was the shortest and quickest north-south connecting route through this region of the Alps.

Into the hinterland: An ancient route also led over the 8,173-ft (2,491-metre) high **Timmelsjoch**. The modern road, completed in 1968, is closed during the winter. It leads into the back country of the Passeier and the small villages of Moos, Rabenstein, Schönau and Blatt. From here, nimble hikers can venture through the remote Pfelderer Valley, over the Eisjöchl Pass of the Hohe Wilde (11,417 ft/3,480 metres), and into the Schnals Valley.

The Passeier residents have always been known as sturdy hikers, especially the legendary *Kraxenträger* (pack carriers). These men carried packs weighing up to 220 lbs (100 kg), transporting such goods as fruit, wine, liquor and vinegar to the Inn Valley and as far as Bavaria. They returned with salt, lard, meat and flax. On their way to the Timmelsjoch Pass the *Kraxenträger* would have passed **Lake Passeier** between Moos and Rabenstein, which was formed by the collapse of a mountain in 1401. This former lake has gone down in history as the "lake of grief". Eighteen years after its formation it flooded the entire Passeier Valley as far as Meran, where 400 people died and the church of the Holy Ghost as well as many other buildings were destroyed. In the following centuries this lake flooded Meran several more times; it was finally drained in 1774.

As yet, the gently undulating Passeier Valley, where some of the more isolated villages still have no electricity, has been spared the damaging effects of mass tourism. But other dangers continue to threaten the valley. Electrical companies are planning to build a tremendous dam in the back country which would greatly disrupt the life of the local farmers. Residents are protesting against the proposed construction.

They want to preserve the original character of their valley – the small villages, mountainside farms and pastures – a peaceful, remote alpine world where towering mountains flank the Austrian border and the **Stuller Waterfall** near the hamlet of Stuls cascades down over 1,122 ft (342 metres), making it Europe's third highest waterfall.

Left, greetings from South Tyrol. Right, not a balcony you could count on.

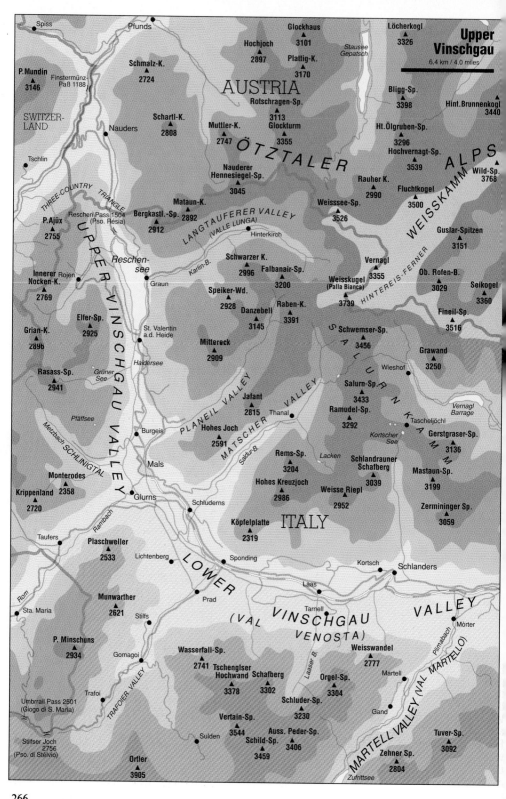

Spiss

Pfunds

Glockhaus
3101

Löcherkogl
3326

Upper Vinschgau

6.4 km / 4.0 miles

Hochjoch
2897

Plattig-K.
3170

Stausee
Gepatsch

Schmalz-K.
2724

AUSTRIA

Rotschragen-Sp.

Bligg-Sp.
3398

Hint.Brunnenkogl
3440

P.Mundin
3146

Finstermünz-
Paß 1188

Schartl-K.
2808

Muttler-K.
2747

3113
Glockturm
3355

Ht.Ölgruben-Sp.
3296

SWITZER-
LAND

Nauders

ÖTZTALER

Hochvernagt-Sp.
3539

ALPS

Tschlin

THREE-COUNTRY TRIANGLE

Nauderer
Hennesiegel-Sp.
3045

Rauher K.
2990

Fluchtkogel
3500

Wild-Sp.
3768

WEISSKAMM

Mataun-K.
2892

Weisssee-Sp.
3526

Guslar-Spitzen
3151

Bergkastl.-Sp.
2912

LANGTAUFERER VALLEY
(VALLE LUNGA)

Hinterkirch

P.Ajüx
2755

UPPER

Reschen Pass 1504
(Pso. Resia)

Reschen-
see

Karlin-B.

Schwarzer K.
2996

Falbanair-Sp.
3200

Vernagl
3355

Ob. Rofen-B.
3029

Innerer
Nocken-K.
2769

Rojen

Graun

Speiker-Wd.
2928

Weisskugel
(Palla Bianca)
3739

HINTEREIS-FERNER

Seikogel
3360

Elfer-Sp.
2925

St. Valentin
a.d. Heide

Danzebell
3145

Raben-K.
3391

Fineil-Sp.
3516

Grian-K.
2896

Mittereck
2909

Schwemser-Sp.
3456

Grawand
3250

Rasass-Sp.
2941

Grüner
See

Haidersee

VINSCHGAU

SALURN

Wieshof

Vernagl
Barrage

Pfäffsee

PLANEIL VALLEY

Jafant
2815

Thanal

Salurn-Sp.
3433

Ramudel-Sp.
3292

Kortscher
See

Tascheljöchl

Gerstgraser-Sp.
3136

Merzbach

SCHLINIGTAL

Burgeis

Hohes Joch
2591

MATSCHER

VALLEY

Saldur-B.

Rems-Sp.
3204

Lacken

Schlandrauner
Schafberg
3039

Mastaun-Sp.
3199

Monterodes
2358

Mals

VALLEY

KAMM

Krippenland
2720

Glurns

Schluderns

Hohes Kreuzjoch
2986

Weisse Riepl
2952

Zermininger Sp.
3059

Rambach

Köpfelplatte
2319

ITALY

Taufers

Plaschweller
2533

Lichtenberg

Sponding

Kortsch

Schlanders

LOWER

Laas

Rom

Sta. Maria

Munwarther
2621

Prad

Tarnell

VINSCHGAU

VALLEY

Mörter

Stilfs

(VAL

VENOSTA)

Weisswandel
2777

Martell

Pilrmbach

MARTELL VALLEY (VAL MARTELLO)

P. Minschuns
2934

Gomagoi

Wasserfall-Sp.
2741

Tschenglser
Hochwand
3378

Schafberg
3302

Orgel-Sp.
3304

Laaser B.

Trafoi

TRAFOIER VALLEY

Schluder-Sp.
3230

Gand

Umbrrail Pass 2501
(Giogo di S. Maria)

Vertain-Sp.
3544

Auss. Peder-Sp.
3406

Tuver-Sp.
3092

Stilfser Joch
2756
(Pso. di Stelvio)

Sulden

Schild-Sp.
3459

Zehner Sp.
2804

Ortler
3905

Zufrittsee

266

VINSCHGAU

Leaving behind the verdant vegetation of the Meran basin and travelling in a westerly direction, our route arrives at **Töll**. Here another world begins. This is the much more austere and harsh world of Vinschgau (Val Venosta), an area stretching some 40 miles (70 km), all the way up to the 4,944-ft (1,507-metre) high Reschen Pass, where the River Etsch, South Tyrol's most important river, has its source, on the Italian-Austrian border.

St Proculus and San Zeno: In Roman times, the Italian-Rhaetian border probably ran through the defile of Töll. During the Middle Ages, the Lombards extended the boundaries of their northern Italian empire as far as Naturns. Lombardian, and later Frankish, margraves had their seat in Verona, where the patron saint San Zeno and St Proculus, celebrated for his daring escape from persecuting heathens over Verona's city walls, held joint status in the people's affections.

These two saints both feature in the village of **Naturns** (Naturno). The **parish church** of Naturns is a Gothic edifice which was constructed in the 15th century. Its Carolingian foundations, however, are rather older. The parish church is dedicated to San Zeno, but, as in Verona, Naturns also looked towards St Proculus for spiritual guidance. The simple church dedicated to him, on the outskirts of town, contains Carolingian wall paintings. These are some of only a few remaining examples of Carolingian art and thus of great importance for art historians.

Proculus is known as the patron saint of cattle. The lovely picture on the interior wall at the entrance of the church is in honour of the saint. It depicts a procession of cows, coloured ochre yellow, reddish-brown and bluish-grey, led by two shepherds in belted frocks and stockings. The shepherd dog driving the cattle has wild eyes and a lolling tongue.

However, one of the most engaging

scenes in these wall paintings, executed around 800, decorates the south wall. It depicts St Proculus in an ingenious swing construction descending from the wall of his diocesan seat in Verona as he makes his escape from the heathens. Onlookers, their heads bent forward and eyes wide with amazement, anxiously watch his escape. But the painting has little sense of drama. The long, egg-shaped faces with their comic triangular noses and round eyes, their mouths painted as a line and the wrinkles of the foreheads drawn as scribbles, are reminiscent of cartoon figures. There is a comedy about the floundering attempts to reach for Proculus. The misdrawn or corrected details and the flatly applied, sharply outlined patches of colour and lightly sketched lines give the work a modern appearance. The angel on the eastern wall of the altar, drawn in blue and black, floating weightlessly in the air, could almost be the work of the Fauvist Henri Matisse.

Gothic frescoes, painted 600 years later, are found on the interior and exte-

Preceding pages: driving the sheep into the Schnals Valley in autumn. **Right,** the winding road up the Stilfser Joch Pass.

rior of the Proculus church. Although these Gothic works are interesting – the picture above the arch of triumph depicts Christ and Mary protecting a group of praying people from arrows being fired by God – they are overshadowed by the Carolingian paintings.

The Schnals Valley: The villages of Partschins, Rabland, Plaus and Naturns all profit from the highly-organised tourism of the Meran basin. The villagers still like to wear the magnificent native costumes of earlier days on holidays and at folk festivals and, as a rule, do not tend to consider themselves true "Vinschgauers".

Beyond these villages, however, there is less and less tourism and the landscape becomes more austere. This is especially true of the **Schnals Valley** (Val Senales) which branches off shortly after Naturns and stretches about 15 miles (25 km) into the Alps of the Ötz Valley. In the tourist village of **Kurzras** (Maso Corto), at the end of the valley, a cable car leads up to the summer ski region on Mt Hochjochferner (9,842 ft/3,000 me-

tres). During the summer international ski champions and members of national ski teams race across the glaciers, in training for the next winter's competitions.

But one of the most interesting events in the Schnals Valley has a much longer history than summer skiing. In early summer the valley's shepherds herd their flocks of 3,000 or so sheep across the 9,898-ft (3,107-metre) Niederjoch Pass, thickly covered with ice, to the mountains of the Ötz Valley. The shepherds have had grazing rights to these highlying pastures since the 13th century. These rights were retained despite the new border drawn between Austria and Italy in 1919.

The main town of the Schnals Valley is **Karthaus** (Certosa). At the end of the 18th century, Emperor Joseph II dissolved the Allerengelberg Monastery, an establishment which had flourished since the Middle Ages but which had been intensely disliked by the native population. The monks were banished, and peasants and craftsmen moved into

A poster advertises a Reinhold Messner slide show.

268

the empty cells, quickly turning the monastery into a village. In 1924, the original monastery burned to the ground but the unusual form of the former cloister can still be discerned in the layout of the town.

The weathered farms of the Schnals Valley tend to be situated at a higher altitude than those in the other regions of South Tyrol, often at levels of 6,500 ft (2,000 metres). Many of them seem to be glued to the steep slopes. These isolated farms symbolise South Tyrolean rural life as it used to be all over the region. The farmers are not discouraged by the extreme difficulties they encounter; in fact, they rather relish the harsh conditions. Reinhold Messner, world famous for his mountaineering expeditions, has purchased Castle Juval at the entrance to the Schnals Valley, thereby returning to his farming roots in the South Tyrol.

Itinerant artists: After passing through Galsaun with its 13th-century ruins of **Castle Hochgalsaun**, and **Kastelbell** (Castelbello), with its recently restored medieval fortress, the road leads to the pleasant village of **Latsch** (Laces), rich in art history. The most notable piece in the church – which once formed part of a medieval hospice of the Maltese knights – is a winged altar-piece created around 1520 by the sculptor Jörg Lederer from Bavaria.

The fact that many works of art from that region ended up in Vinschgau is not as surprising as it might seem. The Benedictine monastery of Marienberg has maintained good contacts with southwestern Germany since its foundation. These contacts were strengthened and supported by the abbots and monks from Ottobeuern and, later, Weingarten. Thus, Gothic altars which were mass produced in German studios were transported along with other trade goods over the Reschen Pass to Vinschgau and the neighbouring region of Grisons in Switzerland.

This particular altar, however, is not one of those which was mass produced. Jörg Lederer carved this altar when he was aged about 50, at the peak of his

Left, carnival mask from the Vinschgau. Right, Reinhold Messner at home at Castle Juval.

career. With it, he took the first steps toward a new formalism: the composition of the retable is more interesting than usual, with a raised middle section and sunken side panels, and the robes of St George and St Florian have a Renaissance elegance.

The paintings decorating the side panels, thought to have been executed by Hans Leonhard Schäufele but possibly the work of another artist from Albrecht Dürer's circle, are more obviously in the style of the Renaissance. These exhibit a much stronger sense of space and the individual figures exude a more self-confident attitude. The northern interior wall of the church contains a series of mediocre, relatively crude 17th-century frescoes depicting the Seven Works of Charity.

Far superior in quality are those in the small **church of St Stephen** in **Morter**. The interior of this former fortress chapel of Upper Montani is completely covered with murals painted by two artists in the 15th century. It is probable that the colourful narrative

frescoes covering the chancel vaults, the barrel vaults, the chancel arch, the eastern wall and a portion of the northern wall were painted by an itinerant Lombardian artist.

About 40 years later, another itinerant artist, this time from southern Germany, painted the north and south walls. His figures, especially those in The Last Judgement, exhibit expressive characteristics and gestures.

Morter is situated at the entrance to the Martell Valley. This high-lying valley stretches for a distance of 12½ miles (20 km) towards the glacier-covered peaks of Cevedale. In earlier times this valley produced iron, smelted near the chapel of St Mary in the Schmelz (translation: foundry), but today its chief product is electricity. The Plima brook, which in former times often overflowed its banks, causing devastating floods in the valley, has today been tamed by the Zufritt Dam.

Refuges at the end of the Martell valley are used as bases by mountain climbers and skiers undertaking expeditions into the surrounding mountains. These peaks, many reaching over 10,000 ft (3,000 metres) in height, mark the border dividing South Tyrol from Trentino and the Lombardian province of Sondrio.

The capital of the region of Vinschgau is **Schlanders** (Silandro). Much of the traditional atmosphere of this town has been lost in the wake of its recent expansion. But among the many new buildings a few structures still serve as reminders of former times, notably the aristocratic residences of Schlandersburg and Schlanderegg and the ruins of the **Schlandersburg Fortress** sited above the town. This fortress was founded in the 13th century and expanded in the 16th century.

The neighbouring village of **Kortsch** (Corces) is a much more attractive place to visit. It stretches across a mound formed by an ancient landslide, a landscape typical to this region and one which is very fertile.

Beyond is **Laas (Lasa)**, famous for its marble deposits and known as the Carrara of South Tyrol. In the 19th

Left, an old woman on her way to gather wood. Right, spinning the glowing disk.

DISC SPINNING

The people of Vinschgau still practise a ritual dating back to Rhaetian times: it is known as spinning the disc (*Scheibenschlagen*) and is a relic of an ancient Rhaetian fire ritual, an element of the pagan cult of sun worship. Ancient Rhaetian fire rituals are still evident in a number of other local traditions in Tyrol, but the most interesting one is disc-spinning.

Today, this ancient tradition is carried on only in Vinschgau, in Grisons and in Friaul. Over the centuries, the function of the ritual has evolved and changed. What may have originally been a fertility or courtship rite gradually came to be associated with the medieval practice of witch burning and the conjuring of spells to banish the plague. In fact, the straw-wrapped pole that forms such an essential part of the disc spinning is even called *Hex* – the Middle High German word for witch.

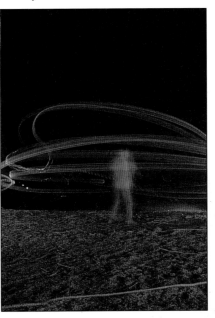

The disc-spinning takes place at the Tartsch Hill, the so-called "navel of the Vinschgau", where the cold winds of the valley converge. This remote and errie setting is a fitting venue for a pagan cult firmly steeped in the supernatural.

As night falls on the first Sunday in Lent, the young men from Tartsch crowd around a special bonfire. Fried bacon, sausages, bread and wine, essential companions to the activity of disc spinning, are passed around the gathering. The men, who will have been working hard all afternoon preparing the bonfire, are ready for refreshment – both liquid and solid. They will also have been busy setting up the straw-wrapped feminine fertility cross known as *Larmstange* – not an easy task when the wind is belting through the valley at a rate of knots.

The huge bonfire beside the cross is then set alight. The discs, made of birchwood with holes bored through the middle, are placed at the edge of the fire or held over the flames with a hazel switch until they become red hot. The discs are then extracted from the fire, and the young men take their position at the outer edge of the Tartsch hill.

They then spin the glowing discs on the hazel switches, making huge circles of light in the pitch black night. The task is tricky and requires athleticism. The patterns made by the red-hot discs are spectacular.

As the young men whip the discs through the air, they make their wishes, uttering them aloud. Traditionally they wish for fertility or for good fortune and happiness in their love lives. Hitting the ground, the switch then sends the glowing disc sailing in a tremendous arc down into the valley. Traditional rhymes, chanted in the local dialect, ask for whom the disc is spinning. Is it for Rosi, or Petra or Heidi? Each of the young disc-spinners will have somebody in mind on this night. In former times, it was also common for any man who already had a sweetheart to hold hands with her and jump over the bonfire.

The disc is intended to symbolise the sun, but it also represents a divine natural principle, symbolised in the colour and design of the disc. For example, the number of lines in the design is symbolic as is the form of the rosettes which decorate the discs.

The disc spinners use two basic kinds of discs: the workaday discs and the Sunday discs. The latter are richly decorated and must be spun with special care and concentration, for it is important that they are not flung off course. They symbolise the cosmic cycle, the four stages of the day, the four phases of the moon, the four seasons. Symbols such as these may also be seen carved on the roof ridges of barns and farmhouses in the area and, inside the home, decorating living rooms and cupboards.

The high point of the disc-throwing ceremony comes at the end of the evening when the female fertility cross is set ablaze, thereby banishing the demon of winter from Vinschgau.

In spite of the pagan atmosphere and the supernatural associations attributed to the ritual through the ages, these days it is approached in a light-hearted manner. If, for example,the wind swirls around the site extinguishing the festivities it is of little concern to the disc-spinners. Nowadays the only thing to really counts are the good intentions of the participants and the aim is to have a good time.

century, it even boasted a school for marble sculptors and developed into a modest centre for the art, supplying tombstones for the cemeteries in the surrounding area and monuments for the cities on the other side of the Alps. The monuments to such famous figures as Bruckner, Grillparzer, Haydn, Mozart and Schubert in Vienna, to Moltke in Berlin and to Schiller in Dresden were carved from Laas's fine-grain marble, of which there are 14 different varieties.

The statue of the poet Walther von der Vogelweide which graces Walther Square in Bozen is also made from Laas marble, as are many of the buildings which were erected in Bavaria during the reign of King Ludwig I (1825–68). Ludwig's favourite court architect, von Schwanthaler, preferred this marble to that of Carrara, referring to the latter as "rubbish, lifeless, blunt".

Recent times have seen a slump in demand for the marble. It is perhaps too beautiful, too highly polished for modern European tastes. But the total decline of the marble industry of Laas has been prevented through increased exports to Japan, the United States (New York's Grand Central Station is encased in this marble) and to some of the wealthy Arab countries.

Closer to home, the Romanesque frieze around the apse of Laas's parish church and the monument to the Emperor Franz Joseph on the Laas village square are also made of the local marble. Outside the village, on the right side of the street at the foot of the Sonnenberg is the **church of Sisinius**, a plain Romanesque edifice of a type common in Vinschgau.

The **church of St John** in **Prad** is another example of medieval Romanesque architecture. Prad is situated along a well-travelled tourist route leading to the **Stilfser Joch Pass** (Passo dello Stelvio). Near the village of Gomagoi, the road forks: the route to the left leads to the resort village of **Sulden** (Solda), lying at 6,257 ft (1,907 metres) at the foot of the Ortler Massif; the road heading straight ahead leads to Trafoi and the Stilfser Joch.

The Marlenberg Monastery in the upper Vinschgau.

Driving round the bends: The road over this pass has a total of 83 bends and is an engineering masterpiece. It was opened in 1825 as the shortest connecting route between the Inn Valley and Lombardy (then part of Austria). Today it is open only from the beginning of June until October, but up until 1859, when Lombardy was separated from Austria, it was open throughout the year. This was quite an accomplishment considering the fact that the highest point is 9,045 ft (2,757 metres).

The Stilfser Joch Pass is the centre of a popular summer ski region. It lies in the **Stilfser Joch National Park**, founded in 1935. This park, which is directly connected to the Swiss National Park in Engadin, spreads over about 334,000 acres (135,000 hectares). Park regulations are in force to protect the magnificent landscapes: the glaciers around the Ortler Massif, Königsspitze and Cevedale, the lush green mountain pastures in the valleys of Sulden, Martell, Ulten, Rabbi, Pejo and Valfurva, a magnificent flora comprising over 2,000 different varieties of plants and a huge number of animals including chamois, ibex and golden eagles. Unfortunately, the interests of the conservationists and those of the tourist industry are often in direct opposition.

Tradition and historic preservation: In Prad and in the former mining village of **Stilfs** (Stelvio), perched high on a mountainside, some of the region's oldest traditions still survive. *Pflugziehen* (pulling the plough), for instance, derives from pagan fertility rites. And every year on the first Sunday of Lent in Upper Vinschgau, the traditional *Scheibenschlagen* (disc spinning) festival is celebrated (*see page 271*). Another tradition which is alive and kicking in this area but extinct elsewhere in the region is the carving of *Reiters*. These are cribriform symbols which are used to subject scorned lovers to public ridicule. Similar symbols are found in the prehistoric cave drawings in Lombardian Valcamonica.

By returning down the pass road you reach Spondinig. Turn left on to the

In the remote Matscher Valley.

main road, where the towering castle ruins of Lichtenberg on the heavily forested Mt. Nörder can be seen to the left. This road leads to Schluderns (Sluderno) with its **Churburg Fortress**, visible from quite a distance. This was founded in the 13th century by the bishops of Chur whose area of influence reached as far as the Upper Vinschgau. The bellicose counts of Matsch, who resided in two fortresses in the Matsch Valley north of Schluderns, soon conquered Churburg. They passed it on to the counts of Trapp who expanded it in the 16th century into a Renaissance residence with an ornamental courtyard of arcades.

The main attraction of this fortress, which is open to visitors, is its arsenal. The Trapps must have paid a small fortune to the famous armourer Missaglia of Milan for the splendid suits of chainmail.

Glurns (Glorenza), with its high walls, three gate towers and four round corner towers is an atmospheric place which has retained much of its medieval character (in fact, it is now protected by a preservation order). It was rebuilt in the 16th century following its complete destruction in the catastrophic battle which the German emperor, Maximilian, lost to the Engadines in May of 1499. Craftsmen conduct their business in the low arcades.

Border land of frescoes: Crossing over the River Etsch and passing Glurn's parish church, which has an amazing Last Judgement from 1496 on its steeple, the road reaches the pleasant village of **Taufers** (Tubre) on the Swiss border. The ruins of three castles high on the mountainside dominating the village and the church of the order of Maltese Knights Hospitaller at the entrance to Taufers are clear indications that in the Middle Ages this was a control station for an important transport route.

The Romanesque frescoes decorating the interior of the **church of St John** and the St Christopher on the exterior wall date from the 13th century. The Gothic paintings have been attributed to an itinerant Lombardian artist of the late 14th century. But the frescoes in the monastery **church** in **Müstair**, located on the Swiss border, date back much further in time. They form the most comprehensive cycle of early medieval painting from the Carolingian period (around 800).

The murals in the tiny **church of St Benedict** in **Mals** (Malles Venosta), dating from the first half of the 9th century, are of a similar style. The figures of the patrons, between the niches along the eastern wall, are impressive portraits of medieval times.

This tour of Vinschgau's churches continues in the crypt of Marienberg Monastery, shining white on the hillside above Burgeis. The 12th-century frescoes – angels (mentioned in every single work about Romanesque murals), the Majestas Domini and the figures of the Apostles – are believed to date from between 1160 and 1185.

Frescoes dating from the late 12th century are also found in the **church of St Nicholas** in **Burgeis** (Burgusio). This village, with its picturesque main square and bulging stone houses jutting over the street, has become a symbol of the Upper Vinschgau – especially for the tourist industry.

More frescoes, this time from the early 15th century, are found in the **church of St Nicholas** in **Rojen** (Roia) which lies in a remote valley west of Lake Reschen, 6,463 ft (1,970 metres) up in the Höfe Massif. The fact that this region offers good hiking and winter sports has attracted a significant tourist industry to the area. Bordered by Switzerland and Austria, it comprises Rojen, Schöneben and Lake Reschen as well as the Langtauferer Valley which leads to the glacier-covered Weisskugel (12,264 ft/ 3,738 metres).

With the advent of tourism, this whole area was hauled into the modern age, and appropriately it is a modern work which completes the list of frescoes in Vinschgau: in the modern **chapel of Mary** in **Alsack**, a tiny hamlet on the windswept Malser Heath, there is a painting of the Virgin Mary as a grieving Vinschgau peasant woman. It was painted by Karl Plattner, an artist born in Mals in 1919.

Aerodynamic headgear.

THE ULTEN VALLEY AND MENDEL PASS

Nestling among the eastern spurs of the Ortler Range, away from the busy road connecting Bozen and Meran, stretches the remote and peaceful Ulten Valley (Val d'Ultimo). Secluded farms, isolated houses and extensive meadows characterise the valley – or so it seems at first glance.

The road enters the valley via the Lana region, a fruit-growing region dubbed the "California of South Tyrol" by the region's tourist board. After leaving the Etsch Valley, the road climbs sharply. Shortly after passing the narrow Gaul Gorge (to the left of the road) it enters the Ulten Valley, a dramatic contrast to the picturesque apple orchards of Lana.

Gothic roots: The Ulten Valley is known as one of the "German" valleys of South Tyrol; even the names of the villages, such as St Pankraz or St Gertraud, reflect this fact. Although there is growing evidence that the region was settled in prehistoric times, the valley was probably first cultivated by the Ostrogoths as they retreated during the great migrations.

As time passed, more and more Baiuvari (Bavarian) settlers arrived in the Ulten Valley. Today the names of some of the farms and fields are still based on Ostrogoth origins, for example Schwienbach (*Swinebach*) or Wegleit (*Wigelite*). Sun symbols or runic inscriptions are often found in the ornamentation on early pieces of ceramics and on the walls of barns, evidence that also points to the ancient origins of the valley.

The history of jurisdiction in the Ulten Valley, first documented around 1140 in connection with the Eppan counts, is unique in South Tyrol. The Ulten Valley residents were allowed to retain their own laws until as late as 1830, when the valley was placed under the jurisdiction of Lana. Later still it came under the authority of Meran, where minor court cases are still heard to this day.

The Ulten Valley inhabitants have always considered themselves German – or rather Tyrolean. Proof of this commitment is found in the jubilant reception accorded Franz Ferdinand, heir apparent to the Austrian throne (whose assassination in Sarajevo was later to trigger World War I), when he visited the valley early in the 20th century.

Under the Nazis, when the residents had to choose between remaining in their native land or migrating over the border to German soil, the valley residents were divided in their loyalties. About 90 percent decided to "opt for Germany", though in the end only about 10 percent actually upped and left. Of these 10 percent, many later returned to their native villages.

The area is fiercely pro-German to this day. The protests by mothers against the closing of the German school under the Italian Fascists and the resulting imprisonment of these women are remembered as vividly as the secret lessons subsequently held in the German language, known as "catacomb lessons". No less striking is the Ulten Valley's

more recent history, which has left deep wounds which still fester.

The lower Ulten Valley: The road from Lana leads past the **Vigiljoch cable car** (on the right-hand side of the road) and, a couple of miles further on, the **Pawigl cable car**. Both take visitors up to Mt Pawigl which offers extensive views over Meran and the Etsch Valley. A number of good hiking paths start from here. Particularly recommended are those leading to Marling, to Meran or into the lower Vinschgau near Naturns. Like everywhere else in South Tyrol, these hiking trails are well marked and maintained.

The Ulten Valley is also very well-geared to winter sports, with several ski lifts and a cross country ski-trail. *Buschen*, comfortable huts offering warming food and drinks, punctuate the paths at regular intervals. The Pawigl Buschen and the inn in St Oswald are especially welcoming. The panorama on clear days from Mt Pawigl, and also from the bends of the northern hiking paths, extends right across the Etsch Valley all the way to the Rosengarten Massif and Latemar.

Commanding the very end of the gorge, at the final bend, is **Castle Braunsberg**, scene of the tragic end of a love affair between a loyal countess and the amorous governor of the castle. In an attempt to salvage her damaged reputation, the countess threw herself out of the window and plunged into the gorge. But as she fell her skirts became entangled on the branches of a tree and she was saved. The governor, deeply moved by his lover's desperate act, likewise threw himself out of the window but he died on impact.

The road leading through the lower Ulten Valley is wide, well-maintained and swift to travel, but it robs the valley of much of its romantic character. After proceeding over a large bridge, it passes the ruins of Castle Eschenloch, first documented as Castle Ulten in 1164. Beyond the castle lies the village of St Pankraz, whose church boasts a 187-ft (57-metre) high pointed steeple. Dominating the end of the valley are the peaks

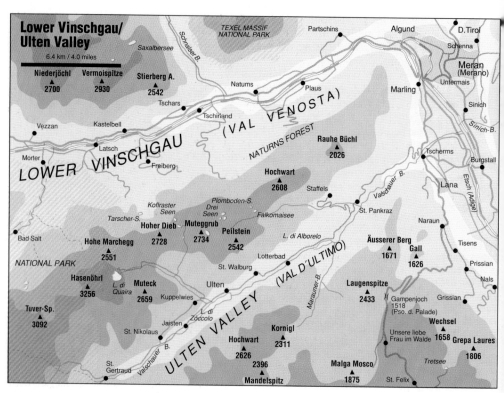

Lower Vinschgau/ Ulten Valley

6.4 km / 4.0 miles

of **Mt Grosser Laugenspitze** (7,135ft/ 2,174 metres) and **Mt Kornigel** (7,582 ft/2,311 metres).

The village of **St Pankraz** (S. Pancrazio) lies at an altitude of 2,395 ft (730 metres). The main route bypasses the village, but it is worth taking the road into the centre and stopping to stroll. It is a delightfully traditional village. At the old entrance a wooden balcony bulges over the road. Such balconies are typical of the Ulten Valley and a source of pride for its Ulten residents, especially during the summer when they are thick with blooming geraniums.

Ausserwirt (outer inn), **Unterwirt** (lower inn) and **Mitterwirt** (middle inn), are three of St Pankraz's oldest buildings. An inscription on the wall of the Innerwirt Inn memorialises Josef Egger, a well-known Tyrolean historian born here in 1839. His most notable work was *The History of Tyrol from Ancient Times to 1815.*

At one time the names of the inns and farms in South Tyrol were used to mark borders; thus St Pankraz's *Pichlerhof* is the farm on the *Pichl* (hill) and the *Eggwirt* is situated on the *Ecke* (corner). The remains of old wooden houses are still clearly visible in front of the **church**. Although this stands on the site of the Ulten Valley's most ancient church, hardly anything of the original edifice now remains.

Beyond the upper limits of the village, a small dirt road high on the hillside connects the farms of the Mariolwerch and the Kirchenwerch, and leads in a roundabout way to **St Helena**, a small pilgrimage church. The *Werche* date from the 12th century and are the ancient administrative bodies of the Ulten Valley. They used to play an important role in legal and tax matters. Each *Werch* was assigned a *Werchbürger* who carried out a variety of minor judicial functions.

The route to St Helena is ideal for hikers (it takes a comfortable two hours to reach the church). Less energetic visitors can travel by road for most of the way, but must complete the last 20 minutes on foot. St Helena, first re-

Home with the shopping.

corded in documents in 1338, is situated on a particularly picturesque site. The nearby Pichler Guesthouse is an agreeable place to stop and enjoy some refreshment.

The main road through the valley leads along the Valschau brook and past Lake Pankraz, one of the valley's five reservoirs. The romantic depictions of these reservoirs in tourist office brochures bear little resemblance to reality. Anyone who argues that the reservoirs fit harmoniously into the landscape should take a look at the gravel pits at **Lake Zogle**. But the amount of electricity produced here is tremendous. The average number of kilowatt hours produced in Weissbrunn per year is approximately 13 million, in Kuppelwies about 32 million, in St Walburg and St Pankraz about 80 million and in Lana near Lake Stallbach approximately 90 million.

The upper Ulten Valley: The next village along the route is **St Walburg** (S. Valburga, 3,904 ft/1,190 metres). The Church of St Walburg, which dates back to the 12th century, lies outside the village centre. The lovely Eggwirt Inn, directly in the centre of the village, serves good Tyrolean, Austrian and Italian cuisine.

Beyond St Walburg a road branches right to the ski region of Schwemmalm below Mt Muteck (8,720 ft/2,658 metres). This ski region has no spectacular runs, but is ideal for families. Residents of the valley are divided in their opinions as to whether the ski resort should be enlarged. Environmentalists, farmers and members of the Alpine Society have formed an alliance to prevent any expansion, but those working in the tourist industry think very differently.

The road proceeding past the ski area leads to the Steinrast and Kuppelwieser meadows, both dominated by the retaining walls of Lake Arzker which lies at the top of the meadows. From this point various hiking trails head off to Hasenöhrl (L'orecchia di lepre, 10,685 ft/3,257) or across to the Vinschgau regions.

In the densely settled village of **Ulten**

This is no South Tyrolean carving, but rather the work of tourists.

(Ultimo, 5,115 ft/1,559 metres), encompassing **St Nikolaus**, is the **Ulten Valley Museum** documenting the lifestyles of Ulten residents over the centuries. Domestic and farming implements, national costumes, jewellery and traditional items are on display.

From St Nikolaus, the old road leads on to St Gertraud. Plans are currently under discussion to widen this road and replace the rustic wooden fences with guardrails in order to ease the way for the endless caravans of vehicles and trailers passing through in summer. But widening this road would destroy just one more of the characteristic Ulten Valley landscapes. With its ancient larch woods and venerable wooden farmhouses, this countryside is the loveliest of the Ulten Valley. Here the Kirchberg and the Klapfberg valleys merge with the main valley, creating the archetypal alpine landscape.

St Gertraud (1,703 ft/519 metres), the last village in the valley, stretches along the steep road. At the upper end is the 14th-century church of St Gertraud.

Here in the upper Ulten Valley, ancient larch forests and stands of birches blanket the mountains up to an elevation of 5,900 ft (1,800 metres). They are particularly beautiful in autumn. The farms of **Pilsen,** below the road to the reservoir, are typical examples of original Ulten wooden farmhouses.

From **Lake Weissbrunn** (6,142 ft/ 1,872 metres), at the end of the main road, a network of trails lead up to Lake Grün, the Lake Grün Refuge (8,297 ft/ 2,529 metres), Mt Weissbrunn (10,673 ft/3,253 metres) and the Haselgrub Refuge (7,956 ft/2,425 metres). According to local legends, the Weissbrunn meadow was formerly a lake containing a dastardly dragon that preyed on the area's livestock.

In fact, these days Weissbrunn is yet another reservoir surrounded by the ugly infrastructure of the electrical company ENEL. The one advantage to this plant is that it provides plenty of parking places for the large crowds of tourists that flock here. One of the easiest hikes from Lake Weissbrunn is the one to Lake

The Church of St Helen above St Pankraz.

Grün. After passing Lake Lang, from whence the Valschau brook springs, the trail leads down to Lake Fischer before returning to the point of departure.

The **Enzian** restaurant Il Godio, is famous far beyond the boundaries of the Ulten Valley and is especially noted for its wide choice of appetisers. Its chef, Giancarlo Godio, has won a number of prestigious prizes.

Other hiking trails (moderately taxing) lead up Mt Hasenöhrl (five hours from St Gertraud) and Mt Tuferspitze (10,161 ft/3,097 metres). Zufrittspitze (Cima Gioveretto, 11,283 ft/3,439 metres) is much more difficult and should be attempted only in the company of an experienced guide. However there are also a number of much easier trails, similar to the one to Lake Grün, leading into adjacent valleys. Several paths, including one from St Nikolaus and one heading across the Zufrittjoch Pass, lead over the ridge into the neighbouring Martell Valley.

Paradise gained: The greater and lesser Laugenspitze Peaks separate the Ulten Valley from the German-speaking communities on Mt Nonsberg. They include **Unsere liebe Frau im Walde** (Senale 4,446 ft/1,355 metres), **St Felix** (S. Felice, 4,150 ft/1,265 metres), **Proveis** (Proves, 4,659 ft/1,420 metres) and **Laurein** (Lauregno, 3,760 ft/1,146 metres). These towns, situated on the outermost ranges of South Tyrol and on the boundary to Trentino, are extremely remote and therefore practically free of tourism and its infrastructure.

They are reached via a number of narrow roads leading across the Gampenjoch Pass (4,961 ft/1,512 metres) or the Mendel Pass (Passo Mendola, 4,472 ft/1,363 metres). The remoteness of this region is likely to suit the kind of hikers who prefer to roam the hills in solitude and don't mind the absence of welcoming inns and huts.

However, this part of South Tyrol could soon become a paradise lost if plans for a connecting route from St Pankraz in the Ulten Valley to Proveis on Mt Nonsberg are realised. These plans highlight the restrictions that en- **The typical Ulten farms have shingle-clad walls.**

snare public projects such as road-building in South Tyrol. It would be much easier, for instance, to reach these remote villages via Senale, but that would mean having to construct the road through the province of Trentino – and permission for this has been flatly refused in the past. Now a tunnel is being considered. In fact, this tunnel already appears on the official road maps, with the optimistic note "under construction".

The village **Unsere liebe Frau im Walde** consists of a collection of individual farms grouped around the pilgrimage church. This village was founded when the salt and trade caravans passed through the Gampen Pass on the way to Brescia.

This was often used as an alternative to the Etsch Valley route, which suffered from regular flooding. Indeed, damage from floods in past years has been so extreme that the lower Etsch Valley frequently suffered from malaria epidemics and transportation was sometimes possible only by boat).

A number of monasteries with hospices attached were founded along this alternative trade route. One of these lies at the foot of the Gampen Pass. The pilgrimage church, whose image of the Virgin Mary is reputed to work wondrous miracles (hence the pilgrims), was first documented in 1184. A statue from the 15th century, remodelled in 1683, reigns in a baroque shrine situated above the main altar.

A lovely tour leads over the Mendel Pass from St Michael near Kaltern. This pass can also be reached via the Mendel cable car. The grand hotels hereabouts are full of faded elegance and evoke memories of Thomas Mann's novel *The Magic Mountain*. The road continues through a richly wooded landscape to Mt Nonsberg and the village of **Unsere liebe Frau im Walde** with its pilgrimage church.

The infrequently travelled Gampen Pass leads back to the Etsch Valley where the alternative route through Nals, Andrian and Hocheppan is also highly recommended.

In the pilgrimage church in the village of Unserer Lieben Frau im Walde.

TRAVEL TIPS

GETTING THERE

BY ROAD

With the exception of the route from the south, through Trient (Trento), all other roads leading into South Tyrol are very winding. Whether you drive over Stilfserjoch or the Stallersattel, up through the Reschen Pass or across Sellajoch you will have to drive up and over one pass or another. The most frequently travelled and well-known of all these thoroughfares is, of course, the Brenner Pass. It is the main connection between Italy and Central and Northern Europe.

There are two separate routes over the Brenner Pass: the toll motorway and the bendy "Old Brenner Road". These two bottle-necks are notoriously overburdened. Traffic jams – whether on the Italian or Austrian side – are the rule rather than the exception. Although blockades like the big lorry blockade of a few years back are fortunately relatively rare, the frustration of the people in the communities affected by the never-ending noise and exhaust fumes increases steadily.

BY RAIL

Bozen/Bolzano and other towns located in the Eisack Valley/Valle Isarco are on the main Italian railway route, the Brenner Line. Most passengers and material cargo are transported north via this line. During peak times in the holiday months trains are often overcrowded and the only way to ensure you find a seat in one of the compartments is to reserve one well in advance. In winter, it is not uncommon for all railway traffic to come to a standstill at the Brenner Pass due to avalanche debris. In such cases, travellers are usually transferred to a commuter bus service, which will then transport them to Innsbruck.

BY AIR

At present, there is no airport in Bozen. The closest airports to South Tyrol are in Verona and Milan in Italy, and in Innsbruck on the Austrian side of the border. There is some concern that South Tyrol should not lag behind other regions due to the absence of an international air connection, but whether or not building an airport in Bozen would be worth the expense is still an open question.

TRAVEL ESSENTIALS

VISAS & PASSPORTS

Visitors from European Community countries, the US and Canada intending to enter Italy must possess either a valid passport or personal identification card. Clearance at border-crossings is a relatively painless operation and motor vehicles from EC countries and Austria – provided that they sport a green "E" sticker – are usually waved through without further ado. The Austrians especially have a penchant for checking nationality stickers; if your car doesn't have one, be prepared to pay a fine. Getting through the border-crossings only becomes a time-consuming ordeal when officials are on strike.

PETS

Visitors entering Italy with dogs or cats are required to produce an official certificate verifying that their pet has been inoculated against rabies. The certificate must have been issued no more than 20 days before the date of arrival.

DRIVING TIPS

Tolls are payable on all Italian motorways. The precise fee depends upon the kind of motorway it is and the distance travelled. The same holds true for the Brenner Motorway in Austria, where the toll can be paid for in German Marks, Austrian Schillings or Italian Lire.

Members of European Community countries intending to rent a car require only their national driver's licence; visitors from other countries are recommended to come armed with an international driver's licence.

Tourists entering Italy in their own motor vehicles are required to have a Green international insurance card.

Up-to-date information regarding road conditions in South Tyrol can be obtained by calling either 0471-978578 or 0471-978577.

PETROL COUPONS

Petrol coupons, once abolished but later reintroduced, are a popular trading item. You can buy petrol coupons at the Italian border (or in advance through motoring organisations such as Britain's

THE COLOUR OF LIFE.

A holiday may last just a week or so, but the memories of those happy, colourful days will last forever, because together you and Kodak Ektachrome films will capture, as large as life, the wondrous sights, the breathtaking scenery and the magical moments. For you to relive over and over again.

The Kodak Ektachrome range of slide films offers a choice of light source, speed and colour rendition and features extremely fine grain, very high sharpness and high resolving power.

Take home the real colour of life with Kodak Ektachrome films.

LIKE THIS?

OR LIKE THIS?

A KODAK FUN PANORAMIC CAMERA BROADENS YOUR VIEW

The holiday you and your camera have been looking forward to all year; and a stunning panoramic view appears. "Fabulous", you think to yourself, "must take that one".

Unfortunately, your lens is just not wide enough. And three-in-a-row is a poor substitute.

That's when you take out your pocket-size, 'single use' Kodak Fun Panoramic Camera. A film and a camera, all in one, and it works miracles. You won't need to focus, you don't need special lenses. Just aim, click

and... it's all yours. The total pictu[r]

You take twelve panoram[ic] pictures with one Kodak Fun Pan[o]ramic Camera. Then put the came[ra] in for developing and printing.

Each print is 25 by 9 centimetre[s] Excellent depth of field. True Kodak Gold colours.

The Kodak Fun Panoramic Camera itself goes bac[k] to the factory, to be recycled. So that others too can capture one of those spectacular phoooooooooootooooooooooooos.

AA and RAC) which will give you a 15 percent discount on petrol in Italy, where prices are considerably higher than elsewhere in Europe.

MONEY MATTERS

As is the case everywhere else in Italy, the unit of currency in South Tyrol is the Lira. You can cash Eurocheques – frequently without even being asked to produce a valid passport or personal identification card – at nearly any bank. The maximum amount you can get in exchange for a single Eurocheque is approximately 300,000 Lire.

If your Eurocheques or EC card should be stolen, immediately report the theft to your hometown bank. That way you will be held responsible for only 10 percent of the amount cashed by a third party; if you fail to follow this procedure, you will end up having to pay the entire sum.

Cash machines have all been converted to the European Four-Number Code during the past few years. At any time of the day or night you can insert your EC card and withdraw money. Most cash machines are quadrilingual (Italian, German, English and French). There is a maximum limit of 300,000 Lira per withdrawal. The machines automatically present you with a receipt.

GETTING ACQUAINTED

GOVERNMENT & ECONOMY

The autonomous provinces of Bozen (Bolzano) and Trient (Trento) together form the region Trentino-South Tyrol, or *Trentino-Alto Adige*, as it is called. The provinces of Bolzano and South Tyrol (*Alto Adige*) are actually one and the same. South Tyrol is subdivided into 116 communities and seven separate valley populations, including Berggrafenamt, Eisack Valley (Valle Isarco), Puster Valley (Val Pusteria), Salten-Schlern, Überetsch-Südtiroler Unterland, Vinschgau (Val Venosta) and Wipptal.

The coat of arms for South Tyrol depicts a red Tyrolean eagle with a golden tongue and extended wings against a silver background. This coat of arms dates from around 1150 when the Counts of Tyrol near Meran/Merano chose the red eagle as their heraldic animal.

According to a population poll taken in 1989, there are 439,765 people living in South Tyrol. According to the national census conducted in 1981,

in which every person was required to cite his or her "linguistic affiliation", 66.4 percent of the population spoke German, 29.39 percent Italian and 4.21 percent Ladin. These percentages are worked out with great precision because they provide the basis for proportional representation in public office.

The *Südtirol Handbuch (South Tyrol Handbook)* proudly proclaims that "of the 430,000 people living in South Tyrol, at least 98 percent are Catholic". Since September 1964 the episcopal seat of the Bozen-Brixen diocese has been in Bozen. Both Bozen and Meran each have an active Protestant congregation and in the latter city there is a Russian-Orthodox and a Jewish community as well.

South Tyrol comprises a total land area of 2,857 sq. miles (7,400 sq. km). Only 3.9 percent of this lies at an altitude of below 1,667 ft (500 metres) above sea level. In contrast to this, 86 percent of the land is situated at an elevation of over 3,333 ft (1,000 metres), with 64 percent of this at an altitude of over (5,000 ft) 1,500 metres. The total surface area can be categorised into 23 percent unproductive land (for instance high mountainous regions), 34.6 percent agricultural land, 38.6 percent forest and 3.8 percent unused land.

The biggest mass-produced agricultural product is fruit, 95 percent of which is apples. More than 50 percent of this comprises the variety Golden Delicious. As much as 60 percent of the entire apple harvest is exported abroad, with Germany receiving a hefty two-thirds of the total.

The second most important agricultural product is wine. The wine yield for the year 1989 amounted to 10.5 million gallons (476,250 hectolitres). About 85 percent of the total harvest is from grapes of "controlled origin" (DOC) and white wine accounts for 28 percent of the entire wine production.

CLIMATE

Because of the widely varying topography, generalisations regarding the climate in South Tyrol are difficult to make. This is clearly illustrated by the following examples: in Vernagt 5,670 ft (1,700 metres) above sea level, in the Schnals Valley, the average temperature is about 40°F (4.8°C) with 25 inches (642 mm) of precipitation during the course of 91 days. In contrast to this, Bozen (850 ft/254 metres) above sea level has a mean temperature of 53°F (11.9°C) and precipitation amounting to 26 inches (660 mm) falling within a period of 77 days.

However, it is these differences which contribute to the attraction of South Tyrol. When the skiing season is in full swing high up in the glaciers, fruit trees are already in bloom down in the Etsch Valley. Within the same week you can stand in line at a chairlift, bundled tightly in a warm parka against the chilly wind, and a day or two later, clad in only a light jacket, stroll through fallen leaves.

A few of the valleys, for instance Schnal Valley or Sarn Valley, are considered regular weather traps, whereas Meran has got the lease on sunshine and the proverbial "golden autumn".

The usually rainless summers are good for tourism but present quite a problem for agriculture. Water sprinklers have become more or less a permanent feature of the landscape.

HEALTH

No special vaccinations are recommended for those planning a visit to South Tyrol. Nevertheless, it's a good idea to consider a few particular points and to take suitable precautions. Any visitors with a known medical problem should consult his or her doctor before travelling. During summer sun-rays can be very strong, especially in areas at high elevations, and should not be underestimated, particularly at the beginning of a holiday. Also make sure your fluid intake (mineral water, fruit juice, etc.) is sufficient.

During the winter and spring seasons, specifically in snowy regions, it's important to pay attention to ultraviolet rays. Because of the relatively cool temperatures, their strength is frequently underestimated. The results are a painful sunburn or what's referred to as a "skier's tan". Don't forget to protect your eyes from the sun and snow too; a good pair of sun-glasses is a must. Visitors used to lowland living may be apprehensive about travelling to areas at rather higher altitudes, but there is no cause for worry; altitude sickness occurs at much higher elevations. One or two days of leisurely acclimatisation are all that's required.

During summer care should taken regarding perishable foods. If it comes to the point where you are in need of medical attention, a traveller's health insurance card will prove helpful. These cards also contain information pertaining to local doctors who work under contract with insurance companies, as well as physicians able to speak other languages.

TIPPING

Tipping, *mancia*, is always a matter of individual discretion, contingent upon the quality of the service rendered and of the recipient's satisfaction. Leaving a really stingy tip is as inappropriate as leaving an outrageously excessive one. In every restaurant operated by Italians there is a cover charge of about 3,000 Lire per person for *pane e coperto* (bread and silverware), no matter how much you may or may not end up eating. This sum doesn't take the place of a tip. As is the case in Austrian and German eating establishments, in Tyrolean restaurants a service charge is included in the price of the meal.

ELECTRICITY

The electricity supply in South Tyrol is AC 220 volts. However, it's a good idea to bring along an adaptor for Italy if you want to be sure of being able to use sockets.

BUSINESS HOURS

With the exception of a few exchange offices located in tourist areas, banks are open from 8am to 1pm and from 2.45 to 4pm Monday–Friday.

As a rule, shops are open from 9am to 1pm and again from 3 to 6.30pm, with grocery stores frequently opening their doors as early as 8am. Many shops and especially those in smaller towns are closed on Wednesday afternoon, but some compensate for this by opening after church on Sunday. Because there is no official closing time, shopkeepers lock their doors at times to suit themselves.

LANGUAGE

Both Italian and German are acknowledged as official languages. For the tourist, this means that a knowledge of one of these two tongues is invaluable. If you speak only English or French, however, you may be in for a bit of a problem as neither is commonly spoken. Ladin is still spoken in the Grödner (Val Gardena) and Gadder Valleys, as well as in a few smaller side-valleys of this region. In this book, places are referred to by their German names; the Italianised versions are generally shown in parentheses on first mention.

COMMUNICATIONS

TELEVISION

The Italian television organisation RAI, represented in Bozen with its own channel, broadcasts programmes in German throughout South Tyrol. You can tune into the Erste österreichische Fernsehen (ORF), the Schweizer Fernsehen and Zweite Deutsche Fernsehen (ZDF) (these last two are broadcast in German), just about everywhere in the region. (The quality of the reception varies depending upon where you are.) In addition to these three, there's the usual mishmash of Italian private stations which operate around the clock.

RADIO

Radio stations are so numerous that it's all but impossible to tune to a particular channel without frequent interference from others. Due to the bilingual nature of the region, radio programmes are broadcast in both German and Italian.

NEWSPAPERS & MAGAZINES

The most important daily newspaper in South Tyrol is *Dolomiten*, which is published in German. Its Italian counterparts are the *Alto Adige* and the *L'Adige*. In addition to these, the usual selection of Italian as well as German daily newspapers and magazines is available. You can even find copies of *Newsweek* and *Time* in Bozen and Meran. For readers of German, the *ff – Südtiroler Illustrierte* provides good reading – more on account of its witty and interesting articles pertaining to specifically South Tyrolean issues than because of its extensive television guide and entertainment tips.

POSTAL SERVICES

Post offices are open from 8am to 1pm Monday–Friday with larger branches maintaining hours from 8.30am to 6.30pm and on Saturday from 8am to 12.30pm. Stamps can also be purchased in *tabacchi* shops designated by a blue sign sporting the words *valori e bollati*.

TELEPHONE

Sit telephone booths are being installed throughout South Tyrol. Calls made from these phones are paid for by special telephone credit cards, available for 5,000 or 10,000 Lire. It is hoped that this method of payment will eventually replace the need to arm oneself with *gettoni* or handfuls of small change in order to make a call. The only disadvantage of the telephone calling cards is that they are not always easy to find, especially in the country.

Dialling codes for the four main districts in South Tyrol are:

    Bozen/Bolzano: 0471
    Brixen/Bressanone: 0472
    Meran/Merano: 0473
    Bruneck/Brunico: 0474

When placing a long-distance call from another country, the "0" of the district dialling code is deleted.

EMERGENCIES

MEDICAL AID

Visitors from European Community countries have the same rights to in-patient and ambulant health care in South Tyrol as they do in their own native lands. To be eligible it is necessary to present an E111 form, which must be obtained in your own country in advance of your trip.

IMPORTANT TELEPHONE NUMBERS

Emergency (Police, Fire Brigade, Emergency Medical Aid): 113
Avalanche Rescue: 0471-77171
Alpine Information: 0471-993 809

THE RED CROSS

Bozen/Bolzano:	tel: 0471-933 333
Brixen/Bressanone:	tel: 0472-313 333
St Christina (Gröden):	tel: 0471-77000
Meran/Merano:	tel: 0473-46666

THE WHITE CROSS

Bozen:	tel: 0471-44444
Brixen:	tel: 0472-24444
Bruneck:	tel: 0474-84444
Deutschnofen:	tel: 0461-616 424
Graun/Vinschgau:	tel: 0473-84691
Innichen:	tel: 0474-73333
Mals:	tel: 0473-81119
Meran:	tel: 0473-30333
Neumarkt:	tel: 0471-812 222
St Leonhard/Passeier:	tel: 0473-86211
Sarntal:	tel: 0471-623 222
Schlanders:	tel: 0473-70212
Seis/Schlern:	tel: 0471-71555
Sterzing:	tel: 0472-765 555
Sulden:	tel: 0473-75428
Waidbruck:	tel: 0471-65444
Welschnofen:	tel: 0471-613 118

CHEMISTS

By dialling the number 192 you can find out the nearest chemist open for emergency duty. You'll also find a list of chemists on emergency duty published in the daily newspapers.

WHERE TO STAY

HOTELS

The tourist board's list of hotels in South Tyrol takes up no fewer than 143 closely printed standard size pages. On the basis of sheer quantity alone, you might think it safe to assume that suitable lodgings are available throughout the year. This assumption is usually justified, but it does not apply to the peak season between July and September and around the Easter and Whitsun holidays. During these times of increased tourist activity, even when it is pouring with rain, every bed, even those in the remotest mountain farmhouse, are occupied.

Since 1985 hotels in South Tyrol have been divided into five categories. The selection runs the gamut from ☆ lodgings where a communal bathroom is located in the hall, to ☆☆☆☆ establishments in which each room is equipped with its own television and telephone, the bed and bathroom linens are changed daily and a doorman stands at the hotel entrance. However, the situation is complicated by the system of taxation. Because a ☆☆☆☆☆ hotel has to pay considerably higher taxes than a ☆☆☆☆ establishment, visitors to South Tyrol can find all the comfort worthy of a ☆☆☆☆☆ hotel in an establishment without an official ☆☆☆☆ designation (nevertheless, room rates are likely to be comparable to what you would pay in a luxury-class hotel). The list of hotels in South Tyrol is available upon request from the Regional Tourist Information Office in Bozen or from the: **Südtiroler Hotelier- und Gastwirteverband HGV**, I-39100 Bozen, Delaistr. 16/1, tel: 0471-971 110.

The following are a few helpful tips for lodgings in the four most frequently visited tourist areas.

BOZEN (Bolzano)

Park Hotel Laurin ☆☆☆☆ Super. Laurinstrasse – Via Laurin. Tel: 0471-980 500; Fax: 047-970 953; Telex: 401 088. Without a question, the best of the luxury hotels in Bozen is the Laurin with its Art Nouveau architecture and heated swimming pool in the hotel's extensive gardens. Rooms: 116,000–155,000 Lire.

Grifone – Greif ☆☆☆☆. Piazza Walther – Waltherplatz. Tel: 0471-977 056; Fax: 0471-980 613; Telex: 400 081. Probably the best-known and most centrally located hotel in Bozen is the

Greif. The hotel's restaurant "Waltherstuben" is also highly rated. Rooms: 66,000–204,500 Lire.

Luna – Mondschein ☆☆☆☆. Piave Strasse-Via Piave 15. Tel: 0471-975 642; Fax: 0471-975 577; Telex: 400 309. The Hotel Mondschein offers its guests comfortable and well-maintained accommodation. Rooms: 75,000–145,000 Lire.

Città di Bolzano – Stadthotel ☆☆☆. Piazza Walther – Waltherplatz. Tel: 0471-975 221; Fax: 0471- 976 688; Telex: 401 434. You'll find the traditional city hotel Città di Bolzano located behind Waltherplatz, on the way to the *lauben* (arcades). Rooms: 36,000–118,000 Lire.

Adria ☆☆. Via Dr. J. Perathoner 17. Tel: 0471-975 735. The Adria is a simple, centrally-located hotel situated directly across from the bus station and only two minutes away from Waltherplatz. Rooms: 32,000–47,000 Lire.

Figl ☆☆. Kornplatz – Piazza del Grano 9. Tel: 0471-978 412. The Figl is another simple hotel which has become a much-loved fixture on Kornplatz. Rooms: 30,000–79,000 Lire.

BRIXEN (Bressanone)

Located in Unterdrittelgasse – called simply Via Terzo Sotto in Italian – are two luxury hotels of the ☆☆☆☆ superclass and ☆☆☆☆ regular variety (the first of these is also a health resort):

Casa di Cura – Kurhaus ☆☆☆☆ Super. Unterdrittelgasse 17. Tel: 0472-35525; Fax: 0472-35 014. Rooms: 145,000–160,000 Lire.

Dominik ☆☆☆☆. Unterdrittelgasse 13. Tel: 0472-30144; Telex: 401 524. Rooms: 80,000–186,000 Lire.

Elefant ☆☆☆☆. Weisslahnstr. 4. Tel: 0472-32 750; Fax: 0472-36579; Telex: 400491. If you want luxurious ambience and excellent dining, this is the place to be. Rooms: 92,000–171,000 Lire.

BRUNECK (Brunico)

All of the leading hotels in this area are to be found in Reischach, located about 2 miles (3 km) from Bruneck itself.

Royal Hotel Hinterhuber ☆☆☆☆. Reischach – Pfaffental Ried 1/A. Tel: 0474-21221; Telex: 400650. The modern, beautifully situated Royal is the best hotel in town. Rooms: 65,000–165,000 Lire.

Rudolf ☆☆☆☆. Reischach – Reischacher Strasse 33. Tel: 0474-21223; Telex: 400 579. Rooms: 50,000–121,000 Lire.

MERAN (Merano)

In Meran visitors can choose from 25 ☆☆☆☆ hotels alone, six of which fall into the ☆☆☆☆ super category. Although it is difficult to try to make any specific recommendations, the following four are obvious choices for visitors The Palace has both an outdoor and indoor swimming pool, the Rundegg is

THE KODAK GOLD GUIDE TO BETTER PICTURES.

Good photography is not difficult. Use these practical hints and Kodak Gold II Film: then notice the improvement.

Move in close. Get close enough to capture only the important elements.

Frame your Pictures. Look out for natural frames such as archways or tree branches to add an interesting foreground. Frames help create a sensation of depth and direct attention into the picture.

One centre of interest. Ensure you have one focus of interest and avoid distracting features that can confuse the viewer.

Use leading lines. Leading lines direct attention to your subject i.e. — a stream, a fence, a pathway; or the less obvious such as light beams or shadows.

Maintain activity. Pictures are more appealing if the subject is involved in some natural action.

Keep within the flash range. Ensure subject is within flash range for your camera (generally 4 metres). With groups make sure everyone is the same distance from the camera to receive the same amount of light.

Check the light direction. People tend to squint in bright direct light. Light from the side creates highlights and shadows that reveal texture and help to show the shapes of the subject. If shooting into direct sunlight fill-in flash can be effective to light the subject from the front.

CHOOSING YOUR KODAK GOLD II FILM.

Choosing the correct speed of colour print film for the type of photographs you will be taking is essential to achieve the best colourful results.

Basically the more intricate your needs in terms of capturing speed or low-light situations the higher speed film you require.

Kodak Gold II 100. Use in bright outdoor light or indoors with electronic flash. Fine grain, ideal for enlargements and close-ups. Ideal for beaches, snow scenes and posed shots.

Kodak Gold II 200. A multipurpose film for general lighting conditions and slow to moderate action. Recommended for automatic 35mm cameras. Ideal for walks, bike rides and parties.

Kodak Gold II 400. Provides the best colour accuracy as well as the richest, most saturated colours of any 400 speed film. Outstanding flash-taking capabilities for low-light and fast-action situations; excellent exposure latitude. Ideal for outdoor or well-lit indoor sports, stage shows or sunsets.

APA
INSIGHT
GUIDES

ARE Going Places:

Asia & Pacific
East Asia
South Asia
South East Asian Wildlife
South East Asia
★ Marine Life
Australia
Great Barrier Reef
Melbourne
★★ Sydney
★ Bhutan
Burma/Myanmar
China
Beijing
India
Calcutta
Delhi, Jaipur, Agra
India's Western Himalaya
Indian Wildlife
★ New Delhi
Rajasthan
South India
Indonesia
★★ Bali
★ Bali Bird Walks
Java
★ Jakarta
★ Yogyakarta
Korea
Japan
Tokyo
Malaysia
★ Kuala Lumpur
★ Malacca
★ Penang
★★ Nepal
Kathmandu
Kathmandu Bikes & Hikes
New Zealand
Pakistan
Philippines
★ Sikkim
★★ Singapore
Sri Lanka
Taiwan

Thailand
★★ Bangkok
★ Chiang Mai
★ Phuket
★ Tibet
Turkey
★★ Istanbul
Turkish Coast
★ Turquoise Coast
Vietnam

Africa
East African Wildlife
South Africa
Egypt
Cairo
The Nile
Israel
Jerusalem
Kenya
Morocco
Namibia
The Gambia & Senegal
Tunisia
Yemen

Europe
Austria
★★ Vienna
Belgium
Brussels
Channel Islands
Continental Europe
Cyprus
Czechoslovakia
★★ Prague
Denmark
Eastern Europe
Finland
France
★★ Alsace
★★ Brittany
★★ Cote d'Azur
★★ Loire Valley
★★ Paris

Provence
Germany
★★ Berlin
Cologne
Düsseldorf
Frankfurt
Hamburg
★★ Munich
The Rhine
Great Britain
Edinburg
Glasgow
★★ Ireland
★★ London
Oxford
Scotland
Wales
Greece
★★ Athens
★★ Crete
★ Rhodes
Greek Islands
Hungary
★★ Budapest
Iceland
Italy
Florence
★★ Rome
★★ Sardinia
★★ Tuscany
Umbria
★★ Venice
Netherlands
Amsterdam
Norway
Poland
Portugal
★★ Lisbon
Madeira
Spain
★★ Barcelona
★ Costa Blanca
★ Costa Brava
★ Costa del Sol/Marbella
Catalonia

Gran Canaria
★ Ibiza
Madrid
Mallorca & Ibiza
★ Mallorca
★ Seville
Southern Spain
Tenerife
Sweden
Switzerland
(Ex) USSR
Moscow
St. Petersburg
Waterways of Europe
Yugoslavia
★ Yugoslavia's Adriatic
Coast

The Americas
Bermuda
Canada
Montreal
Caribbean
Bahamas
Barbados
Jamaica
Trinidad & Tobago
Puerto Rico
Costa Rica
Mexico
Mexico City
South America
Argentina
Amazon Wildlife
Brazil
Buenos Aires
Chile
Ecuador
Peru
Rio

USA/Crossing America
Alaska
American Southwest
Boston
California
Chicago
Florida
Hawaii
Los Angeles
Miami
Native America
New England
New Orleans
★★ New York City
New York State
Northern California
Pacific Northwest
★★ San Francisco
Southern California
Texas
The Rockies
Washington D.C.

★★ Also available as
   Insight Pocket Guide

★ Available as Insight
   Pocket Guide only

INSIGHT
pocket
GUIDES

*Ci VEDREMO·
PRESTO!*

See You Soon! In Italy

located in a castle dating from the 16th century and the Villa Mozart enjoys an international reputation.
Palace Hotel ☆☆☆☆ Super. Via Cavour 2. Tel: 0473-34734; Telex: 400 256. Rooms: 130,000–240,000 Lire.
Schloss Rundegg Kurhotel ☆☆☆☆ Super. Schennastrasse 2. Tel: 0473-34364; Fax: 0473-37200; Telex: 400 256. Rooms: 97,000–220,000 Lire.
Villa Mozart ☆☆☆☆. Markusstrasse 26. Tel: 0473-30 630; Fax: 0473-211 355. Rooms: 150,000–205,000 Lire.
Westend ☆☆☆. Speckbacherstr. 9. Tel: 0473-47654. Rooms: 39,000–98,000 Lire.

CASTLES

South Tyrol has over 350 castles in all. A number of them are privately owned, while others have been turned into museums. A few of them have been converted into hotels, for example:
Fahlburg ☆☆. Tisens. Prissian 83. Tel: 0473-90930. Rooms: 28,000–68,000 Lire.
Friedburg. Barbian. (Private rooms.)
Sonnenburg ☆☆☆. St Lorenzen. Tel: 0474-44099. Rooms: 64,000–120,000 Lire.

HOLIDAY APARTMENTS

Visitors who prefer staying in either a private room or holiday apartment rather than in a hotel should look for something suitable in advance of their trip. Any travel agency should be able to supply a list containing an ample selection. There is a comprehensive catalogue available containing a list of both *privatzimmern* (private rooms) and *Ferienwohnungen* (holiday apartments). It is published by the Association of Private Landlords in South Tyrol and is available at the Regional Tourist Information Office in Bozen. **Verband der Privatvermieter**, Mustergasse 9, 39100 Bozen.

HOLIDAYS ON THE FARM

These have become increasingly popular over the last few years. For families with children a vacation spent at a simple farmhouse often proves less stressful and more relaxing than a stay in a classy hotel.

Over 400 farms are listed in the brochure published by the South Tyrol Farmer's Association. This brochure is available upon request from the Regional Tourist Information Office in Bozen, or directly from the Farmer's Association itself:

Südtiroler Bauernbund, Kennwort "Urlaub auf dem Bauernhof" (Re: Holidays on the Farm), Brennerstr. 7, 39100 Bozen. Tel: 0471-972 145.

FOOD DIGEST

Eating and drinking play an important social role in South Tyrol. As has already been mentioned in the feature on food (*page 93*), the quality of specific inns and restaurants differs greatly and many establishments geared to tourists are interested only in turnover. Consequently many of the region's traditional specialities have become scarce. Bacon, for instance, now generally quick-smoked in large quantities, has suffered just as much as apples, the tastiest of which are being squeezed out of the market by the mass-produced Granny Smiths.

The following tips are intended to give the hungry traveller a few pointers.

WINE CELLARS & RESTAURANTS

EISACK VALLEY

Eisacktaler Kellereigenossenschaft (The Eisack Valley Wine Cellar Co-operative), Laitach 61, 39043 Klausen. Tel: 0472-47553. Located next to the Neustift monastery cellars near Brixen, this is the most important wine cellar co-op in the Eisack Valley.
Restaurant Elefant, Weisslahnstrasse 4, 39042 Brixen. Tel: 0472-32750. The favourite place in Brixen for national and international VIPs.
Fink, Kleine Lauben 4, 39042 Brixen. Tel: 0472-34883. This restaurant is operated by the son of the famous South Tyrolean chef Hans Fink.

BOZEN (Bolzano)

Alois Lageder, Drususallee 235, 39100 Bozen. Tel: 0471-931 577. Guests can enjoy either the nectar of the great wine-virtuoso Lageder or top-quality Italian wines.
Kellereigenossenschaft St Magdalena (St Magdalena Wine Cellar Cooperative), Brennerstr. 15, 39100 Bozen. Tel: 0471-972 944. The name St Magdalena is familiar to anyone who has examined a wine label in South Tyrol; here you have the opportunity to get this wine at source.
Klosterkellerei Gries (Gries Monastery Cellars), Grieser Platz 21, 39100 Bozen. Tel: 0471-282 287. A traditional establishment in the area of Bozen called Gries. It attracts wine lovers and experts alike. Guests are offered the best South Tyrolean wines, for example, the outstanding St Magdalener Classico.

Da Abramo – Zum Goldenen Kreuz (The Golden Cross), Grieser Platz 16, 39100 Bozen. Tel: 0471-280 141. Serves first-rate Italian cuisine. It has a lovely patio for outdoor dining on summer evenings.

Restaurant Greiff – Griffone, Waltherplatz 7, 39100 Bozen. Tel: 0471-977 056. An old, respected and much loved restaurant with an outdoor patio located directly on Waltherplatz.

Zur Kaiserkron (The Kaiser's Crown), Musterplatz 1, 39100 Bozen. Tel: 0471-970 770. International and South Tyrolean cuisine is served here in an exquisite baroque atmosphere.

La Greppia, Claudia-Augusta-Strasse 67, 39100 Bozen. Tel: 0471-271 541. Italian cuisine. Located some distance from the city centre.

Parkhotel Laurin – La Belle Epoque, Laurinstr. 4, 39100 Bozen. Tel: 0471-980 500. A classy establishment in a classy hotel.

MERAN & THE ETSCH VALLEY

Kellereigenossenschaft Andrian (Andrian Wine Cellar Co-operative), Kirchgasse 2, 39010 Andrian. Tel: 0471-57137. A well-known wine cellar co-operative situated on the southern slopes of the Etsch Valley.

Kellereigenossenschaft Terlan (Terlan Wine Cellar Co-operative), Silberleitenweg 1, 39018 Terlan. Tel: 0471-67135. This is the place to come for young white wine, Chardonnay or Sauvignon. Terlan is well-known for these types of wine.

Andrea, Gallileo-Galilei-Strasse 44, 391012 Meran. Tel: 0473-37400.

Villa Mozart, Markusstrasse 26, 391012 Meran. Tel: 0473-30630. Unfortunately the star chef Andreas Hellriegel no longer does the cooking. Nevertheless, his pupils seem to have mastered most of his skills.

Terlaner Weinstuben (Terlaner Wine Bar), Lauben 231, 39012 Meran. Tel: 0473-35571. A respected and well-run restaurant serving excellent white wine (from Terlan) under the *lauben* (arcades) of Meran.

Terlaner Hof, Kirchgasse 15, 39018 Terlan. Tel: 0471-57129. This is the right place for those who would like to taste a bona fide *Weinsuppe* (wine soup), made in the traditional Terlan style.

Andreas, Nationalstr. 114, 39010 Vilpian. Tel: 0471-678 816. Depending on the time of year, the menu offers various game dishes with truffles. The fish dishes are also well worth trying. Located in the Etsch Valley.

Patauner, 39018 Siebeneich, Siebeneich 36. Tel: 0471-918 502. During the asparagus season a culinary festival is held in the Etsch Valley. In this former dining establishment of the "Teutonic Order", guests are served the best of the crop.

UBERETSCH (Upper Etsch)

Bauernkellereigenossenschaft (Farmers' Wine Cellar Co-operative), 39052 Kaltern, Kellereistrasse 6. Tel: 0471-963 124.

Erste & Neue Kellereigenossenschaft (First & New Wine Cellar Co-operative), 39052 Kaltern, Kellereistrasse 5. Tel: 0471-963 122. Wines with any name and reputation at all can be found at this co-operative at the entrance to the city of Kaltern. Extensive and intoxicating tours through the various wine cellars are available.

Marklhof, 39050 Girlan, Marklhofweg 14. A popular out-of-town spot for Bozen natives. Dishes are typically South Tyrolean and run the gamut from *Weinsuppe* to *Strudel*.

Zur Rose, 39057 St Michael-Girlan. Tel: 0471-52249. A well-run restaurant located in the area of the city known as St Michael.

UNTERLAND (Lowlands)

The following establishments are good places to go to sample the famous Gewürztraminer (spiced Tramin wine).

W. Walch, Andreas-Hofer-Str. 1, 39040 Tramin. Tel: 0471-860 126.

Hofkellerei W. & G. Walch (W. & G. Walch Court Cellars), J. von Zallingerstr. 4, 39040 Tramin. Tel: 0471-860 215.

Schlosskellerei Turmhof (Turmhof Castle Cellars), Tiefenbrunner Schlossweg 4, 39040 Entiklar-Kurtatsch. Tel: 0471-880 122. Wine aficionados should make a point of tasting not only the exceptional white wines which are a well-known speciality of Unterland, but also the Blauburgunder (Red Burgundies) from Mazzon and Pinzon. During summer the courtyard provides a romantic spot where guests can sit and drink outside.

Johnson & Dipoli, 39044 Neumarkt, Andreas-Hofer-Str. 3. Tel: 0471-812 923. Not only a place to partake of good wine, but also an excellent place to dine

Andreas Hofer, Andreas-Hofer-Str. 14, 39044 Neumarkt. Tel: 0471-812 155. It's only a few steps from the classy Johnson to this simple inn, where Hofer stopped on his way to Mantua. A place of pilgrimage for admirers of Hofer.

ORGANIC FRUIT GROWERS

Hans Moscon, Tramin. Tel: 0471-860 005.
Marco Mittempergher, Neumarkt.
Tel: 0471-812 402.
Osiris/Bergerhof, Gargazon. Tel: 0473-292 168.
Josef Kröss, Algund. Tel: 0473-40556.
Karl Graiss, Morter/Latsch. Tel: 0473-72008.

CULTURE PLUS

Visitors to South Tyrol can take advantage of a wide variety of cultural attractions, though they may not always be of an international calibre. Nevertheless, in many cases exhibitions and cultural events are of considerable artistic quality.

For those who'd appreciate a general overview of cultural occasions, a calendar of events is available upon request from the Regional Tourist Information Office. You can also find an up-to-date regional programme published in the daily newspaper, *Dolomiten*, or in the weekly magazine *ff*.

Some places also organise festival performances during the peak tourist seasons. The best known include the *Bozen Piano Summer,* the *South Tyrol Unterland Open-air Festival* held in Neumarkt, the *Ritten Summer Festival* which offers a variety of theatre and concert performances, the *Meran Music Week*, a classical music festival, the *Kalter Organ Concerts*, held in the parish church, and the *Lana Festival* in the Gaul Gorge featuring a number of travelling theatre groups.

MUSEUMS & COLLECTIONS

BOZEN (Bolzano)

Municipal Museum, Sparkassenstr. 14: Archeological finds, folkloric costumes, traditional farm rooms, city and regional history.
Museum of Modern Art, Sernesistr. 1: Works from native modern artists.

BRIXEN (Bressanone)

Diocesan Museum, Hofburg: Religious folk art, a cradle museum.
The Cathedral Treasures, Kapitelhaus: Precious textiles, silver busts, altar decorations.
Neustift Monastery: Rococo library housing valuable handwritten manuscripts. Closed: during winter.

DORF TIROL

Tyrol Castle: The Regional Archaeological Museum, an illustrated record of the historical development of South Tyrol, and the castle chapel.
Brunnenburg: Museum of Agriculture containing original implements and tools, an ethnological collection, folklore and folk art.

EPPAN ON THE WINE ROAD

Gandegg Castle, St Michael: Tiled stoves, the oldest organ in South Tyrol, Gothic rooms. Closed: during winter.

KALTERN (Caldaro) ON THE WINE ROAD

The Wine Museum, Goldgasse.

KLAUSEN (Chiusa)

Felsenburg Monastery Säben: Finds dating from the Bronze Age, tombs from the 6th and 7th centuries.
The Gufidaun Town Museum, Schnitzlerhaus: Old utensils and implements used in the country, votive tablets.

MERAN (Merano)

Landesfürstliche Burg (Castle of the Counts), Galileistrasse: Gothic furnishings and *objets d'art*, armour, a collection of stone monuments, musical instruments (closed on Sundays and during winter).
Municipal Museum (Stadtmuseum), Galileistrasse: Prehistory, mineralogy, paintings by old and new Tyrolean masters, arts and crafts, Gothic sculptures.

ST KASSIAN IN THE ABTEI VALLEY

Pic Museo Ladin: Fossil collection, the remains from "ursus spelaeus", taken from the bear caves in the Conturines Group, agricultural implements and tools.

ST LEONHARD IN THE PASSEIER VALLEY

Andreas-Hofer Commemorative Room, near Sandwirt: A small collection of written documents, clothing, etc belonging to the heroic South Tyrol freedom-fighter.

ST ULRICH IN GRÖDEN

Cesa di Ladins, Reziastr. 83: The Gröden Museum houses works by native woodcarvers, wooden toys, a mineral collection, finds dating from the Bronze and Stone ages as well as the last Ice Age.

ULTEN

Talmuseum (The Valley Museum), St Nikolaus: South Tyrolean folk art, furnishings (closed during winter).

THERMAL BATHS

Spa City Meran: When it comes to health resorts, South Tyrol offers a variety of conventional and unconventional options.

Head and shoulders above all of them is the spa city of Meran, which first gained its reputation during the time of Elisabeth of Bavaria, "Sissy", who came to enjoy the city's good, clear air. Although the city cannot necessarily be recommended for its air today, certain health treatments, for instance *Fangopackungen* (mudpacks), baths and inhalations to alleviate rheumatic disorders, arteriosclerosis or chronic inflammations of the respiratory tract still draw visitors. Somewhat less well-known is the Meran *Traubenkur* (Grape Cure), available during the autumn. The freshly pressed juice of these curative grapes is said to have an especially fortifying effect on the system. For more information contact: Kurverwaltung Meran, Freiheitstr. 45, I-39012 Meran. Tel: 0472-35223.

Bad Salomonsbrunn: Located in the Antholzer Valley. This spa hotel, its waters fed by a lively, effervescent spring, has existed since the Middle Ages. Common ailments treated here include various gynaecological and circulatory complaints, metabolic diseases and rheumatism. During the 18th century Bad Salomonsbrunn enjoyed a reputation for being a "general ladies' bath", due to its efficacy in healing gynaecological disorders. Both internal and external (i.e. drinking and bathing) treatments are administered here. For further information contact: Bad Salomonsbrunn, Antholz Niedertal 1, 39030 Rasen-Antholz. Tel: 0474-42199.

Kurhaus Dr Guggenberg (Dr Guggenberg's Health Resort): On the Unterdrittelgasse in Brixen. It was established in 1890 by Otto von Guggenberg, a colleague of the internationally famous Sebastian Kneipp. The resort has remained loyal to its original mentor and treatments offered still follow the teachings of Kneipp. For more information contact: Casa di cura – Kurhaus Dr von Guggenberg, Unterdrittelgasse 17, 39042 Brixen. Tel: 0472-21525.

Bad Kochenmoos: In the Vinschgau/Val Venosta, just a few miles from Meran, is the very last of the traditional "farmers' baths". The waters here are rich in sulphur and are said to help in treating metabolic and abdominal disorders as well as rheumatism. For further information contact: Bad Kochenmoos, Staben, 39025 Naturns. Tel: 0473-87106.

SPORTS

With the exception of deep-sea diving, it's possible to partake in just about every kind of sport imaginable in South Tyrol. The wide choice of athletic activities extends far beyond the alpine programme generally associated with the region.

The following tips are intended to give an idea of the varied sporting activities that can be found.

CYCLING

Really serious mountain bikers like to tackle one of the mighty passes – for example, the Stilfser Joch. However, the majority of cyclists are content with less taxing routes. There is a host of marked paths and trails to choose from many leading through forests and often continuing on up to high pass elevations.

Some places offer what are referred to as "Bicycle Touring Weeks", for example Lana (Hotel Schwarzschmied, tel: 0473-52800; Hotel Eichhof, tel: 0473-51196), Prags (Dolomite Mountain Bike Tours, conducted in September and October; Tourist Information Centre, tel: 0474-78660), Rasen, Schluderns, Sexten, Sand in Taufers and Tramin (Cycling Weekend, conducted in spring; Tourist Information Centre, tel: 0471-860131).

Further information is available by contacting each of the respective local tourist information agencies directly.

GOLF

One of South Tyrol's two golf courses is located close to Steinacherhof am Petersberg, about 20 miles (30 km) outside of Bozen. (To get there, take the motorway exit marked Auer/Ora.) This 9-hole course, open from May until November, is situated at an altitude of 4,000 ft (1,200 metres) above sea-level and extends for about 8,500 ft (2,550 metres). The course is classified at par 34 and has a club house, restaurant and bar. There is a golf pro available for instruction and the green fee is about 35,000 Lire. Steinacherhof, Deutschnofen. Tel: 0471-615 122 or 615 627.

The second of South Tyrol's 9-hole golf courses, situated above Lake Karer in the shadow of the Rosengarten, was completed in 1991. Further information is available in Welschnofen. Tel: 0471-613 126.

RAFTING & HYDROSPEED

River-rafting is a thrilling sport. In South Tyrol it is available in Sand in Taufers. Rivers are tackled in rubber rafts holding either 8 or 10 persons. Trips are organised by Hermann's Skistadl, tel: 0474-678 422; and Club Nr. 1 for Fun, tel: 0474-679 188.

SKIING

In the weeks after the Christmas holidays and outside the peak season hotels run what what are called "White Weeks", offering especially attractive ski-lift and hotel rates.

DOLOMITI SUPERSKI

"Ultimate Skiing" is the motto of Dolomiti Superski, the biggest ski network in the world. A network of connected ski lifts around the Grödner Valley (Val Gardena) and in the Dolomites has grown over the years to include 450 separate lift facilities and nearly 690 miles (1,100 km) of ski runs. It connects 38 different ski areas in 11 valleys. Some 270 snow and ski-run maintenance vehicles to maintain optimum conditions. There are also good bus connections within certain areas, for instance in the Grödner Valley. The ski pass for Dolomiti Superski may be used in the following regions:
Kronplatz (Plan de Corones), near Bruneck
Hochabtei Valley (Alta Badia), near Corvara
Gröden and Seiser Alm (Val Gardena, Alpe di Suisi)
Fassa Valley and Lake Karer (Val di Fassa, Carezza)
Arrabba, at the foot of Sella
Hochpuster Valley (Alta Val Pusteria)
Obereggen (Fiemme), at Latemar
San Martino and Passo Rolle
Eisack Valley with the Plose, (above Brixen)
Tre Valli, near Moena

In addition to these areas, the superski pass is also valid in Austria in Zell am See-Kaprun, Gasteinertal, Dachstein-Tauern, Dachstein-Krippenstein and Schladming.
In the 1992 season, the price for adults was about 33,100 Lire per day and 393,100 Lire for a 21-day pass, with rates increasing during the peak season (23 December–5 January and 3 February–1 April) to 39,000 Lire and 462,300 Lire respectively. Children are given a discount of about 30 percent. A season's pass costs around 600,000 Lire and if purchased prior to the beginning of the season (before 22 December) 520,000 Lire. Further information is available directly from: **Dolomiti Superski,** I-39048 Selva/Wolkenstein. Tel: 0471-795 397 or 795 398; Fax: 0471-794 282.

ORTLER SKIARENA

The second largest ski network association is the Ortler Skiarena, but this is not nearly as extensive as Superski. The Ortler Skiarena encompasses 12 ski areas, 68 lifts (of which 5 are funiculars), and around 125 miles (200 km) of ski-runs. Unlike Superski, the Ortler Skiarena is composed of a number of unconnected areas including:
Meran 2000 – Hafling
Pfelders in the Passeier Valley
Vigiljoch near Meran
Schnalstal Valley
Reschen – Graun – Schöneben
Langtaufers
Haider Alm – St Valentin
Watles – Höfer Alm
Trafoi
Sulden on the Ortler
Latsch – Tarscher Alm
Schwemmalm in the Ulten Valley

Prices are somewhat lower than those of Superski. Adult rates lie between 78,000 Lire for 3 days and 326,000 Lire for 20 days, with a season's pass costing 370,000 Lire. Children's rates run from 59,000 Lire for 3 days to 215,000 Lire for 20 days.

MOUNTAIN CLIMBING

A number of well-known mountain climbers hail from South Tyrol. Reinhold Messner is the most famous of them all. But many ordinary South Tyroleans are also keen climers. For intrepid climbers bent on giving the precipitous Dolomites a try, the following addresses should prove useful. General information and mountaineering guides are available through the **Verband der Südtiroler Berg- und Skiführer**, Poststrasse 16, 39100 Bozen. Tel: 0471-977 317.

MOUNTAINEERING SCHOOLS

Alpinschule Catores, 39046 St Ulrich. Tel: 0471-78037
Kletterschule Gröden (climbing school), 39047 St Christina. Tel: 0471-76302
Grödner Bergführer, 39048 Wolkenstein. Tel: 0471-74133
Alpinschule Eggental-Rosengarten, 39056 Welschnofen. Tel: 0471-613 365
Alpin-Kletterschule Schlern, 39040 Seis am Schlern. Tel: 0471-71285
Alpinschule Südtirol, Lauben 37, 39100 Bozen. Tel: 0471-974 033
Alpinschule Taufers, 39032 Sand in Taufers. Tel: 0474-68514
Bergsteigerschule Meran (school of mountaineering), Laubengasse 6, Reisebüro Alpina, 39012 Meran. Tel: 0473-33022
Bergsteigerschule Sulden-Ortler, 39029 Sulden. Tel: 0473-75404

PHOTOGRAPHY

South Tyrol offers both professional and amateur photographers an extensive and exciting variety of subject matter. It's advisable to bring photographic materials with you from home, as film in general is quite expensive in Italy.

There are some photo labs which will develop colour negatives quickly, but if your standards are high, you're advised not to use them. In Bozen, however, there is a photo lab located in Bindergasse which will develop excellent, professional-quality slides in just a few hours.

USEFUL ADDRESSES

TOURIST INFORMATION

Both local tourist information centres throughout South Tyrol and the Regional Tourist Information Centre in Bozen are excellent. Information is obtainable in person as well as by telephone and post. The Regional Tourist Information Centre publishes a large number of brochures and other materials, although information tends to be in Italian and German.

Visitors with specific questions should address their queries to the tourist information centres located in the particular area or city they are interested in. All questions can be addressed to the central information office: **Landesverkehrsamt Südtirol**, Pfarrplatz 11/12, I-39100 Bozen. Tel: 0471-993 808.

ABTEI (Alta Badia)

39030 Stern-La Villa.	Tel: 0471-847 037
39036 Pedratsches.	Tel: 0471-839 695
39030 St Kassian.	Tel: 0471-849 422

AHRN VALLEY

39030 Luttach.	Tel: 0474-61136
39030 St Johann-Weissenbach.	Tel: 0474-61257
39030 Steinhaus.	Tel: 0474-62198
39040 Aldein.	Tel: 0471-886 800
39022 Algund.	Tel: 0473-48600
39040 Altrei.	Tel: 0462-82022
39010 Andrian.	Tel: 0471-57300

ANTHOLZER VALLEY

39030 Antholz, Mitteltal.	Tel: 0474-42116
39030 Rasen, Niederrasen.	Tel: 0474-46269
39040 Auer.	Tel: 0471-810 231
39040 Barbian.	Tel: 0471-654 411
39100 Bozen, Waltherplatz.	Tel: 0471-975 656
39100 Bozen, Bahnhofstr.	Tel: 0471-85722
39031 Bruneck.	Tel: 0474-85722
39014 Burgstall.	Tel: 0473-291343
39033 Corvara.	Tel: 0471-836176
39030 Colvosco-Kolfuschg.	Tel: 0471-836 145
39050 Deutschnofen-Eggen.	Tel: 0471-616 567
39057 Eppan/Weinstrasse.	Tel: 0471-52206
39043 Feldthurns.	Tel: 0472-45290
39050 Freienfeld.	Tel: 0472-67390
39030 Gais-Uttenheim.	Tel: 0474-54220
39010 Gargazon.	Tel: 0473-292 244
39020 Glurns.	Tel: 0473-81097
39041 Gossensass.	Tel: 0472-62372
39030 Gsiesertal.	Tel: 0474-78436
39010 Hafling.	Tel: 0473-99457
39038 Innichen.	Tel: 0474-73149
39050 Jenesien.	Tel: 0471-54196
39052 Kaltern am See.	Tel: 0471-963 169
39020 Kastellbell-Tschars.	Tel: 0473-624 193
39043 Klausen.	Tel: 0472-47424
39043 Kurtatsch/Weinstrasse.	Tel: 0471-880 100
39040 Kurtining/Weinstrasse.	Tel: 0471-817 388
39023 Laas.	Tel: 0473-73613
39040 Lajen.	Tel: 0471-654 633
39011 Lana an der Etsch.	Tel: 0473-51770
39030 Lappach.	Tel: 0474-63220
39040 Laurein.	Tel: 0463-30108
39055 Leifers.	Tel: 0471-950420
39040 Lüsen.	Tel: 0472-43750
39024 Mals.	Tel: 0473-81190
39040 Magreid/Weinstrasse.	Tel: 0471-817 292
39020 Marling.	Tel: 0473-47147
39020 Martell.	Tel: 0473-74523
39012 Meran.	Tel: 0473-35223
39037 Meransen.	Tel: 0472-50197
39010 Mölten.	Tel: 0473-668 001
39040 Montan.	Tel: 0471-819 747
39013 Moos im Passeier.	Tel: 0473-643 558
39010 Nals.	Tel: 0471-678 619
39025 Naturns.	Tel: 0473-87287
39040 Natz-Schabs.	Tel: 0472-42440
39044 Neumarkt.	Tel: 0471-812 373
39030 Olang.	Tel: 0474-46277
39020 Partschins-Rabland.	Tel: 0473-97157

39030 Percha.	Tel: 0474-41155
39030 Pfalzen.	Tel: 0474-58159
39026 Prad am Stilfser Joch.	Tel: 0473-76034
39029 Sulden.	Tel: 0473-75415
39020 Trafoi.	Tel: 0473-611 677
39030 Prags.	Tel: 0474-78660
39040 Proveis.	Tel: 0463-30106
39040 Ratschings.	Tel: 0472-66666
39010 Riffian.	Tel: 0473-41076

RITTEN

39054 Klobenstein.	Tel: 0471-56100
39059 Oberbozen.	Tel:0471-55245
39037 Rodeneck.	Tel: 0472-44044
39040 Salurn.	Tel: 0471-884 279
39032 Sand in Taufers.	Tel: 0474-68076
39047 St Christina-Gröden.	Tel: 071-73046
39015 St Leonhard/Passeier.	Tel: 0473-86188
39030 St Lorenzen.	Tel: 0474-44092
39010 St Martin in Passeier.	Tel: 0473-85810
39030 St Martin in Thurns.	Tel: 0474-53175
39010 St Pankraz in Ulten.	Tel: 0473-78171
39046 St Ulrich in Gröden.	Tel: 0471-76328
39030 St Vigil in Enneberg.	Tel: 0474-51037
39040 San Lugano.	Tel: 0462-87136
39058 Sarntal.	Tel: 0471-623091
39017 Schenna.	Tel: 0473-95669
39028 Schlanders.	Tel: 0473-70155

SCHLERN

39040 Kastelruth.	Te: 0471-71333
39040 Seis am Schlern.	Tel: 0471-71124
39058 Schluderns.	Tel: 0473-75858
39020 Schnals.	Tel: 0473-89148
39030 Sexten.	Tel: 0474-70310
39050 Steinegg.	Tel: 0471-676 574

39049 Sterzing.	Tel: 0472-765 325
39036 Taisten.	Tel: 0474-74010
39030 Terenten.	Tel: 0474-56140
39018 Terlan.	Tel: 0471-57165
39050 Tiers.	Tel: 0471-642 127
39010 Dorf Tirol.	Tel: 0473-93314
39010 Tisens-Prissian.	Tel: 0473-90888
39034 Toblach.	Tel: 0474-72132
39040 Tramin.	Tel: 0471-860131
39040 Truden-Kaltenbrunn.	Tel: 0462-87078
39010 Tscherms.	Tel: 0473-51015
39016 Ulten, St Walburg.	Tel: 0473-79987
39010 Unsre liebe Frau i. W.	Tel: 0463-86103
39040 Vahrns.	Tel: 0472-24958
39040 Villanders.	Tel: 0472-53121
39040 Villnös.	Tel: 0472-40180

VINSCHGAU

39020 Graun.	Tel: 0473-832 333
39027 Reschen.	Tel: 0473-83101
39030 Vintl-Pfunderertal.	Tel:0472-49100
39050 Völs am Schlern.	Tel: 0471-72047
39040 Waidbruck.	Tel: 0471-654321
39056 Welsberg.	Tel: 0474-74118
39035 Welschnofen-Karer See.	Tel: 0471-613 126
39030 Wengen.	Tel: 0471-84139
39040 Wiesen-Pfatsch.	Tel: 0472-765 730
39048 Wolkenstein-Gröden.	Tel: 0471-75122

ART/PHOTO CREDITS

INDEX

A
B
D
E
F
G
H
I
J
a
b
c
d
e
f
h
i
j
k
l